JESUS
AND FAITH

JESUS
AND FAITH

A Conversation on the work of
John Dominic Crossan

EDITORS
Jeffrey Carlson
Robert A. Ludwig

ORBIS BOOKS

Maryknoll, New York 10545

The Catholic Foreign Mission Society of America (Maryknoll) recruits and trains people for overseas missionary service. Through Orbis Books, Maryknoll aims to foster the international dialogue that is essential to mission. The books published, however, reflect the opinions of their authors and are not meant to represent the official position of the society.

Library of Congress Cataloging in Publication Data

Jesus and faith : a conversation on the work of John Dominic Crossan /
  editors, Jeffrey Carlson, Robert A. Ludwig.
      p.   cm.
  Contains revised and edited papers originally prepred for the
conference "Jesus and Faith" held Feb. 1993 in DePaul University.
  Includes bibliographical references and index.
  ISBN 0-88344-936-6 (pbk.)
  1. Jesus Christ—Historicity—Congresses. 2. Crossan, John
Dominic. Historical Jesus—Congresses. 3. Jesus Christ—Biography—
Congresses. 4. Jesus Christ—Biography—History and criticism—
Congresses. I. Carlson, Jeffrey Daniel, 1956- . II. Ludwig,
Robert A.
BT303.2.J455   1993
232.9'01—dc20
[B]   93-39117
                                                    CIP

Contents

Introduction

JEFFREY CARLSON and ROBERT A. LUDWIG

In February of 1993, DePaul University hosted a conference entitled "Jesus and Faith: Theologians in Conversation with the Work of John Dominic Crossan." The conference brought together scholars, students, teachers, and pastoral ministers to explore the relationship between historical studies and theology. The conference focused on Crossan's work, particularly his 1991 book, *The Historical Jesus: The Life of a Mediterranean Jewish Peasant*. Those attending the conference included Dutch filmmaker Paul Verhoeven (*Basic Instinct, Total Recall, The Fourth Man*), who plans to make a film about the historical Jesus, and a graduate student from South Africa, who is developing a doctoral dissertation on Crossan's work.

This volume contains, in revised and edited form, the papers from that conference, as well as several others that we solicited. Both the conference and this book are, in a sense, a tribute to Crossan's premier scholarship. We feel fortunate to have Dominic as a colleague at DePaul, and celebrate *The Historical Jesus* as a culmination of over twenty years of research. The book has received much deserved praise and has sparked a great deal of controversy, both inside and outside academic circles. It sold 25,000 copies in its first six months, has already been through multiple printings, and is translated for publication into several languages. Crossan's new book, *Jesus: A Revolutionary Biography* (scheduled for publication by HarperSanFrancisco in January 1994) will make his thought available to an even wider audience, since it presents a briefer and more popularly-written interpretation of the program of the historical Jesus.

Our collection of essays is offered as a resource for those who are concerned with the implications of Jesus research for the life of faith. Those who claim to follow Jesus, to believe in him, to see him as the source of spiritual truth and meaning, will be interested in the results of historical research into the social worlds inhabited by Jesus and the literary traditions that provided the earliest interpretations of his life and teachings. In the Epilogue of *The Historical Jesus*, Crossan raises the question of "permanent relevance" of "an understanding of the historical Jesus" for the ongoing Christian tradition and those who make it their spiritual home. One who believes in Jesus and confesses him as "Christ" or "Son of God" can never be indifferent to the efforts to discover the historical Jesus, even when, as Crossan would admit, we can never have more than *an understanding* or *an interpretation* of the historical Jesus.

Jeffrey Carlson's essay raises the key questions that the conference and now this book seek to explore:

> *Do* scholarly reconstructions of the "historical Jesus" — Crossan's or anyone else's — play a role in theology? *If* such scholarly reconstructions *do* play a role, then in what specific ways should contemporary Christian theology be revised in the light of *new* scholarship? What happens when the data for developing a historical Jesus reconstruction *includes,* as it does in Crossan's case, material previously *excluded* from the New Testament canon, such as the *Gospels of Thomas* and *Peter,* and other texts? If such data is deemed theologically relevant today, then what does that say about past theological *decisions to exclude it*? . . . What happens if, and, indeed, when the "program" of the historical Jesus seems to contradict many beliefs and practices that have developed within traditional Christianity? If, for instance, Jesus proclaimed a "brokerless kingdom," then is there an ultimate betrayal in the very establishment of a hierarchical Church? If the Jesus movement was deliberately itinerant and radically egalitarian, are there betrayals in the moves to fixed residency in Jerusalem (or Rome) and fixed leadership roles for exclusively male bishops, presbyters, and deacons? . . . Finally, what happens if, and *certainly* when, the historical portrait of Jesus' life and death seems to violate the delicate, heartfelt, life-sustaining piety of many contemporary Christian men and women?

These are only some of the questions that readers will find creatively explored in the following pages.

In this volume's opening chapter, *John Dominic Crossan* argues that "earliest Christian faith" had four possibilities: Thomas, Pauline, Q, and Exegetical Christianity. The first, exemplified in Thomas, Gnostic Christianity, would negate the importance of the historical Jesus, but each of the other three would in its own way affirm Jesus' crucial historicity. This leads Crossan to argue that non-Gnostic Christian faith is always (1) an act of faith (2) in the historical Jesus (3) as the manifestation of God.

Bernard Brandon Scott provides a rich analysis of Crossan's intellectual development from *In Parables* (1973) through *The Historical Jesus*. Scott argues that Crossan's work has balanced a Darwinian historicism of the diachronic with a Sausseran synchronicity, but with a preference for the latter. Scott argues that Crossan's method, refined in his most recent work, "brings the quest [for the historical Jesus] into the new sciences."

Jeffrey Carlson reflects on the means by which Crossan arrives at his "reconstruction" of Jesus, and argues that religious identity is inevitably the product of a process of dynamic interaction and selective reconstruction. This insight, Carlson suggests, is appropriate to the boundary-crossing program of Crossan's Jesus, and may lead beyond "narrowly Christian" confines, to influence and evoke other religious identities, the "syncretic amalgams" yet to be.

Sheila Greeve Davaney reads Crossan against the background of several modern theological models, namely postliberalism, deconstructionism, and revisionist theology. Davaney proposes her own fourth model, pragmatic historicism, which she sees as similar to Crossan's work in its commitment to a "thick" reading of history's "multilayered dimensions, . . . internal tensions and conflicting possibilities in every historical moment," and in its "acknowledgment of the value- and interest-laden role of the interpreter."

Robert A. Ludwig's essay explores the similarities between contemporary Catholic christology (European revisionist and Latin American liberation theology) and Crossan's historical portrait. These combine to offer a critical correction to the Christ who emerges after Constantine in the early councils. The latter produced "a dysfunctional christology," which today provides theological legitimacy to "a dysfunctional church." Crossan's reconstruction, on the other hand, provides a credible Jesus worthy of our best religious instincts and spiritual hungers.

Catherine Keller sees parallels between Crossan's Jesus and movements in today's feminist theology and "postcolonial Christianity." She finds traditional christology's "heroic individualism" and understanding of kingdom—which is focused on an ever-receding horizon—problematic, finding Crossan's emphasis on wisdom, egalitarian protest movement, and *"basileic presence"* to be very close to developments in feminism and Salvadoran Christian praxis. Both provide, simultaneously, a deconstruction and a reconstruction.

Frans Jozef van Beeck compares Crossan's *The Historical Jesus* to the exegesis of the New Hermeneutic from the 1950s and 1960s. This chapter raises a number of significant criticisms of Crossan's book, particularly the latter's use of social-scientific ideal types, his understanding of orality, and his tendency to, as van Beeck puts it, engage in "projection" under the guise of historical reconstruction.

Marc H. Ellis reflects on histories "covered in blood," histories of "1492" and of "Auschwitz." Ellis sees Crossan's Jesus as a potential way forward in the struggle against Christian theological triumphalism and the violence of empire, as well as against contemporary Israel's oppression of Palestinians. This Jesus symbolizes, for Ellis, the contemporary challenge to "do what needs to be done," in "a practice that opens the person and the community to the world in all its dimensions," and to become liberated from "a self-definition of Jew and Christian . . . that is increasingly irrelevant in the world."

Charles R. Strain compares Crossan's Jesus with "socially engaged Buddhism" and with Christian liberation theology. Strain criticizes liberation theology's future orientation, favoring instead the "utterly available kingdom of God" offered by Crossan's Jesus. The dualism of "oppressed vs. oppressor," which for Strain leads to the violence of "ethical cleansing," is undone by Buddhist interdependence and by Jesus' radical egalitarianism. Faced with the challenge of enacting these extreme messages, Strain proposes the metaphor of "working the linkages" between egalitarian communities and the enveloping social structures. "Linkages between communities and powerful institutions," Strain argues, "are necessary to leverage social change."

Dennis P. McCann argues that "Crossan's Jesus is far less hostile to modern business than the partisans of one or another form of the Social Gospel have presumed him to be." McCann's thesis is "that Christianity's perennial bias against moneymaking in general and modern business in particular rests less on the teachings of Crossan's Mediterranean Jewish peasant and more on the aristocratic prejudices of Plato and Aristotle." The "brokerless kingdom" of Crossan's Jesus, McCann maintains, challenges the conventions of *all* brokered forms of human interaction, both pro- and antibusiness.

Finally, *John Dominic Crossan* offers extensive "responses and reflections" on each of the other essays in this volume. In this piece, really another full essay, Crossan extends his thinking in a number of crucial areas. He reflects on his early life in Ireland and explores its impact on his later work, answers numerous questions about the method and content of his reconstruction of the historical Jesus, and postulates an "earliest Christian" dialectical tension between Christian *itinerants* who faithfully imitated Jesus, and Christian *householders* who faithfully compromised his radical program.

We conclude with two points. First, just as the conference was intended to reach beyond a closed academy of rarified scholarly debate into the world of contemporary believers, who seek a credible Jesus and a meaningful spirituality, so with this volume. We want to address a broad audience at the place where faith and understanding, fact and meaning, meet. Crossan's work, we believe, needs a hearing in a wide arena—by ordinary but thoughtful Christians who struggle today to make sense of their lives *and* their tradition, their experience *and* their inherited beliefs. Too often, this kind of research is kept from those in the pew, supposedly because "the people couldn't handle it" or "they're not ready for it." After our conference at DePaul an article appeared in *The Milwaukee Sentinel* (February 13, 1993, page 9A), which illustrates this. Reporter Mary Beth Murphy raises the precise question:

Can research into the historical Jesus be taught to those in the pew? If it's done slowly and carefully, said Crossan. A Catholic priest who leads a parish in Kansas said he wouldn't even attempt it. He said he attended the conference for his own enrichment and spiritual growth, not to take anything back to his congregation. "That's terrible," Crossan said when told about the priest's remarks. "That he would want it [this knowledge] for himself, but never use it, that would be very sad."

Second, finally, a word of thanks to all those who supported this project. We are particularly grateful to those persons in the sponsoring departments of University Ministry and Religious Studies who worked to make the DePaul conference a success. We also want to express our gratitude for the financial support provided by the University Research Council, the College of Liberal Arts and Sciences and Dean Richard Meister, and the Provost's Office. Mostly, however, we want to thank the scholars who have contributed their work to this volume. The reader will find their essays stimulating and provocative. Certainly, Dominic Crossan himself is at the top of our list. His diligent scholarship, his clever mind, his courageous spirit, and his commitment to truth-telling—combine to present us with a monumental work about a topic that lies at the center of Christian faith: Who is this Jesus? Who do *you* say he is?

Clearly, while *The Historical Jesus* and *Jesus: A Revolutionary Biography* are summary works, they are but the present high-water mark in a career that continues to hold much promise for those of us who have always found Dominic Crossan's work so compelling. He is already involved in still another exciting project, attempting to explore *what happened* after the historical Jesus was crucified. His new book has been tentatively titled *After the Crucifixion: The Search for Earliest Christianity*. We sense another conference . . . and another collection of essays to offer to the public.

1.

The Historical Jesus in Earliest Christianity

JOHN DOMINIC CROSSAN

Prologue: Radical Egalitarianism and Contemporary Democracy

The Historical Jesus: The Life of a Mediterranean Peasant proposed that the historical Jesus proclaimed and performed the Kingdom of God, and empowered others to do likewise, as a community of radical egalitarianism negating not only the ancient Mediterranean's pivotal values of honor and shame, patronage and clientage, but culture and civilization's eternal round of hierarchies, discriminations, and exclusions. That vision and program was focused, as it had to be for a peasant talking primarily even if not exclusively to other peasants, on the body. It emphasized free healing, or the egalitarian sharing of spiritual and religious resources, and open commensality, or the egalitarian sharing of material and economic resources. I used commensality rather than table-fellowship because, as an anthropological term, it means table-fellowship precisely as a microcosm of societal discrimination. I presume all of that discussion in what follows and add only one postscript to it before turning to my present subject.

Radical egalitarianism should not be confused with contemporary democracy, as if I were simply and crudely retrojecting the latter back into the first common-era century. Three points, one anthropological, one historical, and one philosophical.

First, those who, like peasants, live with a boot on their neck can easily imagine two different dreams. One is quick revenge, of a world in which they might get, in turn, to put their boots on those other necks. Another is reciprocal justice, of a world in which there would never again be need of necks and boots on either side. Thus, for example, the anthropologist James C. Scott (1977: 226) moves from Europe to Southeast Asia, notes the popular tradition's common reaction to such disparate elite traditions as Christianity, Buddhism, and Islam, and argues very persuasively that peasant culture and religion are actually an anticulture, qualifying alike both the religious and political elites that oppress it. It is, in fact, a reflexive and reactive inversion of the pattern of exploitation common to the peasantry *as such*:

> The radical vision to which I refer is strikingly uniform despite the enormous variations in peasant cultures and the different great traditions of which they partake. . . . At the risk of over generalizing, it is possible to describe some common features of this reflexive symbolism. It nearly always implies a society of brotherhood in which there will be no rich and poor, in which no distinctions of rank and status (save those between believers and non-believers) will exist. Where religious institutions are experienced as justifying inequities, the abolition of rank and status may well include the elimination of religious hierarchy in favor of communities of equal believers. Property is typically, though not always, to be held in common and shared. All unjust claims to taxes, rents, and tribute are to be nullified. The envisioned utopia may also include a self-yielding and abundant nature as well as a radically transformed human nature in which greed, envy, and hatred will disappear. While the earthly utopia is thus an anticipation of the future, it often harkens back to a mythic Eden from which mankind has fallen away.

That is the ancient peasant dream of radical egalitarianism. It does not deny the other dream, that of brutal revenge, but neither does that latter one negate the former's eternal thirst for reciprocity, equality, and justice. In the words of an unnamed peasant woman from Piana dei Greci, province of Palermo, Sicily, speaking to a north Italian journalist during an 1893 peasant uprising, as cited by Eric J. Hobsbawm (1965: 183):

> We want everybody to work, as we work. There should no longer be either rich or poor. All should have bread for themselves and for their children. We should all be equal. I have five small children and only one little room, where we have to eat and sleep and do everything, while so many lords have ten or twelve rooms, entire palaces. . . . It will be enough to put all in common and to share with justice what is produced.

Second, if all members of some group are equally eligible for office or equally due some goods or services, then the only absolutely fair human way to decide is by lot, leaving the choice up to chance or God, fate or Providence. That was how Saul, the first Jewish king, was elected from "all the tribes of Israel," according to 1 Samuel 10:21. And that was how the early Christians chose a replacement for the traitor apostle Judas from among "the men who have accompanied us" since the beginning, according to Acts of the Apostles 1:21-26. Obviously, of course, as in the implicit and presumed male exclusivity of that former case and the explicit and very deliberate male exclusivity of that latter one, discriminations can still be present even in a lottery. They are there, too, in electing a High Priest only from a certain family. But lottery is how the peasant Zealots elected a new High Priest after they had been swept into Jerusalem as Vespasian's forces tightened the noose around the doomed city in the fall of 67 and winter of 68 CE. Josephus, as an aristocratic priest, can hardly contain his rage as he tells that story in his *Jewish Antiquities* 4.147–207.

Finally, to appreciate the distinction between contemporary democracy and radical egalitarianism one can read the political philosopher Barbara Goodwin's futuristic description of the island-continent of Aleatoria with its Total Social Lottery (1992: 6):

> The Aleatorian system is nothing if not consistent. Just as the task of government [Lotrep] is allocated randomly, so are the various public duties which any state requires to be carried out. The bureaucracy, judiciary, our juries, the police, and our fighting forces are all composed of people chosen by lot for a five-year period. The advantages are similar to those which we enjoy in our Lotrep system. No one holds office long enough to develop a professional ethos, or to invent professional secrets, or to be corrupted.

In contemporary America, for example, every appropriate person has a vote *in electing* the President but, although every appropriate person has also a legitimate right *to be* President, we are not yet ready for a national lottery instead of a presidential campaign. But lottery is precisely what egalitarianism looks like in practice. In my book, in summary, I spoke of radical egalitarianism and, whether one likes that message from Jesus or that interpretation from me, it is not the same as contemporary democracy. It is something infinitely more terrifying than that.

Be that as it may, this paper asks a wider question. Is any historical investigation or any historical reconstruction of importance for Christian faith? By historical study I mean an analysis whose theories and methods, evidence and arguments, results and conclusions are open, in principle and practice, to any human observer, any disciplined investigator, any self-conscious and self-critical student. Abstracting, then, from my own or anyone else's analysis, is such work mere background scenery, mere optional detail, or is it part and parcel of the whole? Granted, of course, that the historical Jesus is always an interpretive construct of its own time and place, but open to all of that time and place, is such a construct always in dialectical tension with faith itself? Bluntly: is Christian faith always (1) an act of faith (2) in the historical Jesus (3) as the manifestation of God? Imagine, for example, these responses from different observers all of whom have heard and seen exactly the same phenomena in the life of Jesus.

> He's dumb, let's ignore him.
> He's lost, let's leave him.
> He's dangerous, let's fight him.
> He's criminal, let's execute him.
> He's divine, let's worship him.

That last response, I propose in this paper, is Christian faith and it was there as soon as it was uttered or performed — before any death or resurrection, just as well as after it.

What I intend to do is locate ourselves in the fifties of that first common-era century and look at four groups, four early Christian groups for whom we have adequate documentation to see something of their faith. I look at how they are responding or not responding to the historical Jesus. I intend to see if the questions we ask here today may have been asked and answered by others long, long ago.

I ask you, however, to observe one methodological discipline in reading this paper. Imagine that you have never known the last chapters of any of the gospels, that you have never been told what happened on that first Easter Sunday. Try, if you can, and, of course, it is almost impossible, to erase that data from your minds. Although those texts seem to tell what happened forty to sixty years before they were written, I ask you to bracket them as we focus instead on what was there in the fifties when, for the first time, we have adequate documentation to discern divergent patterns of Christian faith. I hold that those final chapters in our present gospels have nothing whatsoever to do with the *origins of Christian faith* but have everything to do with the *origins of Christian authority*. Faith, however, must have preceded authority, belief must have preceded power, and questions about who was to lead the communities must have presumed some communities there to lead. In any case, and whether you accept my reason or not, I ask you to bracket what you "know" about Easter Sunday for the duration of this paper. I look, then, within that bracketing, at four types or modes or groups or aspects or emphases (is that adequate hedging?) of earliest Christian faith to see how they are responding to the historical Jesus.

I: Thomas Christianity

By Thomas Christianity I mean the vision of faith expressed in the *Gospel of Thomas* discovered near Nag Hammadi, Upper Egypt, in 1945 (Meyer). This document, terminally called a gospel, contains only sayings, parables, or short dialogues, and has no actions, incidents, miracles, or passion and resurrection accounts. Some scholars have dated the text's original composition between the fifties and seventies of the first century and, while I agree both with a quite early date and a definite independence from the four New Testament gospels, my present location of Thomas faith in the fifties rests on another argument. Those Christians whom Paul is strongly opposing during the winter of 53 to 54 CE in writing 1 Corinthians make eminent sense as Thomas-type Christians. That suggestion was made over a decade ago by Helmut Koester (1980a: 113-119; 1980b: 244-50; 1990: 55-62) and has recently been emphasized once again by Stephen Patterson (1991). In what follows, then, I am watching both that *Gospel of Thomas* and Paul's opponents in 1 Corinthians. Notice, as just one example, this saying in both 1 Cor 2:9-10a and *Gos. Thom.* 17:

> But, as it is written, "What no eye has seen, nor ear heard, nor the heart of man conceived, what God has prepared for those who love him," God has revealed to us through the Spirit. For the Spirit searches everything, even the depths of God.

> Jesus said, "I shall give you what no eye has seen, what no ear has heard, what no hand has touched, what has not arisen in the human heart."

A word of background before proceeding. I imagine early Christianity developing with three major wings, as it were, and my descriptions of them are to be taken neutrally. To the right is a conservative Legal Christianity remaining extremely close to Torah-observant Judaism. To the left is a radical Gnostic Christianity accepting Gnosticism's vision of a Good God of Spirit and an Evil God of Matter locked in mortal combat within the human being, which was but a spiritual spark trapped in a physical prison. In the center is Catholic or Universal Christianity claiming that name as wider than either of those alternatives and compromising with them, on its right by keeping the Hebrew Scriptures, and on its left by approving dietary, sexual, and material asceticism as acceptable for some but not mandatory for all.

Articles, books, and theses have argued that the *Gospel of Thomas* is thoroughly and completely Gnostic and other articles, books, and theses have argued a completely opposite position (Patterson 1990). It seems to me that the gospel is primarily concerned with asceticism rather than Gnosticism and while such a document could easily be read within Gnosticism or even drawn more and more deeply into its sphere, in itself the *Gospel of Thomas* still stands on the borders between Catholic and Gnostic Christianity. In terms of what actually happened, however, Thomas Christianity would eventually move much more fully into the orbit of Gnostic Christianity. I emphasize three major themes in that form of Christian faith.

Wisdom Speaking

Thomas Christianity used no titles except "the Living Jesus" who, yesterday, today, and tomorrow speaks as Wisdom in the midst of an unheeding world, in *Gos. Thom.* 28:

Jesus said, "I took my stand in the midst of the world, and in flesh [with the Greek loan-word *sarx*] I appeared to them. I found them all drunk, and I did not find any of them thirsty. My soul ached for the children of humanity, because they are blind in their hearts and do not see, for they came into the world empty, and they also seek to depart from the world empty. But now they are drunk. When they shake off their wine, then they will repent."

There is not a hint in the *Gospel of Thomas* of any interest in death or resurrection and such would probably have been irrelevant to Jesus as Wisdom *speaking*. Notice, of course, that one *might* be able, by insisting on that *sarx*, to pull Thomas off a trajectory into Gnostic Christianity but such never happened historically.

Paradise Regained

Next, Thomas Christianity is polemically antiapocalyptic. It is enthralled not by the arrival of the end but by the return of the beginning. Its vision is of paradise regained. Whenever "the disciples" ask Jesus questions, for example, they are usually in the wrong and receive corrective answers. Corrections about the end of time appear in *Gos. Thom.* 18, 51, 113 and corrections about the nature of Jesus appear in *Gos. Thom.* 24, 37, 43, 52, 91 (Davies 1983: 82-84; 1992: 678). Both sets of corrections coalesce to say that what they seek is already before their eyes if they can but see it. The polemical overtones of those corrections are also quite evident, in fact derisively so, in *Gos. Thom.* 3:

Jesus said, "If your leaders say to you, 'Behold, the kingdom is in heaven,' then the birds of heaven will precede you. If they say to you, 'It is in the sea,' then the fish will precede you. Rather, the kingdom is within you, and it is outside you."

The Kingdom is, like wisdom, both inside and outside the believer, both an internal gift and a cosmic presence. Or again, in *Gos. Thom.* 18:

The disciples said to Jesus, "Tell us how our end will be." Jesus said, "Have you discovered the beginning, then, that you are seeking after the end. For where the beginning is, the end be. Blessed is one who stands at the beginning: that one will know the end and will not taste death."

Sexual Asceticism

Finally, Thomas Christianity insists on sexual asceticism. This third major theme flows directly from that second one. Here is paradise regained in practice. In *Gos. Thom.* 4, 11, 16, 22, 23, 49, 75, 106 there are a series of sayings extolling the "single one" or the "solitary." This derives from Jewish speculation on the androgynous nature of that first created human being before *it* was split into Adam as Male and Eve as Female. The original "single one" has become "two" by becoming male and female. Thomas Christianity seeks a return not only to Eden before sin but, even earlier, to Eden before sex. The practical result of this vision is, of course, celibate and preferably virginal existence. You can see this stated neutrally in *Gos. Thom.* 22:

> ... when you make male and female into a single one, so that the male will not be male nor the female ... then you will enter [the kingdom].

And you can see it stated with ineffable chauvinism in *Gos. Thom.* 114:

> For every female who makes herself male will enter the kingdom of heaven.

One returned to the dawn of creation, back before that sexual split led to disaster in the Garden of Eden, through nude baptism in which one temporarily took off those garments of shame decreed there after sin and rose from the waters a new creation to live permanently a life of abstention from the world and sexuality.

Such a faith, focused on the hidden meaning of Jesus' esoteric sayings as invitations to asceticism from heavenly wisdom herself, could find the earthly Jesus important but only with increasing difficulty. If and as Thomas Christianity moved steadily into Gnosticism, the historical Jesus would become steadily more and more irrelevant to faith.

II: Pauline Christianity

During the winter of 53 or 54 CE, as we have just seen, that is, from twenty to forty years before the New Testament gospels gave us their last chapters, Paul was writing to the church at Corinth and defending the possibility and actuality of bodily resurrection. I have two main points to make.

The First Fruits of Them That Sleep

As you hear 1 Corinthians 15:12-20 watch very carefully the logic of Paul's argument and pay special attention to the emphasized verses:

> Now if Christ is preached as raised from the dead, how can some of you say that there is no resurrection of the dead? *But if there is no*

resurrection of the dead, then Christ has not been raised; if Christ has not been raised, then our preaching is in vain and your faith is in vain. We are even found to be misrepresenting God, because we testified of God that he raised Christ, whom he did not raise if it is true that the dead are not raised. *For if the dead are not raised, then Christ has not been raised*. If Christ has not been raised, your faith is futile and you are still in your sins. Then those also who have fallen asleep in Christ have perished. If for this life only we have hoped in Christ, we are of all men most to be pitied. But in fact Christ has been raised from the dead, the first fruits of those who have fallen asleep.

Paul never argues that Jesus' resurrection was a unique privilege afforded only to him. That would have been a perfectly possible proposal since ancient Judaism believed that Elijah, for example, had been taken up to heaven but never presumed that privilege applied to all others as well. Why was Jesus not just another special case, another individual prerogative with no wider application than himself? Why, as those italics emphasize, is Jesus' resurrection actually dependent on the general resurrection?

It has often been said that Paul believed the end of the world was at hand. It is more accurate to say that he believed *it had already begun* for that is his logic in the preceding passage. As a Pharisee he believed in the general resurrection at the end of time. But Jesus, he claims, has already risen as the start of the general resurrection. Notice his metaphor. Jesus is the "first fruits," that is to say, the beginning of the harvest, the start of the general resurrection. That is why he can argue in either direction: no Jesus resurrection, no general resurrection, or, no general resurrection, no Jesus resurrection. They stand or fall together and Paul presumes that only the mercy of God delays the final consummation, the ending of what has already started. The *Titanic* has, as it were, already hit the iceberg and Paul's mission is to wake the cabins as far and as wide as possible. While God gives time. In such a theological vision, resurrection is the only possible way to articulate the presence of Jesus for Paul, but it is also inextricably linked to the imminent general resurrection at the end of the world.

If you focused just on those verses and that argument, you could persuasively argue that the historical Jesus is as irrelevant for Pauline Christianity as it was and would be for Thomas Christianity. Granted, of course, that one must die in order to resurrect but that is surely the bare minimum true of every human being. One lives and, without being told, we know what comes next: one dies. If that is the faith of Pauline Christianity, then *how* Jesus died is totally irrelevant. Only death was required, the type and mode would be irrelevant. He could be the "first fruits" of the general resurrection, no matter how he died.

The Folly of the Cross

Notice that it is precisely in 1 Corinthians where Paul is debating with a Thomas-type faith, although of course other places as well, that he insists inaugurally on the mode and not just the fact of Jesus' death. He did not just die, he was executed; he was not just executed, he was crucified. Here, as just one example, are some quotations from the famous section in 1 Corinthians 1:17-31:

> For Christ did not send me to baptize but to preach the gospel, and not with eloquent wisdom, lest the cross of Christ be emptied of its power.
>
> For the word of the cross is folly to those who are perishing, but to us who are being saved it is the power of God. For it is written, "I will destroy the wisdom of the wise, and the cleverness of the clever I will thwart." Where is the wise man? Where is the scribe? Where is the debater of this age? Has not God made foolish the wisdom of the world? For since, in the wisdom of God, the world did not know God through wisdom, it pleased God through the folly of what we preach to save those who believe. For Jews demand signs and Greeks seek wisdom, but we preach Christ crucified, a stumbling block to Jews and folly to Gentiles, but to those who are called, both Jews and Greeks, Christ the power of God and the wisdom of God. For the foolishness of God is wiser than men, and the weakness of God is stronger than men.
>
> For consider your call, brethren; not many of you were wise according to worldly standards, not many were powerful, not many were of noble birth; but God chose what is foolish in the world to shame the wise, God chose what is weak in the world to shame the strong, God chose what is low and despised in the world, even things that are not, to bring to nothing things that are, so that no human being might boast in the presence of God. He is the source of your life in Christ Jesus, whom God made our wisdom, our righteousness and sanctification and redemption; therefore, as it is written, "Let him who boasts, boast of the Lord."

Martin Hengel's 1977 book, *Crucifixion*, is the terrible commentary on that passage as it would have been understood by first-century hearers. It is a catalogue of horror and a concordance of terror citing text after text concerning crucifixion. It was an execution primarily for the lower classes or for those who were being deliberately degraded to that level by its imposition. It was intended as a theater of deterrence especially for those who threatened in any way imperial Roman power. Along with fire and the beasts, it was one of three *supreme* penalties that were *supreme* precisely because there would not be anything left to bury. This is Hengel's summary (86-88):

> Crucifixion as a penalty was remarkably widespread in antiquity. It appears in various forms among numerous peoples of the ancient

world, even among the Greeks. . . . [It] was and remained a political and military punishment. While among the Persians and the Carthaginians it was imposed primarily on high officials and commanders, as on rebels, among the Romans it was inflicted above all on the lower classes, i.e., slaves, violent criminals, and the unruly elements in rebellious provinces, not least in Judaea. The chief reason for its use was its allegedly supreme efficacy as a deterrent; it was, of course, carried out publicly. . . . It was usually associated with other forms of torture, including at least flogging. . . . By the public display of a naked victim at a prominent place — at a crossroads, in the theatre, on high ground, at the place of his crime — crucifixion also represented his uttermost humiliation, which had a numinous dimension to it. With Deuteronomy 21.23 in the background, the Jew in particular was very aware of this. . . . Crucifixion was aggravated further by the fact that quite often its victims were never buried. It was a stereotyped picture that the crucified victim served as food for wild beasts and birds of prey. In this way his humiliation was made complete. What it meant for a man in antiquity to be refused burial, and the dishonour which went with it, can hardly be appreciated by modern man.

Crucifixion meant being left on the cross for croaking raven and scavenging dog who permanently hovered or prowled those set places of public execution attracted by the smell of sweat and blood, urine and excrement. Maybe one's friends or relatives might get permission to bury what was left but, in general, if one had such influence, one was not crucified, and if one was crucified, one did not have the influence to get a proper burial. And *if* (a very big if) pagan soldiers in the Jewish homeland actually observed Deuteronomy 21:22-23 and buried crucifieds by sunset, it was not much more than a nearby shallow grave and still the dogs were watching and waiting. That is what Paul means by the folly of the cross, the absurdity of preaching a crucified savior.

I conclude, first, that, for Paul, the historical Jesus, particularly and precisely in the terrible and servile form of his execution, is part of Christian faith. It is to the historical Jesus so executed that he responds in faith.

There is also a second conclusion. A vision of the resurrected Jesus was absolutely significant in Paul's case. Visions will not be operative in either of the next two cases. They may have been there, of course, but Q Christianity was primarily interested in living like Jesus and Exegetical Christianity was primarily interested in searching the scriptures. Their faith was there before Jesus died and, for them, Easter meant not creation but continuation.

Here, for example, is a model for Christian faith intended not to deny the validity of Paul's experience but to question strongly its exclusive normativity. There is this story in Mark 14:3-9:

And while he was at Bethany in the house of Simon the leper, as he sat at table, a woman came with an alabaster flask of ointment of pure nard, very costly, and she broke the flask and poured it over his head. But there were some who said to themselves indignantly, "Why was the ointment thus wasted? For this ointment might have been sold for more than three hundred denarii, and given to the poor." And they reproached her. But Jesus said, "Let her alone; why do you trouble her? She has done a beautiful thing to me. For you always have the poor with you, and whenever you will, you can do good to them; but you will not always have me. She has done what she could; she has anointed my body beforehand for burying. And truly, I say to you, wherever the gospel is preached in the whole world, what she has done will be told in memory of her."

Why is this unnamed woman so important? Why does she get that absolutely stunning accolade from Jesus at the end? Why is this precise action and none other in any other gospel singled out for such an extraordinary comment?

As Jesus and his male disciples journeyed to Jerusalem and his death, he told them three times that he would die and rise again. I consider those three prophecies in Mark 8:31, 9:30-32, 10:32-34 to have been created by Mark himself just as are the reactions of the disciples after each one. They ignore, deny, dismiss, or avoid discussing those fatal predictions. But now, in the home of Simon the Leper, for the first time somebody believes that Jesus is going to die and that unless it is done now, his body can never be anointed.

Earlier commentators often discussed whether that unnamed young man fleeing naked into the night from the Garden of Gethsemane in Mark 14:51-52 might be Mark himself obliquely and indirectly signing his narrative. It is just as possible, even more credible, but unfortunately quite as unprovable, to suggest that the unnamed woman in Mark 14:3-9 is "Mark" herself obliquely and indirectly signing her narrative. That, however, is not the point. We cannot ever be sure whether Mark was a woman or a man. We can, however, be absolutely sure that the author of this gospel placed on Jesus' lips the choice of an unnamed woman for the supreme model of Christian faith, for that faith that was there before, despite, and even because of Jesus' death. For Paul, Easter came late that year. For Her, Easter came early that year.

III: Q Christianity

A third type of earliest Christian faith is that of the community behind the document scholars call Q, an abbreviation for the German word *Quelle* or source. A more proper title that treats it in its own right and not just as a source or Quelle might be the *Synoptic Sayings Gospel* or, more simply, the *Q Gospel*. It is not a document presently available in manuscript copy, as in the two preceding cases, but a hypothetical reconstruction from those places where Matthew and Luke agree with one another in order and content but do not derive such data from their other main source, Mark (Jacobson; Mack 1993).

Into Whatever House You Enter

This faith shows no interest in the death and resurrection of Jesus, but sees him as speaking for Wisdom, or better, living according to Wisdom and empowering others to do so, then, now, and always. Although its apocalyptic expectation is not as fundamental for its faith as is Paul's, it uses it again and again to warn and threaten those who are refusing its message. I focus on one key text, best seen at Luke 10:2-11, and I ask you to recognize the reciprocity of eating and healing that is basic to it:

> And he said to them, "The harvest is plentiful, but the laborers are few; pray therefore the Lord of the harvest to send out laborers into his harvest. Go your way; behold, I send you out as lambs in the midst of wolves. Carry no purse, no bag, no sandals; and salute no one on the road. Whatever house you enter, first say, 'Peace be to this house!' And if a son of peace is there, your peace shall rest upon him; but if not, it shall return to you. And remain in the same house, eating and drinking what they provide, for the laborer deserves his wages [in Luke; but food, in Matthew]; do not go from house to house. Whenever you enter a town and they receive you, eat what is set before you; heal the sick in it and say to them, 'The kingdom of God has come near to you.' But whenever you enter a town and they do not receive you, go into its streets and say, 'Even the dust of your town that clings to our feet, we wipe off against you; nevertheless know this, that the kingdom of God has come near.' "

In what follows I make two points to understand the faith of the community behind the *Q Gospel*.

Two by Two

We are told in Luke 10:1 that those messengers or missionaries were sent out "two by two." Why? We know that the rabbis often traveled on official business in twos but that was much later, after the destruction of Jerusalem's Temple in 70 CE. There is no evidence of such a procedure at the time of Jesus. There are two other texts that may clarify what is happening. One is that highly symbolic story, in which two followers of Jesus travel from Jerusalem to Emmaus on Easter Sunday. One of them is identified as Cleopas, a male, the other is left unidentified. I presume, in such a combination of named and unnamed pairs, especially in Mediterranean society, that the second person was a woman. She is not, however, specified as *his* wife. Another text is this one in 1 Corinthians 9:5, in a context where Paul is discussing his own missionary activities:

> Do we not have the right to be accompanied by a believing wife (*adelphēn gynaika*), as the other apostles and the brothers of the Lord and Cephas?

That translation makes the problem a simple one of support for both the missionary and his wife, with the literal Greek "sister wife" collapsed into the English "wife." But is Paul talking about real, married wives, and, if so, how exactly are we to imagine what happened to their children in such situations? And, more specifically, how could the unmarried Paul be accompanied by his wife? My proposal is that a "sister wife" means exactly what it says: a female missionary who travels with a male missionary as if, for the world at large, she was his wife. The obvious function of such a tactic would be to furnish the best social protection for a traveling female missionary in a world of male power and violence. If society, by the way, got wind of it, the term for such women would be "whores," the standard description for any women outside normal social convention or outside normal male control. Jesus, of course, would then be consorting with "whores."

Turning now from persons to places, to where exactly were those followers of Jesus sent? What I am watching here is the move from visiting *houses* grouped together as tiny *hamlets* near the fields, to visiting *towns* with some market capacity, and on to visiting *cities* with public buildings and possibly walls. In the first half of our text, for example, at Luke 10:5-7, a "house" destination is mentioned four times, but in the second half, at Luke 10:8-11, a "town" (literally *polis*, a city) is mentioned twice.

Recent scholarship on the *Q Gospel*, and especially the work of John S. Kloppenborg, has argued for two distinct layers in the composition of that Gospel. An earlier one emphasized primarily a lifestyle and missionary activity that, despite the expectation of opposition and even persecution, was remarkably open and hopeful. Later came a second one, far more dark and defensive, threatening dire apocalyptic vengeance against "this generation" for refusing to accept their witness. What happened to change the community's vision may possibly be seen in that very change from *house to town*, from Luke 10:5-7 to 10:8-11. What may well have happened to the communities of the *Q Gospel* was that a relatively successful mission to the small *houses* of the villages and countryside turned into a comparatively obvious failure as they moved into *towns* such as, for example, Chorazin, Bethsaida, and Capernaum.

Carry No Knapsack

Recall that the *Q Gospel* at Luke 10:4 commanded those messengers to "Carry no purse, no bag, no sandals; and salute no one on the road" (Vaage; Downing 1987). I focus here on just one of those elements: no bag or knapsack. Why that injunction? The answer involves a look at some other radical missionaries who, in the first century, preached to the ordinary people a message both by what they said and how they lived, both by what they taught and how they dressed. Enter the Cynics (Dudley; Sayre).

Cynicism was a Greek philosophical movement founded by Diogenes of Sinope who was born on the mid-southern coast of the Black Sea and lived between 400 and 320 BCE. The term itself means Dogism, coming from *kyon*, the Greek word for dog, and it was used, as if quoting a well-known nickname, of Diogenes by Aristotle. It was originally a derogatory term for the provocative shamelessness with which Diogenes deliberately flouted basic human codes of propriety and decency, custom and convention. We use cynicism today to mean belief in nothing or doubt about everything, but what it means philosophically is theoretical disbelief *and* practical negation of ordinary cultural values and civilized presuppositions.

The classic Cynic story is that of the encounter between Diogenes and Alexander the Great at Corinth in 336 BCE. The latter is just setting out to conquer the world through military power, the former had already done so through disciplined indifference. This oft-told tale was already known to Cicero in his *Tusculan Disputations* 5.92 (King: 518-19) from 45 BCE:

> But Diogenes, certainly, was more outspoken in his quality of Cynic, when Alexander asked him to name anything he wanted: "Just now," he said, "stand a bit away from the sun!" Alexander apparently had interfered with his basking in the heat.

That story is a calculated questioning of power, rule, dominion, and kingship? Who is the true ruler: the one who wants everything, or the one who wants nothing; the one who wants all of Asia, or the one who wants only a little sunlight? And just as Cynicism had a first flowering after the conquests of Alexander, centuries before Jesus, so it had another after those of Augustus, at the time of Jesus. Both times were ripe for a fundamental questioning of power and the Cynics did it not only in abstract theory among the aristocratic elites but in practical street theater among the ordinary people. They were populist preachers in marketplace and pilgrimage center, and their life and dress spoke as forcibly as their speech and sermon. Cynicism was, in other words, the Greco-Roman form of that universal philosophy of eschatology or world-negation, one of the great and fundamental options of the human spirit. For wherever there is culture and civilization, there can also be counterculture and anticivilization.

One striking difference, however, between Jesus missionaries and Cynic missionaries is in that knapsack. The Cynics wore it proudly and programmatically to symbolize their complete self-sufficiency. They carried their homes with them. They needed nothing that could not be carried in a simple knapsack slung over their shoulders. But the Jesus missionaries, in contrast, are told precisely to carry no knapsack. Since a reciprocity of healing and eating is at the heart of the Jesus movement, no knapsack is symbolically correct for them. They are not urban like the Cynics, preaching at street corner and marketplace. They are rural, on a house-mission to rebuild peasant society from the grassroots upward. Since commensality is not just a technique for support, but a demonstration of message, they could not and should not dress to declare itinerant self-sufficiency but rather communal dependency.

The faith of the Q community is faith in the historical Jesus in an almost physical sense of the term. They are living and acting in continuity with his life to the point where faith and imitation are indistinguishable. Except, of course, that they are not just imitating Jesus, they are imitating, like him, Wisdom's truest lifestyle. To believe that the Wisdom of God appeared performancially in Jesus' life meant, for them, to live likewise. That faith was there before he died and continued not so much despite, but because of, it. He had warned them to expect refusal and even persecution, to live the life of Wisdom spurned. I wonder if anyone ever told them that they had lost their faith on Good Friday and had it restored by visions on Easter Sunday?

IV: Exegetical Christianity

My fourth, and final, example, comes from the world of scribal learning, exegetical dexterity, and even hermeneutical gymnastics. I refer to those individuals and groups who, after the execution of Jesus and probably in Jerusalem, began to search their scriptures not just to find apologetical or polemical ammunition against others but to find foundational and textual understanding for themselves. A word of background, to begin with.

The Jewish sect of the Essenes, whose home at Qumran was destroyed during the First Roman-Jewish War and whose hidden library has given us the Dead Sea Scrolls, applied prophetic writings from the Hebrew Scriptures to their own past history and present situation. They were a priestly-led group who withdrew from Jerusalem's Temple to a "monastery" on the Dead Sea's northwest coast. They judged that the Temple was polluted after the usurpation of the High Priesthood by Jewish rulers of the Hasmonean dynasty, Jonathan and Simon, between 152 and 134 BCE. Their biblical applications evince a dense intertextual weave between old and new, past and present, a work of skilled exegetes and learned scribes where intense concentration is often needed to distinguish Bible from Commentary (Crossan 1991: 368-70). If your eyes spin in reading those laminated texts or your heads spin in hearing them read, that is precisely the point. You should not be able too easily to take them apart and see how they were constructed.

I maintain that Jesus' first followers knew almost nothing whatsoever about the details of his crucifixion, death, or burial. What we have now in those detailed passion accounts is not *history remembered* but *prophecy historicized*. We have, in other words, Exegetical Christianity.

In testing this hypothesis, forget all you "know" about Easter Sunday from accounts written in our Gospels between forty and sixty years after the event. Bracket even what you know from 1 Corinthians 15 written twenty years after the event (but you can cheat a little and recall from there that Paul said "Christ died *for our sins* in accordance with the scriptures" [emphasis mine]). Imagine, instead, learned followers of Jesus beginning to search their scriptures *immediately* after the crucifixion. Imagine what preceded those gospels of forty to sixty years later and without which they might never have existed.

Locate yourself on the first Holy Saturday, *a day which is going to last about, say, five or ten years*. You are among certain followers of Jesus who are not at all peasants, are not at all interested in miracles, are not at all interested in collecting, preserving, or creating Jesus-sayings, but are very, very interested in studying the scriptures to understand your past, reclaim your present, and envisage your future. What do you find, what do you produce? You know, first of all, exactly what you are looking for. You search for texts that show death not as end but as beginning, not as divine judgment but divine plan, not as ultimate defeat but postponed victory for Jesus. You are, therefore, especially looking for texts with a certain duality, a certain hint of two stages, two moments, two phases, or two levels.

One such text is the ritual of the Jewish Day of Atonement, which has *two* goats, one driven out into the desert carrying the sins of the people, and the other presented for sacrifice in the Temple (Crossan 1988: 114-59; 1991: 376-83). The basic text is in Leviticus 16:7-10 and 21-22 describing the ritual as mandated by God to Aaron, the first High Priest.

> He [Aaron] shall take the two goats and set them before the LORD at the entrance of the tent of meeting [the predecessor of the Temple during the desert period of the Exodus]; and Aaron shall cast lots on the two goats, one lot for the LORD [this goat is to be sacrificed within the Temple itself] and the other lot for Azazel [this goat is to be driven out to Azazel, demon of the desert]. Aaron shall present the goat on which the lot fell for the LORD, and offer it as a sin offering [in the Temple]; but the goat on which the lot fell for Azazel shall be presented alive before the LORD to make atonement over it, that it may be sent away into the wilderness to Azazel . . . Then Aaron shall lay both his hands on the head of the live goat, and confess over it all the iniquities of the people of Israel, and all their transgressions,

all their sins, putting them on the head of the goat, and sending it away into the wilderness by means of someone designated for the task. The goat shall bear on itself all their iniquities to a barren region and the goat shall be set free in the wilderness.

You, as a Jerusalem Jew, have probably seen that actual ritual and are not just imagining it from the biblical text alone. We, however, also know four precise details about that ritual's actual process from the *Mishnah*, the rabbinical code of law organized around 200 CE by Judah the Patriarch. The two goats had to be alike and equal, scarlet wool was placed on the scapegoat's head, it was abused by the people as it was hurried towards the desert, and, before it was killed there the scarlet wool was attached between a rock and its horns. You would have known that the scarlet wool recalled Isaiah 1:18 and God's promise: "though your sins are like scarlet, they shall be as like snow; though they are red like crimson, they shall become like wool." And, as long as you were thinking about Isaiah, that abuse in which the people symbolically and emphatically transferred their sins to the poor doomed animal reminded you of Isaiah 50:6, "I gave my back to those who struck me, and my cheeks to those who pulled out the beard; I hid not my face from insult and spitting." You knew that the people spat their sins onto the scapegoat and that they used reeds to poke and hurry the poor animal towards its desert fate. Such spitting and poking or piercing was not, of course, just cruelty but a physical participation in the ritual itself.

Your choice of the Day of Atonement and its twin goats was not, to be quite frank, a very happy choice. Jesus could easily be interpreted as the scapegoat, the goat driven and killed outside the city as an atonement *for the sins* of the people (you may now cheat and recall "for our sins" in 1 Cor 15:3). But that second goat is also sacrificed, albeit in the Temple itself, and that sounds just like another but different version of the passion. Something more was clearly needed and it was there, as far as we can see, from the beginning.

As you read Leviticus 16 or recalled the ritual you would must have noted that Aaron is told in 16:23-24 to change his garments:

Then Aaron shall enter the tent of meeting, and shall take off the linen vestments that he put on when he went into the holy place, and shall leave them there. He shall bathe his body in water in a holy place, and put on his vestments; Then he shall come out and offer his burnt offering and the burnt offering of the people, and making atonement for himself and for the people.

And that change of garments by the High Priest, Aaron, easily reminded you of Zechariah 3:3-5, where, in the late sixth-century BCE just after the

Jewish leadership had returned from the Babylonian Exile, the High Priest, Joshua, is imagined having his garments changed by an angel:

> Now Joshua was dressed with filthy garments as he stood before the angel. The angel said to those who were standing before him, "Take off his filthy clothes." And to him he said, "See I have taken your guilt away from you, and I will clothe you with festal apparel [in Greek: a long robe]." And I said, "Let them put a clean turban on his head." So they put a clean turban on his head and clothed him with the apparel; and the angel of the LORD was standing by.

Now your search is starting to get somewhere. Of the twin goats, the first or scapegoat worked best as a prophetic or interpretative type of the cross, the second was a little redundant. But those twin garments, one filthy and one clean, worked much better as a prophetic type of Jesus, first dishonored at the cross, and then triumphant at his second coming. And, as long as you were in Zechariah, and thinking along those lines, it was easy enough to go from 3:1-5 on to 12:10:

> And I will pour out a spirit of compassion and supplication on the house of David and the inhabitants of Jerusalem, so that, when they look on the one whom they have pierced, they shall mourn for him, as one mourns for an only child, and weep bitterly over him, as one weeps over a firstborn.

You have now arched beautifully and completely from past to future, from passion to parousia, from Jesus crucified to Jesus triumphant, from the day of piercing to the day on which those who pierced Jesus would mourn for him and for what they had done.

Here, finally, is a Christian document which shows that entire exegetical procedure. It combines all four strata: the TWO GOATS of Leviticus 16 from Bible and *Mishnah*, in underlined text; the CROWNING and ROBING of Zechariah 3, in bold roman text; the SEEING and PIERCING of Zechariah 12, in bold italic text; and the SPITTING of Isaiah 50, in ordinary italic text. These are all laminated into one demonstration that Jesus' past crucifixion pointed inevitably toward his future victory. The section is developed through four questions based on the actual ritual of the Day of Atonement. This is in the *Epistle of Barnabas* at 7:6-12, a book written toward the end of the first-century CE but showing no knowledge of the New Testament Gospels (Lake: 1.340-409).

> Note what was commanded: "Take two goats, goodly and alike, and offer them, and let the priest take the one as a burnt offering for sins."
> [1] But what are they to do with the other?

"The other," he says, "is accursed." Notice how the type of Jesus is manifested: *"And do ye all spit on it,* **and goad [pierce] it,** and bind the scarlet wool about its head, and so let it be cast into the desert." And when it is so done, he who takes the goat into the wilderness drives it forth, and takes away the wool, and puts it upon a shrub [instead of the rock] . . .

[2] What does this mean?

Listen: "the first goat is for the altar, but the other is accursed," and note that the one that is accursed is **crowned** because then *"they will see him on that day"* with the long scarlet robe *"down to the feet"* on his body, and they will say, "Is not this he whom we once crucified and rejected *and pierced and spat upon?* Of a truth it was he who then said that he was the Son of God."

[3] But how is he like the goat?

For this reason: "the goats shall be alike, beautiful, and a pair," in order that when they see him come at that time they may be astonished at the likeness of the goat. See then the type of Jesus destined to suffer.

[4] But why is it that they put the wool in the middle of the thorns? It is a type of Jesus placed in the Church, because whoever wishes to take away the scarlet wool must suffer much because the thorns are terrible and he can gain it only through pain. Thus he says, "those who will see me, and attain to my kingdom must lay hold of me through pain and suffering."

If, by the way, our eyes or heads are now spinning, that is part of the process. We are persuaded of the validity of the argument by the sheer difficulty in taking it apart. It is almost easier just to listen and nod, or read and agree than to analyze, explore, and disentangle.

Exegetical laminations such as the above were what certain learned followers of Jesus were doing in the years immediately after his death and it was passion-parousia rather than passion-resurrection on which they were concentrating. That, and other similar examples, is what the *prophetic passion* looked like for years and still continued to do so for skilled exegetes long after the next stage, the *narrative passion*, developed and separated from it.

Imagine the faith of those learned exegetes. They are certainly in a social class above the Q Christians and they have an interest in the Hebrew Scriptures that the *Gospel of Thomas* would find absolutely inappropriate, as in *Gos. Thom.* 52 (with "the disciples" wrong once again):

His disciples said to him, "Twenty-four prophets have spoken in Israel, and they all spoke of you." He said to them, "You have disregarded the living one who is in your presence, and have spoken of the dead."

But how does one express the relationship of Exegetical Christianity to the historical Jesus? Their faith in the historical Jesus was so strong that they were constantly inventing more of it all the time, more of the history, that is, so that there could be more of the faith! A large amount of the *words* of Jesus were preserved because communities like those of the *Q Gospel* or the *Gospel of Thomas* were trying to live by them. That is to say, they remembered he said no sandals because their feet hurt and not just because they had memorized it well. But a large amount of the *deeds* of Jesus were created within Exegetical Christianity. They believed in the historical Jesus so much that they kept creating more and more of him out of biblical type and prophetic text.

Epilogue: Historical Jesus and Christian Faith

Those four examples are all I have and three of them express faith in the historical Jesus, a faith differentiated indeed by divergent emphases and aspects and understandings of that historical Jesus. I draw two conclusions, at least as challenges for further discussion.

First, it is certainly possible to have Christian faith without any constitutive reference to the historical Jesus. It is called Gnostic Christianity and its possible trajectory is already latent, at least with hindsight, in the *Gospel of Thomas* and those Thomas-style Christians Paul knew at Corinth in the early fifties. And I presume it is still with us today. Apart from that, however, Christian faith, at least in Catholic Christianity, is *belief in the historical Jesus as the manifestation of God*. I think, in other words, that at the heart of any form of Catholic Christianity there is always a dialectic between an historically-read Jesus and a theologically-read Christ. But any analysis of an historical Jesus must be open to the disciplined historical methods of its *contemporary* world and must be able to stand up to its judgments without special pleading. I presume that there will always be divergent historical Jesus-s, that there will always be divergent Christ-s built upon them, but I argue, above all, that the structure of a Christianity will always be: *this is how we see Jesus-then as Christ-now*. I am proposing that the dialectic between Jesus-s and Christ-s (or Sons, or Lords, or Wisdoms, or Whatevers) is at the heart of both tradition and canon, that it is perfectly valid, has always been with us and probably always will be, at least in Catholic Christianity.

Second, about three hundred years after the crucifixion of Jesus, on the twenty-eighth of October in 312 CE, the Roman Emperor Constantine, believing that victory over his imperial rival Maxentius near Rome's Milvian Bridge had been obtained by Christ's power, converted to Christianity. It is interesting, by the way, that we know that event to the day but we know the date of Jesus' death only as sometime within a decade of years, from 26 to 36 CE. In any case, Constantine, wanting a unified Christianity as the

Empire's new religion, ordered the Christian bishops to meet, under imperial subsidy, in lakeside Nicea southeast of Constantinople and there erase any major theological disagreements between them. Even if one is not already somewhat disquieted at imperial convocation, presence, and participation, it is hard not to become very nervous in reading this description of the imperial banquet celebrating the Council of Nicea's conclusion, from Eusebius' *Life of Constantine* 3.15:

> Detachments of the body-guard and troops surrounded the entrance of the palace with drawn swords, and through the midst of them the men of God proceeded without fear into the innermost of the Imperial apartments, in which some were the Emperor's companions at table, while others reclined on couches arranged on either side. One might have thought that a picture of Christ's kingdom was thus shadowed forth, and a dream rather than reality.

A Christian leader now writes a life, not of Jesus, but of Constantine. The meal and the Kingdom still come together but now the participants are the male bishops alone and they recline, with the Emperor himself, to be served by others. Dream or reality? Dream or nightmare?

It is, of course, an example of that dialectic just proposed between historical Jesus and confessional Christ, of peasant Jesus grasped now by imperial faith. Still as one ponders that progress from open commensality with Jesus to episcopal banquet with Constantine, is it unfair to regret that it all happened so fast and moved so swiftly, that it was accepted so readily and criticized so lightly? Is it time now, or is it already too late, to conduct, religiously and theologically, ethically and morally, some basic cost-accounting over Constantine?

2.

to impose is not / To Discover

Methodology in John Dominic Crossan's The Historical Jesus

BERNARD BRANDON SCOTT

John Dominic Crossan's *The Historical Jesus: The Life of a Mediterranean Jewish Peasant* is the achievement of a lifetime of reflection on the historical Jesus and the Jesus tradition. In responding to such an ambitious work, the temptation is to pick away at the small points and miss the real meat. I want to situate this book within the context or trajectory of Crossan's own work. By following such a path I hope to show the development of his method and summarize the methodological contribution of this new book. I take as a guidepost in judging these methodological developments these lines from Wallace Stevens: "to impose is not / To discover" (Stevens 1990: 403). Stevens' warning is appropriate in discussing method since sometimes the glittering method hides the data it seeks to expose. Method should produce insight, not just rearrange the data. Wallace Stevens also makes an appropriate, though ironic, guide since *The Historical Jesus* is one of the few books of Crossan's that does not have a poetic title.

Throughout his career, John Dominic Crossan has engaged in a series of ongoing experiments in both formal method and theology. These experiments culminate in his *The Historical Jesus: The Life of a Mediterranean Jewish Peasant*. I do not believe for a minute that this current point is terminal, but it does represent a significant apex of a life's work. My concern is primarily Crossan's methodology, although at the end I want to turn my attention to a significant theological current that runs throughout Crossan's work. I might even be cajoled at the end of this paper to predict Crossan's next work.

The Three Bears

New Testament scholarship reflects the currents of the wider intellectual world of which it is part. Charles Darwin and Ferdinand de Saussure can

22

stand as the two great emblems of modern science. Darwin, the father of evolutionary biology, bequeathed to us as part of his unintentional legacy the model of historical development. This idea has proven so fecund that it has led us to view biblical criticism under the model of archaeology, using historical tools to examine the layers of the text and early Christianity. At the turn of the century Saussure began a quieter revolution, a revolution that has now triumphed in the intellectual world. Saussure rejected the explanatory power of the diachronic to explain the particular and instituted the science of the synchronic, which examines the particular as part of a system. For Saussure we understand the particular, not by knowing where it comes from, but by how it functions within its current context. With one notable exception, Crossan has followed Saussure.

In one of Crossan's earliest books, *In Parables: The Challenge of the Historical Jesus,* he demonstrated an almost surgical skill in the use of the newly developed redaction criticism to separate redaction from tradition in the reconstruction of various parables. This surgical tool, while greatly modified over the years, has remained a practiced one in Crossan's craft. Reconstruction is one of three methodological steps that are typical of Crossan. While *In Parables* methodologically remains well within the Darwinian tradition of New Testament criticism, it experimented in its use of redaction criticism to advance form-critical efforts and Martin Heidegger's categories of time to organize the parables. This latter issue provides the second clue to Crossan's methodology: formalism. Even though Crossan is not particularly attracted to Platonic forms, he frequently engages in a formalism that allows him to systematize historical particularity. His use of Heidegger to create a formal order for the parables is an early example of this tendency.

In Parables was both a beginning and an end. It marked not only Crossan's entrance into parable studies but also, in a real sense, was the last "traditional" book he would write. Its methodology fell well within the bounds of traditional historical criticism. From this point on, he began to experiment with a variety of methodological perspectives, especially those drawn from secular literary criticism. The earliest of these methodologies, which left an indelible cast on his work, was structuralism. With this turn toward Saussure, he began to move away from a Darwinian understanding of the sciences. This influence may well derive from his participation in the Parables Seminar of the Society of Biblical Literature, a seminar which he chaired.

Two aspects of structuralism that have most affected his work are synchronicity and the formalistic assumptions of structuralism, a tendency he already had. I do not think that Crossan can be classified a structuralist, or poststructuralist or something else. He is in many ways *sui generis*. He might even be described as a scholarly *bricoleur*, to borrow Claude Lévi-Strauss's term for the mythmaker. This is not to impugn inconsistency, eclecticism, or syncretism to his methodological choices, but to point out that the data to be analyzed drives his methodologies, the need to account for the anomalies that he confronts.

Crossan's influential *The Dark Interval: Towards a Theology of Story* illustrates this new shift in his work. Structuralism evidences itself not only in the use of A.J. Greimas's model of actants, but more importantly in the use of parable and myth as formal models, not just literary types. One might even argue that myth and parable function for Crossan as epistemological types. Formalism combines with synchronicity to incline Crossan to view myth and parable as systems. Yet Crossan always remains true to his original training as a historical critic, and so what he actually produces is a synchronic analysis of a diachronic phenomenon. He traces, for example, the diachronic tradition of the synchronic model parable through the Hebrew Bible (the Book of Ruth) and the modern examples of Franz Kafka and Jorge Borges. He vigorously pursued this way of thinking in his *Raid on the Articulate: Comic Eschatology in Jesus and Borges*.

The King Is in His Counting House

In terms of experiments leading directly to his *The Historical Jesus*, Crossan's *Finding Is the First Act* plays an extremely important role. The entire treasure-trove tradition forms the basis for a synchronic analysis. Theoretically, all folk treasure-trove stories form the context for the analysis of the one parable in Matthew (13:44). Practically, the analysis depends on as many treasure-trove stories as Crossan could collect. This is intertextuality on a wide scale. As a parable interpreter myself, I found this methodology both convincing and daunting, since it would have demanded an encyclopedia as the appropriate model for writing a book on all the Jesus parables. Crossan also derives from his synchronic analysis of treasure-trove stories a formal model for the telling of the story. This model then serves to illustrate how the Jesus parable deconstructs or defamiliarizes the formal structure. This totalizing synchronicity is an important model for Crossan's *The Historical Jesus*.

Crossan's next move, *In Fragments: The Aphorisms of Jesus*, is equally daring and advanced his project along similar lines. Only the synchronic construct shifts from a single story to a form: Form criticism (*Formgeschichte*) had studied these sayings diachronically and individually. Now Crossan subjected them to a synchronic analysis. This method allows Crossan to deal with an aphoristic core that not only grew and developed diachronically, but, more importantly, has its own internal rules of transformation. Thus, the whole aphoristic tradition becomes a system with formal rules. This development is critical for the methodology underlying *The Historical Jesus*, since it enables Crossan to construct the inventory on which the selection of the data for analysis depends. *In Fragments* clearly demonstrates Crossan's three methodological moves: reconstruction of the system; formalism in the development of the aphoristic model; and synchronicity in the functioning of the aphoristic tradition as single system.

Equally important, though unnoticed, is Crossan's *Sayings Parallels: A Workbook for the Jesus Tradition*, for here he began the inventory that underlies *The Historical Jesus*. Significantly, this inventory included noncanonical sayings.

A final formal step involved his analyses of the gospels. His *Four Other Gospels: Shadows on the Contours of Canon* and *The Cross That Spoke: The Origins of the Passion Narrative* led him to develop a theory of stratification that involves a careful reconstruction and a formalization of the gospel tradition. These two works continue Crossan's passion for reconstruction and layering based on the model of biblical studies as archaelogy. At the same time, he does not view the texts individualistically, but as parts of a system. Since Crossan understands the whole of early Christianity as a synchronic system, categories like canon play no evaluative function. While this has been controversial, it is surely the correct step since the canon is a theological and ecclesial evaluation and not a historical judgment.

Crossan's previous work is a series of experiments that lead up to the book under discussion and the methodology used to build and sort the inventory of the data of the Jesus tradition. *The Historical Jesus* is the culmination of those experiments.

All the King's Horses and All the King's Men
Cannot Put Humpty Dumpty Together Again

In Appendix 1 of *The Historical Jesus* (434-450) Crossan arranges the data of the tradition into complexes, and each complex contains all the attested versions of a saying/theme. These complexes are the smallest functioning synchronic units. For the most part, they are readily constructed and are not controversial. Only a very few times did I find myself questioning whether a particular saying belongs to a complex, and while one could debate these issues, they are not critical to Crossan's overall argument. Crossan then evaluates each complex on the basis of two interlocking criteria. How many times does it have independent attestation, and at what levels within the stratification does it occur? Crossan sorts the database according to these criteria.

Before critiquing this methodology, its significance should be noted. The quest for the historical Jesus has floundered because it lacked a sure base. The great merit and eventual undoing of E.P. Sanders's *Jesus and Judaism* was his effort to find a sure foundation, something that could not be debated, the facts (3-5). He settled on Jesus' temple action, which has turned out to be very debatable. He disparages the sayings tradition because it is so open to multiple interpretations and controversy about authenticity (13-18). Crossan has chosen a much wider base on which to build. He has basically set up two criteria—multiple attestation and stratification.

At this point the controversy truly begins, since these two criteria are interlocked. Crossan sees as early and independent, items that many scholars would see as late and dependent. Among the many items of debate one could list the following: Crossan's use of the *Gospel of Thomas*, the stages of development in *Q*, the Cross Gospel (a gospel that some might accuse Crossan of authoring), and Secret Mark. While Crossan has been building his case for stratigraphy for several years, this area remains controversial. Nevertheless, Crossan's reconstruction of the historical evidence does not depend on idiosyncratic or unproven stratification. Much of his stratification is dependent on the work of others, such as John Kloppenborg for *Q-The Synoptic Sayings Source* and Stephen Patterson for the *Gospel of Thomas*. Furthermore, since he does not depend on any single cluster or single item from a cluster, a rearrangement of the stratification would not drastically affect his argument. In fact, Crossan's argument would survive even if Thomas were shown to be dependent on the synoptics. His arguments might make less sense at some points, but they would survive.

More important is the method's validity. Has Crossan broken through and proposed a sound method, regardless of execution? While this is perhaps a premature judgment, I think he has. While the two criteria are not without problems, used jointly, multiple attestation and early stratification should weigh in favor of the authenticity for a cluster's core. That is, a cluster that has both multiple attestation and early stratification should be presumed authentic. Of course, if this is a correct methodology, it will lead to an intense debate on the stratification of the tradition. The debate is already well underway in the various studies on *Q*, the *Gospel of Thomas*, or the recent work of Helmut Koester, *Ancient Christian Gospels*. Koester comes very close to arguing that the earliest stratum of Q and Thomas is the historical Jesus (for example, 95, 156). Furthermore, Crossan's proposal resituates the problematic of the historical Jesus as the core problem for early Christian history and may be the final death knell for Martin Kähler's distinction between the Jesus of history and the Christ of faith. Although it would take us far afield, this rejection of Kähler's dialectic in view of a more analogical understanding of the place of Jesus in New Testament theology is a distinctively Catholic move on Crossan's part (Tracy).

Even granted Crossan's methodology and assuming his stratification, the method does not produce automatic or unambiguous results. A high number of attestations and an early stratification produces only an assumption of authenticity for a cluster's core; it does not guarantee it. For example, Crossan rejects the cluster with the second highest score, "Jesus' Apocalyptic Return." In his reconstruction, it is an early postcrucifixion development that employs Daniel 7:13 as a way of understanding how the scenario of the death and resurrection will play itself out. Crossan's analysis of this complex (243-47) exhibits the consistency of his method. The whole complex is understood as a system; the complex is reconstructed as a functioning system with its own inner dynamic, i.e., the use of Daniel 7:13 and Zechariah 12:10; synchronicity and formalization allows the complex to operate as a system; reconstruction leads to a core that demands a post-resurrection situation.

Crossan eschews the use of the negative criterion or criterion of dissimilarity: "the earliest form of a saying we can reach may be regarded as authentic if it can be shown to be dissimilar to characteristic emphases both of ancient Judaism and of the early Church" (Perrin 1967: 39). Rather he relies on reconstruction of the strata and synchronic functioning of the cluster.

Under this methodology Crossan sometimes evaluates positively what previously had been evaluated negatively. This demonstrates the openness of his method since he takes what is presented to him, not just what would build a case. His fascinating treatment of the miracle tradition is a case in point, although such a discussion is too complex for a simple summary. A simpler example will have to suffice. The parable of *The Planted Weeds* has two attestations, one in Thomas and one in Matthew. One of those attestations comes from Crossan's first level (Thomas). In Crossan's methodology, this gives it high consideration. On the other hand, most modern parable scholars, including myself, have evaluated this parable negatively (Scott 1989: 68-70). Many have seen it as Matthew's creation, although that option was unavailable to me, because I am convinced that Thomas is independent of the synoptics.

Nevertheless, I was persuaded by the arguments of Burton Mack that it deals with the issues of community building and, therefore, could not be a Jesus parable. Crossan's method frees him in certain ways I was not. Since for him only the core is authentic, not any particular extant example, he can argue that the core is authentic and coheres with those other parables in which Jesus pictures the kingdom as weeds (following the very intriguing suggestions of Douglas Oakman [1986: 116-18]). On the other hand, my need to reason to or reconstruct an originating structure trapped me, because I could not see my way clear to do so. Furthermore, I found unacceptable Oakman's uncritical acceptance of the extant Matthean version as authentic. What Crossan reconstructs is the trajectory of the cluster; what I wanted to reconstruct was the originating structure. My question is whether Crossan's method at this point, as attractive as it is, is a sleight of hand? Is the core an illusion? Is one positing the existence of an authentic parable because the method demands such a parable to account for the two extant nonauthentic parables? Or is the method properly honoring the oral, and therefore temporary, nature of the Jesus tradition prior to the writing of the Gospels? This needs much more theoretical work, but it is an interesting suggestion. Even more, Crossan's use of the clusters demands interpretation; the meaning of a cluster is not obvious and this of course will lead to even greater controversy.

Crossan at times also uses the evidence of attestation and stratigraphy negatively. For example in dealing with the apocalyptic Son of Man Sayings, the fact that they only have single attestation, and then not from the early stages, is a strong indication that they are inauthentic (243). A strong criticism of the negative criterion, which Crossan eschews, was that it produced an eccentric Jesus, one at odds with his culture and the tradition that followed. One could also question whether Crossan's dual reliance on early stratigraphy and multiple attestation does not reward the atypical and useful. Or to paraphrase Walter Ong, folks in an oral culture must think memorable thoughts (1982: 34). Nevertheless, while all efforts to deal with the criteria for authenticity have been tricky, the patterning that results from the use of a stratigraphy and attestation is potentially very promising and the results convincing.

My Kingdom, My Kingdom for a Horse

What is new methodologically in Crossan's *The Historical Jesus* is his engagement with the social sciences. Let me limit my remarks to how this fits into the volume's overall methodological thrust. Crossan has taken seriously the nearly unanimous results of New Testament criticism that the Kingdom of God was the central topic of the teaching of Jesus. But most studies that begin with *hJ basileiva tou' Qeou'* situate Jesus' discussion within Judaism. Crossan, true to his synchronic instincts, begins by situating it within the largest available system, the Roman Empire. That larger system remains the focus throughout the book, and in many ways gives the volume its distinctive character. As a direct result of this situation, Jesus becomes a very political, almost liberationist, character.

This system explains the threefold division of the book. "Part I, The Brokered Empire" indicates the primary system, Empire, and shows how it functions through brokerage. The second part, "Embattled Brokerage," deals with breakdowns in the Empire as brokerage fails, and the final section, "Brokerless Kingdom," concerns Jesus' response to this system, an egalitarian peasant society, characterized by an open table and commensality. As Crossan says, "They [the missionaries] share a miracle and a Kingdom, and they receive in return a table and a house. Here, I think, is the heart of the original Jesus movement, a shared egalitarianism of spiritual and material resources" (341). The system in which Jesus fits, according to Crossan, is the Roman Empire. Thus, neither Judaism nor Jesus nor primitive Christianity are viewed as separate and distinct items, but as part of a larger social, literary, and historical synchronicity. Crossan does not reconstruct them from their diachronic outcome, i.e., Christianity from the point of view of canon and Chalcedon or Judaism from the point of view of the Mishnah, but from the point of view of the contemporary system in which they exist. Whether or not Crossan has the content right, he has certainly made the correct methodological step.

Even more, Crossan now joins several others in what might become a new unified methodology in which the methodological rooms are no longer separate. He attempts to combine as equal and coexistent three vectors, as he refers to them: historical, literary, and social methods. This cross-pollination is a great advance.

There Was an Old Woman Who Lived in a Shoe

I began by noting that over the years Crossan has engaged in a series of ongoing experiments in both formal method and theology. This paper has dealt almost exclusively with the issues of formal method. Yet there is a strong interplay between method and theology in Crossan's work. In his earliest work on Jesus, *In Parables*, he maintained "an intrinsic and inalienable bond between Jesus' experience and Jesus' parables." By paying careful attention to the poetic language of the parables, one could actually have access to "what is most important about Jesus: his experience of God" (22). Crossan links Jesus' experience of God with the parable so that his own exegesis of the parables, of Jesus' language, is an exploration of Jesus' experience of God. In *In Parables* a romantic ideology, which was soon to disappear from Crossan's work, forges the link.

As Crossan played with notions of story in *The Dark Interval*, he likewise explored how God could be present in story and how story could threaten that experience. "If there is only story, then God, or the referent of transcendental experience, is either inside my story and, in that case, at least in the Judaeo-Christian tradition I know best, God is merely an idol I have created; or, God is *outside* my story, and I have just argued that what is 'out there' is completely unknowable" (40-41). The link between method and the experience of God continues, only Crossan would appear to have boxed himself in. He tries to wiggle out of the box by arguing that the parables "shatter the deep structure of our accepted world" and thereby at least open us to God (122).

In *Raid on the Articulate* and *Finding Is the First Act*, Crossan begins to explore a way out of the box with his powerful metaphor of the aniconicity (no image) of God. God has no image, not even the image of parable, and this profound paradox drives the peculiar linguistic form the parables take. The parable of the Treasure becomes, in Crossan's hands, a parable about parables (metaparable) and a parable about the experience of God as no image. The aniconicity of God in parable destroys our absolutes, the efforts to make an idol of God, "and in the space cleared by their absence offers us a freedom for human responsibility, personal and social decision" (117). The aniconicity of God even subverts our efforts at ethics, our efforts to make ourselves Godlike.

Crossan has long been criticized for falling into Albert Schweitzer's well, at the bottom of which Schweitzer claimed was the image of the interpreter, not Jesus. I myself thought that his Jesus seemed too close to Kafka or Borges. His Jesus seemed too individualistic, too modern, too clever with words. Yet in *The Historical Jesus* Crossan once again forges a link between method and theology. By situating Jesus in the context of the Roman Empire, Jesus' concerns become those of the underclass of the Empire. Even more, his methodology of stratigraphy and multiple attestation draws Crossan to miracle and meals as the most basic core. In what he calls "a perfect circle of victimization" (324), sickness, sin, and taxation are all tied together. The excessive taxation of the period left poor people hungry and desperate. However, the power structure could never argue that its taxation was the cause of the people's despair, so it blamed the people's sinfulness. The forgiveness of sins was the monopoly of the temple, which required more taxation of the people. Thus, when Jesus heals, he forgives sins and challenges the religious and political structure of the empire. "All of this was religiopolitically subversive" (324). So also is the eating in common, the sharing of all things. "Here, I think, is the heart of the original Jesus movement, a shared egalitarianism of spiritual and material resources" (341). Such, again, is a radical challenge to the established empire and the building of a new peasant kingdom of equals. While the aniconicity of God is not explicitly invoked, it runs underneath the argument like a mighty river. The no image God has broken out of language and shattered transcendence based on the empire's image of hierarchy in favor of a pure aniconicity of egalitarian commensality. Once again, Crossan's method profoundly drives his theology.

Let me conclude with three observations:

(1) I began with two lines from Wallace Stevens, "to impose is not / To Discover." The great ignorance of the nontheoretical is their trust in common sense, which almost inevitably leads to a positivism. The great problem of method is that it can become a straightjacket, distorting the data; its great promise is that it can function as a lens that allows the data to appear in significant arrangements. Methodologically, Crossan has not imposed but discovered, and rearranged the data, and more data than most, in an interesting and innovative new configuration.

(2) While perhaps unfair, a comparison with the recent work of John Meier, *A Marginal Jew: Rethinking the Historical Jesus*, is almost unavoidable. If we return to the model with which I began, Meier is much more in the line of Darwin. His is a historicism of the diachronic. It is the book that should be written to follow out the old quest. Crossan's *The Historical Jesus* is a work of Sausseran synchronicity. It brings the quest into the new sciences.

(3) I said at the beginning I might hazard a guess as to what Crossan's next book might be. If he continues on this same path, it would seem to me that he would have to do for the Gospels what he has done for the fragments of Jesus tradition.

3.

Crossan's Jesus and Christian Identity

JEFFREY CARLSON

Introduction: The Question of Religious Identity

Every religious person and community must find ways to clarify the particular religious identity they embody. What is "the Buddhist thing," "the Muslim thing," "the Christian thing," that makes individuals and communities recognizably and distinctively Buddhist or Muslim or Christian? Is it located primarily in a specific ethical approach? In a core ritual? In a foundational story? In a set of beliefs about the nature of reality? Whichever "candidates" for "the core thing" are proposed, the central questions remain the same: What is my, what is our, religious identity, and how do we come to know what it is?

Christian theology has sought and continues to seek creative and authentic answers to these questions. Christian theology, perhaps best defined as critical reflection on the meaning, truth, and contemporary relevance of the symbols, stories, beliefs, and practices of the ongoing tradition, must seek continually to clarify the nature and content of Christian religious identity. As Christians "do" theology, therefore, they have tended to concern themselves with two foci: the Christian "message" and the contemporary "situation." In some way or another, theologians have sought to correlate these twin concerns. Debates have raged on (1) the content and method of representing the "message"; (2) the content and method of representing the "situation"; and (3) the appropriate "weight" given to each.

Jesus as Norm?

In asking after "the Christian thing," it might seem that "Jesus" is an obvious candidate for the norm, criterion, or "essence" of Christianity, the core thing that forms the basis for Christian religious identity. However, access to "Jesus" is only available through multiple and often conflicting sources: the literature found within the Bible, as well as the many ancient texts not included in the biblical canon. Even within the New Testament alone, there are *four* "biographies," which show marked disagreement with one another. What, for instance, were the last words of Jesus before his death? How does Jesus die—*with serene confidence that he is in the hands of his Father* ("Father, into your hands I commend my spirit")? This is indeed the Jesus of Luke, but not the Jesus of Matthew or Mark, for whom Jesus cries "My God, My God, why have you forsaken me?" Then he dies, abandoned. Was Jesus born in a manger? Yes, but only in Luke. Were there wise men following a star? Yes, but only in Matthew. John and Mark tell nothing of Jesus' birth at all. Peter the "rock of the church?" Pilate washing his hands? Guards at Jesus' tomb? Yes, but only in Matthew. (Only there, as well, do the onlookers cry out, at Jesus' trial, "His blood be on us and on our children!" And on our *children*.)

In the latter part of the eighteenth and early part of the nineteenth centuries, the "quest for the historical Jesus" was in full swing. Scholars like Matthew Tindal, Gotthold Ephraim Lessing, Hermann Samuel Reimarus, and David Friedrich Strauss were asking whether and how one might discover the "real" Jesus behind the "veil" of the evangelists and their conflicting stories. This task even haunted Thomas Jefferson, who wrote *The Philosophy of Jesus of Nazareth* while president in 1804, and then the even more ambitious *The Life and Morals of Jesus of Nazareth Extracted Textually from the Gospels in Greek, Latin, French & English* in 1820. Seeking the authentic Jesus, Jefferson wrote of his attempts at "abstracting what is really his from the rubbish in which it is buried, easily distinguished by its lustre from the dross of his biographers, and as separable from that as the diamond from the dung hill" (Pelikan: 190).

Unfortunately—at least for those who believed in the project—it seemed that there would be as many "historical Jesuses" as there were interpreters, as each portrayal reflected the would-be historian's own philosophy of life. As Albert Schweitzer put it, the so-called "historical Jesus" was, in each case, "a figure designed by rationalism, endowed with life by liberalism, and clothed by modern theology in an historical garb" (Pelikan: 398). Equally unfortunately—at least for those who still believe in the project—the situation has not really changed very much in our own time. As John Dominic Crossan has pointed out, Jesus has been portrayed recently as a political revolutionary, as a magician, as a Galilean charismatic, as a Galilean rabbi, as a Hillelite or proto-Pharisee, as an Essene, and as an eschatological prophet. As Crossan notes, "that stunning diversity is an academic embarrassment" (Crossan 1991: xxviii). Contemporary interpreters should take heart, however, since they are not alone. Jaroslav Pelikan prefaced his brilliant study of the interpretations of Jesus through the centuries with the observation that, when one seriously considers the Christian tradition of witness to Jesus, "it is not sameness but kaleidoscopic variety that is its most conspicuous feature" (Pelikan: 2). What is "the Christian thing," given the multiple Christs of Christianity?

Challenges of Crossan's Work

Crossan's new book, *The Historical Jesus: The Life of a Mediterranean Jewish Peasant*, attempts to move beyond what he considers to be an embarrassing impasse by developing a more rigorous methodology for historical Jesus research. Crossan's method involves what he calls "a triangular focus of multicultural social anthropology, Greco-Roman and Jewish history, and an acute literary sensitivity to the difference between literal and metaphorical language" (Crossan 1992). He focuses not only on biblical, but also on noncanonical texts, in developing what he calls a "reconstruction" of the program of the historical Jesus. Crossan proposes that Jesus was "a peasant Jewish Cynic," whose strategy was

> ... the combination of *free healing and common eating*, a religious and economic egalitarianism that negated alike and at once the hierarchical and patronal normalcies of Jewish religion and Roman power. ... Miracle and parable, healing and eating were calculated to force individuals into unmediated physical and spiritual contact with God and unmediated physical and spiritual contact with one another. He announced, in other words, the brokerless kingdom of God (Crossan 1991: 422).

In the Epilogue of his book, and in his essay found in this volume, Crossan reflects on the question of the "permanent relevance" of "an understanding of the historical Jesus" for the ongoing Christian tradition. He offers this challenge: Dismiss the quest for the historical Jesus, and you are a Gnostic. This, he notes, was an option in the first century, and remains one today! Who has "ears to hear" *that*? Crossan, ever the advocate of Catholic Christianity, commends *its* approach, namely, that of expressing one's faith in the historical Jesus as "the manifestation of God," by engaging in a dialectic between "an historically-read Jesus and a theologically-read Christ." He provides us with three "earliest Christian" examples of such dialectical engagement: Pauline, *Q*, and exegetical forms of Christianity.

Crossan's fascinating work raises a host of questions and challenges, which one might consider under the headings of "method" and "content." First, on method: *Do* scholarly reconstructions of the "historical Jesus" — Crossan's or anyone else's — play a role in theology? *If* such scholarly reconstructions *do* play a role, then in what specific ways should contemporary Christian theology be revised in the light of *new* scholarship? What happens when the data for developing a historical Jesus reconstruction *includes*, as it does in Crossan's case, material previously *excluded* from the New Testament canon, such as the *Gospels of Thomas* and *Peter*, and other texts? If such data is deemed theologically relevant today, then what does that say about past theological *decisions to exclude it*? Furthermore, what does this very *reconstructive process* suggest about the nature of religious identity, about the nature of "belonging," at any given time, to any particular "religious tradition"?

And what about the *content* of historical Jesus reconstructions? What happens if, and, indeed, when the "program" of the historical Jesus seems to contradict many beliefs and practices that have developed within traditional Christianity? If, for instance, Jesus proclaimed a "brokerless kingdom," then is there an ultimate betrayal in the very establishment of a hierarchical church? If the Jesus movement was deliberately itinerant and radically egalitarian, are there betrayals in the moves to fixed residency in Jerusalem (or Rome) and fixed leadership roles for exclusively male bishops, presbyters, and deacons? One may not have to wait for Constantine to begin the cost-accounting. One may need to begin with Jesus' own family, starting with James. Or is all of this somehow inevitable? Do all *movements* either die out or become *institutions*? Finally, what happens if, and *certainly* when, the historical portrait of Jesus' life and death seems to violate the delicate, heartfelt, life-sustaining piety of many contemporary Christian men and women? *How can they*, as Professor Crossan put it with such excruciating clarity, "follow the dogs?"

Needless to say, I will not attempt to answer each of these questions in turn—other contributors to this volume will consider a number of them in greater depth. Instead, in what follows, I will focus primarily on questions of "method." More precisely, what can we learn, from Crossan's work, about the nature of Christian, indeed religious identity? I am, in this paper, less concerned with the "content" of that identity, than with the *process* by which it is constituted, and the lesson we might learn from attending carefully to the dynamics of that process. I will conclude, however, with a brief reflection on one aspect of the "content" of Crossan's portrait of the historical Jesus, namely, Crossan's depiction of the crucifixion.

There Is Only Reconstruction

In the Epilogue to *The Historical Jesus*, Crossan describes the ongoing work of the "Jesus Seminar," in its attempt to detect and determine historical Jesus material:

> After presenting papers and discussing arguments, [scholars] voted on each item. . . . Colored beads and ballot boxes were intended, no doubt, to catch the media's attention, since one of the Seminar's purposes was popular education about the problems and difficulties, results and conclusions of contemporary historical Jesus research. But actual objections, from laity and scholars alike, often spoke against the whole idea of voting on Jesus or against the legitimacy, validity, or usefulness of any reconstructed historical Jesus. . . . Yet scholars

know, even if the laity does not, that the very Greek text of the New Testament on which any modern translation must be based is itself a reconstruction and the result, however executed, of a scholarly vote in a committee of experts. . . . This book, then, is a scholarly reconstruction of the historical Jesus. . . . But one cannot dismiss it or the search for the historical Jesus as *mere* reconstruction, as if reconstruction invalidated somehow the entire project. Because there is *only* reconstruction. . . . If you cannot believe in something produced by reconstruction, you may have nothing left to believe in (Crossan 1991: 424-26).

Crossan's work, through the means by which it arrives at its reconstruction of Jesus, both suggests and exemplifies a process of selectivity that, I believe, has immense implications and applications. Allow me to develop some reflections, meditations on the theme "there is only reconstruction."

Many academic, social, and ecclesiastical programs advocate "multiculturalism" or "pluralism" as a remedy to the misunderstanding and violence so characteristic of our age. "We," advocates insist, must learn to respect and understand "them." The "self," they say, must encounter, with new openness, the "other." "Christianity," according to many, should enter into dialogue with "non-Christian religions." The virtues of tolerance, respect, and mutual understanding are, of course, laudable. The benefits resulting from programs of multiculturalism and pluralism are, arguably, many. However, I suspect that many such programs proceed from a dubious assumption, namely, a view of personal and cultural identity as fixed, reified, and static. "Pluralism" often suggests, for many interpreters, two or more discrete, bounded systems, each with its own stability, and an unchanging "core identity." Similarly, "multiculturalism" often suggests two or more discrete, bounded cultures, each with its own "purity."

I am deeply suspicious of these assumptions. I believe that most advocates of multiculturalism and pluralism overlook the radical plurality *within* the systems and cultures they name as "Western," "Christian," etc. It is my contention that a more accurate analysis of the nature of identity would view it as a dynamic, interactive process. On this reading, the "multi" of "multiculturalism" and the "plural" of "pluralism" refer to the ongoing processes of selective reconstruction from among many possibilities. Identity is never "fixed," "in just this way," "once and for all." It is inevitably the product of a series of syntheses in which, to borrow a phrase from the mathematician/metaphysician Alfred North Whitehead, "the many become one, and are increased by one" (Whitehead 1978: 21). Individual and communal religious identities are patchwork products of just this process.

There Is Only Syncretism

In an address to Brazilian bishops in 1990, the present pope warned of the dangers of *"syncretism,"* according to which, as he put it, certain "mythic and demiurgic aspects arising from beliefs with the most diverse origins and meanings have intermingled in a confused fashion with *the basic mysteries* [emphasis mine] of Christian faith." Syncretism, in the pope's view, ranges in varieties from "the constant recourse to superstition to an *incomplete* [emphasis mine] presentation of *genuine* [emphasis mine] doctrine" (Pope JPII: 410). Reaffirming what was said in 1986 at the Assisi celebration of the Interreligious Day of Prayer for Peace, the pope wrote that it is necessary to avoid "not only syncretism, but also any appearance of syncretism which is totally contrary to real ecumenism." Legitimate indigenous traditions, he concluded, may have

> ... excellent values ... and can also constitute a kind of 'evangelical preparation'. . . . However, it would be quite another thing to welcome them and incorporate them in to the content of the Christian message. . . . It is necessary *to duly purify* [emphasis mine] all elements which, for example, are clearly incompatible with the mystery of the oneness and absolute transcendence of a personal God, or connected with the economy of salvation, in which Christ is the only way for people to be redeemed. . . . The efforts towards *a genuine inculturation of the Gospel message* [emphasis in text] are certainly valid and needed, in the sense of finding new forms for its proclamation, with new, *properly purified* [emphasis mine] elements drawn from the cultures of peoples who are being evangelized (Pope JPII: 411).

Over against this voice of caution before the threatening other, and this need to conserve the purity of one's unchanging core identity, I would juxtapose three other voices. The first is that of African bishop Anselme T. Sanon. He writes:

> Here we are, evening pilgrims finally come to this place where Jesus is being kept. Bending down like John to peer into the tomb, or following Peter there, we see that everything, even the shroud, *has been folded* [emphasis mine] and placed to one side. The generations that have followed, since that day, have placed labels on everything, to arrange everything in good order and classify it all: a careful inventory and list. What can be said of Jesus of Nazareth that has not been said? ... What stranger is this, this latecomer, this evening companion come to trouble the disciples of Emmaus in their joy? Yes, we are of the race of this stranger, the only person in Jerusalem not yet to have understood what everyone else in his cultural universe is seized by. ... Two thousand years of manifold readings by hearts and eyes eager to understand the truths of faith have opened many a way leading to the Lord. By what right may one see in Jesus a chief of initiation? ... Is this not rather to disfigure, to mutilate him? Perhaps indeed. But our intention deserves a hearing: for us it is a matter of presenting

the Savior under other aspects (Mark 16:12), to lend him other faces, in cultural humanities that he surely could not refuse. [To do this is a] legitimate right of ours . . . [and] it is the Lord who grants it to us—that Lord who wills to be manifested to us in the appearances, the faces, in which we are more apt to discover him (Sanon: 92-94).

The second voice is that of Raimon Panikkar, the self-proclaimed "multireligious self," who describes his religious journey as follows: "I 'left' as a Christian, I 'found' myself a Hindu and I 'return' a Buddhist, without having ceased to be a Christian" (Panikkar: 2). On the issue of religious identity, Panikkar writes:

After much effort and many painful misunderstandings, Christian theology has accepted as fact what in certain theological circles is called the development of dogma. This seems to be a good starting point, but it would hardly suffice if interpreted merely as a kind of explication of *something already there*. Were religious consciousness static, our task would be only to *unfold* what was already there nicely *'folded'* [my emphases]. . . . [But] *growth* [emphasis in text] is perhaps the most pertinent category to express [the actual] situation, which is more than simple development or explication. In growth there is continuity as well as novelty, development as well as a real assimilation of something that was outside and is now incorporated, made one body. In growth, there is freedom. . . . I repeat: Growth means continuity and development, but it also implies transformation and revolution. . . . We do not know where we are going. Yet in this common ignorance genuinely religious people experience real fellowship and fraternal communion (Panikkar: 70-72).

The third voice is that of anthropologist James Clifford. He writes that what anthropologists call "cultures" are inevitably ethnographic collections (Clifford: 230). He goes on to note that

. . . the concrete activity of representing a culture, subculture, or indeed any coherent domain of collective activity is always strategic and selective. . . . [D]iverse experiences and facts are selected, gathered, detached from their original temporal occasions, and given enduring value in a new arrangement. . . . Anthropological *culture collectors* [my emphasis] have typically gathered what seems 'traditional'—what by definition is opposed to modernity. From a complex historical reality (which includes current ethnographic encounters) they select what gives form, structure, and continuity to a world. What is hybrid or 'historical' in an emergent sense has been less commonly collected and presented as a system of authenticity. . . . [As an example of anthropological selectivity, Clifford notes, Margaret Mead and others] chose not to study groups that were, as Mead wrote in a letter, 'badly missionized'. ... The experience of Melanesians becoming Christians for their own reasons ... did not seem worth salvaging. ... Mead found Arapesh receptivity to outside influences 'annoying.' *Their* culture collecting complicated hers (Clifford: 231-32).

Another anthropologist, André Droogers, defines "syncretism" as "religious interpenetration, either taken for granted or subject to debate" (Droogers: 20). The thesis I wish to advance is that all religion is, inevitably, a form of syncretism. The phenomenon of religious interpenetration, of the "mixing" of elements from two or more different systems to produce something new, is inevitable, and is at the very heart of personal and communal religious identity. To have a religious identity is, inevitably, to be a "syncretic self," the product of a process of selective appropriation, internalizing elements drawn from vastly varied pools of possibility. We are this amalgam, this ever-changing assemblage of diverse elements, brought together out of freedom and amid a certain destiny, an array of cultural-linguistic influencing factors we cannot control completely.

Christian Identity Reconsidered

Crossan's work makes valuable contributions to any discussion concerning the nature of religious identity. He maintains that there is not one single unambiguous and objectively certain norm or essence of Christianity. The "historical Jesus" is clearly, for Crossan, no such thing. The "historical Jesus," Crossan does not hesitate to admit in his book, is a scholarly reconstruction, *a version, a product* of a process of informed judgment and therefore, like all scholarly hypotheses, ever open to revision and correction. Recall Crossan's claim that there have been and will continue to be *"divergent historical Jesuses."* This is *not* the nineteenth-century quest for the historical Jesus! This is not the Enlightenment's dream of value-free objectivity, nor liberal theology's dream of the unchanging essence of Christianity that will enable us to, once and for all, separate the "kernel" of authentic Christianity from the "husk" of corrupt Christendom.

While admitting, therefore, that his reconstructed Jesus is an interpretive construct, a matter of probability and not certainty, Crossan notes, with Bishop Butler, that "probability is the very guide of life." But this is *not* the nineteenth-century's quest, and Crossan's Jesus is *not* the "essence of Christianity."

If there is not one unchanging version of the historically-read Jesus, neither is there one single and unambiguous "theologically-read Christ." Crossan has described *multiple* "earliest Christian" options. Of course, there have been multiple Christs *throughout* the Christian tradition. In worshiping the Jesus who is rabbi, turning point of history, light of the gentiles, king of kings, cosmic Christ, son of man, true image of God, crucified savior, monk, mystical bridegroom, universal man, prince of peace, teacher of common sense, poet of the spirit, and liberator, to use some of Jaroslav Pelikan's categories; or the Jesus who is master of initiation, chief, ancestor, elder brother, and healer, to use some categories developed by contemporary African theologians, Christians have resisted the temptation to parrot simply and uncritically an inherited version of religious identity. Instead, in developing their christologies, they have critically appropriated those stories, songs, beliefs, laws, and practices that *they* have found to be true. They have been evening pilgrims, engaging in growth, collecting a culture. They have selectively internalized elements from vastly varied pools of possibility. They have been authentic, that is, syncretic selves. "Ask my hearers," Jesus says in John's Gospel, "they know what I said." My plural hearers.

In asserting, therefore, that Christian faith inevitably involves a dialectic between "*an* historically-read Jesus and *a* theologically-read Christ" [my emphases], Crossan is, I believe, moving beyond the old quests for the historical Jesus, and offering theology an important way forward. His work suggests that Christian identity is inevitably the product of a process of dynamic interaction and selective reconstruction.

On my reading, personal authenticity *demands* that individuals and communities continuously detect, reclaim, and creatively appropriate renewed reconstructions of their own religious identities. My thesis regarding the inevitably syncretic nature of religious identity challenges religious men and women to inventory honestly and assess critically the multiple elements comprising their religious identities. It also challenges them to reflect on the very nature of "belonging" to "a tradition." Once we recognize explicitly the selectivity such belonging entails, we will be challenged to rethink our notions of "insider" vs. "outsider," and even the very distinctions between "the world religions." I am not suggesting that there is "a common essence" shared by all religions, in terms of the "content" of the elements selectively appropriated. I am suggesting, however, that there is a structural, formal constant: Each of our "inventories" shows the influence of *many* places and times. We are all, and each, intrinsically plural. Together we share that formal complexity, that syncretic identity. There is no *inter*religious common essence, but there is an *intra*religious common experience: each "one" of us is "many." As Michael Pye has argued, syncretism

> ... is a natural *moving* aspect of major religious traditions ... and indeed, I would venture to suggest, of all religious traditions. It is part of the dynamics of religion which works its way along in the ongoing transplantation of these religious traditions from one cultural context to another whether geographically or in time (Pye 1971: 92).

One must be wary of Søren Kierkegaard's chilling observation: "Frequently, when I am most convinced that I understand myself, I am assaulted by the uneasy feeling that I have really only learned someone else's life by rote" (Kierkegaard: 37). Facing up to the syncretic nature of religious identity is, I believe, the best way to address the spiritual malaise, banality, and superficiality so characteristic of our American culture, where persons seldom are encouraged to appropriate critically their own authentic identities, mimicking instead the desires and goals of others. It is also, I would suggest, the best way to begin dialogue with another. We begin as authentic, that is, as self-consciously and explicitly syncretic selves. This much, we share.

When the present pope warns against the dangers of syncretism, he is joined by a host of theologians. Jon Temme, for instance, writes that the "core" of Christianity must remain untouched and undamaged, and that a "syncretized Christ must be rejected if the Church is to retain the core element of its existence" (Temme: 32). In the light of this combination of scorn and fear, it is useful to recall Droogers' observation that the label "syncretism" is itself, in cases like the ones just noted, a pejorative name used by the powerful. He writes that

> . . . exclusivist claims will give rise to accusations of syncretism (in the negative subjective sense) as their necessary complement. . . . The exclusive claims are often maintained by a class of religious specialists who monopolize, with more or less success, the definition of truth, and spend a lot of time eliminating possible contradictions and oppositions. . . . [So called] syncretists rarely call themselves by that name. Syncretists are always the others (Droogers: 16).

In the face of those "religious specialists" who would demarcate, once and for all, the boundary of orthodox Christian identity, I offer the suggestion that there is no permanent and singular core of Christianity or any "religion." There are only the multiple products of ongoing processes of selective reconstruction. Any and every candidate for "the core thing" is, inevitably, yet another version, another instance of selectivity, partiality, and particularity. Articulating one's religious identity is an act of courage and authenticity, an example of the process of "growth" to which Panikkar refers. It is also, like all things human, ambiguous. In any reconstructed version of religious identity, Christian or otherwise, much that might have been included is excluded. Voices are silenced and oppressed. Robert Schreiter writes of what he calls "the price of shaping traditions: traditions are formed in acts of violence that demand the repressions of certain themes, and those submerged themes will continue to stalk the tradition" (Schreiter: 14). One must beware, therefore, of mystifications, of so-called pristine "inaugural moments" that are deemed normative and that are held to be fixed foundations for all who follow. Scholars and ecclesiastics can work beautifully and creatively within such "hoops" as canon or creed or dogma, but the very status of each of these circumscribed realities must be recognized as yet another, perhaps still compelling product of the process of selective reconstruction. And one must be prepared to take that "per-haps" quite seriously. Past versions do not necessarily constitute the content of my present religious identity, and I am not bound to accept them uncrit-ically. They are, instead, marvelous examples of daring to designate a cen-ter, to name, to reconstruct from among the many, to articulate one's identity. In considering creative reconstructions from the past, one should do *as* they did, but not necessarily *what* they did. One should participate in the process of selective reconstruction, as they did, with courage and creativity, but what is produced by that process must be one's own. It must be creative and not destructive, liberative and not oppressive.

In my opinion, there are two grave crises to which interpreters of religion must attend: the crisis of inauthenticity, to which I have already referred, and the crisis of conflict. Religious men and women must respond creatively to the interreligious and intercultural violence characteristic of every age, but so rampant in ours that the philosopher Edith Wyschogrod has named this the era of "man-made mass death" (Wyschogrod: 165). If violence involves the "other," perhaps a new vision, in which the self is already plural, already "other," and thereby united with every person by virtue of the syncretic nature of each of our identities, will provide a way to hope and a way to move toward a future that is creative and liberating. To the extent that any theory can make a difference in practice, we have reason to hope that this theory may help. If we can think the point of "plurality within," then the very distinction "within/between" begins to blur. Where does x end and y begin, when so much of y is in x?

Theologians may have much to learn from social scientists like Arjun Appadurai, who describes an emerging "global culture" by focusing on five interconnected dimensions of cultural flow. He calls these dimensions: (a) "ethnoscapes," meaning "the landscape of persons who constitute the shift-ing world in which we live: tourists, immigrants, refugees, exiles, guestwork-ers, and other moving groups and persons"; (b) "technoscapes," meaning the flow of mechanical and informational technology across "previously impervious boundaries" through multinational corporations; (c) "finan-scapes," meaning the rapid flow of money through currency markets, national stock exchanges and commodity speculations; (d) "mediascapes," meaning the "distribution of the electronic capabilities to produce and disseminate information (newspapers, magazines, television stations, film production studios, etc.)"; and (e) "ideoscapes," meaning the flow of ideas, terms and images often organized around such "keywords" as, for instance, "freedom," "rights," "sovereignty" and, with particular power these days, "democracy" (Appadurai: 296-300). Given the significance of these fluid realities, Appadurai suggests that "deterritorialization" is "one of the cen-tral forces of the modern world" (Appadurai: 301). Appadurai does not wish to claim that there no longer exist "relatively stable communities and networks, of kinship, of friendship, of work and of leisure, as well as of birth, residence and other filiative forms," to which I would add, of course, belonging to particular religious communities. Nor could one deny the bloody and horrifying consequences of ongoing "tribalisms" around the world today. But, Appadurai concludes, "the warp of these stabilities is everywhere shot through with the woof of human motion" (Appadurai: 297). Can we think the point of religious deterritorialization, so that our reflection makes a difference in practice? Appadurai's analysis and others like it are clues, I believe, toward a fuller understanding of the very nature of the selective appropriation of diverse possibilities that characterizes the development of authentic religious identity. Such ideas will help us to face the challenge of responding creatively to violence in this the "death age." When identity is inevitably syncretic, under whose banner should we fight? And who are they, our enemies?

A Historically-Read Jesus

What about Crossan's claim that, at least for non-Gnostic Christianity, the historically-read Jesus, now seen in terms of our best current scholarly *version*, is an integral component of Christian faith? Crossan, I believe, makes a good case for his argument that Paul, the Q community, and exegetical Christianity exemplify a faithful concern with *a* historical Jesus. And one could easily make the case that Christianity has, over the centuries, done the same thing. Crossan is right—the Christ of faith, however portrayed, intends to be a legitimate interpretation of the meaning and significance of the person and work of the very Jesus who lived then and there. The fact that Christianity has been concerned with *a* historical Jesus, of course, does not mean that past Christians have known *Crossan's reconstructed Jesus*. This *new* version was, quite literally, not possible until now. But now that it is here, *theology should attend to it*. Crossan's Jesus may serve, in the words of David Tracy, to "check, refine, develop, correct or confront all christological formulations by comparing them critically with the earliest memory images of the community" (Tracy 1981: 320). The radical egalitarianism of Crossan's Jesus may spur a renewed "deideologization" of the scriptural texts, to use Schubert Ogden's term (Ogden: 166), just as Bultmann's program had sought to "demythologize" them. This new reconstructed version of the historical Jesus may also play a role in the development of new christologies, shaping future Christian identities. It may even, in a manner *most* appropriate to the boundary-crossing program of Crossan's Jesus, lead beyond "narrowly Christian" confines, to influence and evoke other religious identities, the syncretic amalgams yet to be. Such developments, if authentic, would occur in ways we cannot currently predict—unless, when confronted with this new Galileo, we refuse to look through the telescope, or wait 400 years to do it.

Dogs at the Cross

Allow me to conclude by citing 2 Kings, Chapter 9 (vs. 10, 36):

The dogs shall eat Jezebel in the territory of Jezreel, and no one shall bury her. . . . In the territory of Jezreel the dogs shall eat the flesh of Jezebel; the corpse of Jezebel shall be like dung on the field in the territory of Jezreel, so that no one can say, this is Jezebel.

This is Elijah's prophecy about a "cursed woman," as Gale Yee calls her (Yee: 848), a foreign wife of the king of Israel who used her power to support the worship of Canaanite fertility deities. Biblical texts paint a thoroughly negative picture of her, and Elijah's prophecy is fulfilled. In his paradoxical theology of the cross, Paul had said that Jesus, like all who "hung on a tree," was "cursed" by God. One of the most profoundly unsettling results of any historical Jesus reconstruction concerns the conflict between historical investigation and inherited beliefs. In his survey of classical and contemporary christologies, Richard McBrien notes that one thing is historically certain—Jesus was buried in a tomb owned by Joseph of Arimathea, "a distinguished member of the Sanhedrin," and that the tomb was later discovered to be empty (McBrien: 416). Crossan's analysis of the nature of crucifixion explodes such assurance and no doubt forces, for many, a rethinking of the meaning of "resurrection." How might the religious sensibilities of Christians be affected by Crossan's hypothesis that the corpse of the historical Jesus was most likely devoured by wild beasts? I must admit that I find the imagery horrifying and haunting and also inspiring. It *magnifies* the power of the Christian symbol of the cross. It extends and deepens Paul's astonishing claim, "We preach Christ crucified." Its pathos is incalculable. I can well imagine someone meditating on this image, stepping off a bus in a snowstorm, halfway home, finding oneself saying, "My Lord and my God."

4.

A Historicist Model for Theology

SHEILA GREEVE DAVANEY

It has become commonplace in the contemporary period to assert that human existence is thoroughly historical in nature. This assertion entails both the recognition that human beings are situated in particular historical locales, circumscribed by place and time and that these specific contexts are themselves the product of complex historical processes and contemporary responses to them. This acknowledgment of radical historicity has raised questions for numerous academic disciplines about the character of knowledge, claims to validity and the norms by which such competing claims might be adjudicated. And theology, perhaps more than most disciplines, has been compelled to reconsider its nature and task as well as the status of its proposals. These reconsiderations have been comprehensive in scope, leaving no aspect of theological inquiry unscrutinized, and have resulted in an unprecedented diversity of positions with little prospect of consensus. But if the end products of theological reflection are disparate today nonetheless the recognition of historicity has focused renewed attention across the theological spectrum on the question of how the present should understand its relation to the past, both as a whole and in particular to that past that is taken to be the originating locus of the specific religious tradition with which the theologian is concerned. It is on this question of the relation of the present to past history and the significance of this relation for theology that this paper will focus.

The question of the relation of past and present is not a new concern for theological reflection. It has been present throughout Western theological thought. However, while it is not an entirely new question, it has nonetheless taken on unique contours in our day that require some understanding of our own period and of the preceding modern period in order to understand its particular character.

The Legacy of Modernity

The modern period to which we are heirs was no monolithic affair but was religiously, politically, culturally and cognitively pluralistic. Its various strands, while supporting an emerging "modern" conception of the world, also increasingly challenged one another so thoroughly that according to many thinkers today we now stand at the threshold of a new postmodern era whose hallmark is the acknowledgment of modernity's contradictions, limitations and failures. The modern period, for its own part, grew out of the demise of its preceding eras, of the medieval world and the developments commenced during the Renaissance and Reformation. In particular the breakdown of ecclesial authority, the advent of Protestantism and the religious conflicts of the sixteenth and seventeenth centuries, the rise of modern science and the scientific method, the emergence of national states with centralized governments, technological advances and economic and social reorganization all ushered in a new era, fraught with new challenges and possibilities, that was decisively different from earlier times.

The results of these developments were profound. The breakdown of authority and of societal consensus, especially as these were manifested in religious conflicts, indicated the need for public norms and criteria, not tied to particular traditions, that could be utilized to resolve disputes among groups and individuals. At the same time, advances in the sciences suggested that precise forms of knowledge could be formulated and publicly demonstrated to be true. Thus while old forms of authority and adjudication fell asunder resulting in cultural crises, concurrently new possibilities for seemingly secure knowledge and clear norms gained ascendancy; born in a crisis of authority, modernity issued forth in a new confidence in reason's capacities and the conviction that such reason led to emancipation from superstition and the dismantling of authoritarian structures whether they were religious, political or economic.

This modern drive for objectivity and certitude in knowledge had many consequences. One of particular note for this paper is that the repudiation of seemingly heteronomous authority implied for many early moderns, especially Enlightenment thinkers, a suspicion of the past and what Hans-Georg Gadamer has called a prejudice against prejudice. Jeffrey Stout, writing about Descartes, states, "the crisis of authority made an absolutely radical break with the past seem necessary. Methodical doubt therefore sought complete transcendence of situation. It tried to make the inheritance of tradition irrelevant, to start over again from scratch, to escape history" (Stout 1981: 67).

This desire to transcend the authority of the past found expression not only in rationalistic philosophy and science but also in a wide variety of new disciplines of inquiry that emerged during the Enlightenment and its aftermath, including those of biblical criticism, hermeneutics and the study of non-Western traditions. Van Harvey, in his book *The Historian and the Believer*, argues that during modernity these forms of inquiry came to understand themselves as founded upon "a new morality of critical judgment" that stood in sharp contrast to what he terms the "ideal of belief" (Harvey: 38-39). In this new morality the historian or other critical thinker is not the mediator of a taken-for-granted tradition, but a critical thinker who seeks demonstrable facts defensible in the arena of public debate. Ironically, however, in their very practice, these disciplines would come to embody the questioning of reason's universality, neutrality and capacity for objectivity. For, through their focus on concrete and material existence, insistent and far-reaching questions began to be raised about the role of the knower in any inquiry, the status of the past and the grounds for determining criteria. Eventually, these inquiries contributed to the historicizing of Christianity, the repudiation of its traditional appeals beyond history to support its claims to uniqueness and superiority and the radical circumscription of what Christianity's own past could be understood to yield in support of its assertions.

Not only did disciplines committed to Enlightenment ideals come, through their analyses, to undermine central assumptions of modernity, but there arose as well countertraditions that stood as alternatives to these presuppositions and commitments. Hence, romanticism celebrated history, tradition and nature over against an arid reason. And, the masters of suspicion—Marx, Freud, Nietzsche and Feuerbach—made their appearance linking knowledge and claims to truth not to a universal rationality, functioning publicly, but to often hidden economic and psychological processes and to the operations of power.

Critiquing the Enlightenment

Thus, modernity has bequeathed us not a singular heritage but a diverse and conflictual legacy. The twentieth century, for its part, has witnessed the continuation and transmutation of these various strands of modern thought. For many persons the Enlightenment ideals of reason and confidence in reason's capacities endure, despite both internal and external challenges. But, increasingly, it appears that the more historicist insights of modernity have gained credence in our day challenging modernity in its Enlightenment form. Across many disciplines from literary criticism to philosophy of science, from political theory to anthropology the understanding of reason espoused by the Enlightenment has been thoroughly criticized and, by many, rejected. Assumptions of neutrality, of the capacity to ascertain sure and indubitable foundations for knowledge, of reason's transcendental character and universal nature all seem problematic today. Moreover, the accompanying notions of the self as autonomous, independent of tradition and only incidentally historical are equally under attack.

There are many debates about how this critical turn has taken place. For some thinkers the critical stance toward Enlightenment modernity is interpreted as the extension and radicalization of historical consciousness as it developed in the nineteenth century and into the twentieth century. For others, it represents a more radical break and the rejection of even those earlier historicist orientations. And even if historicity is a current way of conceiving of human existence, how such historicity should be defined is not nearly as clear.

There are many different interpretations of humanity's historical nature, and a variety of emphases within those interpretations. Yet, despite those debates, a tentative definition might be ventured to further conversation in this context. That provisional definition can be stated as follows: Human beings are inhabitants of neither nowhere nor everywhere, but are situated within particular temporal and spacial locales, demarcated by distinctive languages, worldviews, political and economic structures, and social, religious and ethical systems. Hence, human existence is always particular, concrete and pluralistic. Moreover, the acknowledgment of the localized character of experience entails the further recognition that any contemporary context is the product of the complex historical processes that have preceded it *and* of the contemporary responses to these processes. Hence, to be historical is not only to be concrete and particular, but to be so by virtue both of being shaped within a specific lineage of historical development *and* by the creative transmutation of that heritage. The present is, thereby, always a product of its history but can never be merely reduced to or explained exhaustively by that history. Continuity and difference both, therefore, mark the historical process.

Postmodern American Theology

On the North American scene today a number of theological responses have emerged to the widespread challenges to modernity and to the accompanying shift to a more historicist orientation. Prominent among these alternatives are currently postliberalism, deconstructionism and revisionist theology. In each case, these theological perspectives have joined in the repudiation of any search for certain and incontestable knowledge be that found in reason, experience or revelation and have instead insisted upon the local, social and political character of all theological claims. Yet, while the logic of this historicist sensibility has led much of theology away from Enlightenment modernity and, indeed, nineteenth-century liberalism, it has not issued forth in any theological consensus. In particular, while theology has turned its attention to history, there have emerged competing and disparate accounts of how the past should be understood, how its role and status in shaping the present should be conceived, and what relative weight should be given to continuity and creativity.

For postliberals, identified predominately with Yale University and the work of George Lindbeck, the insights of contemporary historicism lead to a recognition that human beings are thoroughly traditioned beings, existing within particular historical lineages that provide the basic interpretive categories that make human life possible at all. Theology, in this view, is essentially an intrasystematic affair in which the past is understood to provide the founding narrative framework within which life, in particular traditions, takes place. For postliberals, thus, the originating claims of a tradition, what Lindbeck calls its depth grammar, are endowed with normative weight, and theological adequacy is, therefore, judged in terms of how well a theological position coheres with and embodies the encompassing narrative of that historical tradition. The present may creatively and diversely give expression to originating claims of a tradition but it is the past that is the site of authority.

In contrast, for deconstructionists, such as Mark C. Taylor, this privileging of the past is a blatant contradiction of postmodern sensibilities, a nostalgic longing for some still place of certainty. Instead, deconstructionists argue that the past is unavailable to us in such a manner. Moreover, neither the past nor, indeed, even any present text, doctrine, narrative or person can make authoritative claims upon us, but rather all are open to reinterpretation. Theology, in this view, has interest in offering definitive construals of neither reality nor faithful renderings of the past. Rather, theology should be engaged in endless play, opening up new possibilities, deconstructing earlier interpretations and uncovering the contradictions and ambiguities that past ones have hidden. Here the past has no privileged status; it is an arena for play that makes no claim on our loyalties and sets no boundaries to our creativity.

Revisionist theology, for its part, has proposed a more mediating line, especially in the increasingly postmodern thought of David Tracy. This postmodernist form of revisionist theology has, on the one hand, asserted the traditioned nature of experience and the inescapability of struggling with the past. On the other hand, it has argued that being so traditioned leads neither to being cut off from other traditions nor to a rigid notion of the authority of the past. Instead, Tracy and other revisionists have stressed an understanding of theology as a hermeneutical enterprise in which contemporary thinkers creatively engage the classics of their traditions out of their present-day situations in order to ascertain insights for the current moment.

Now each of these understandings of the past—as site of authority, field of play and context for hermeneutical engagement—reflects the repudiation of the Enlightenment ideals of neutrality and objectivity, and its goal of certitude and each represents the turn to historically circumscribed experience and knowledge, albeit in very different ways. But how, in fact, do these theological interpretations of the nature and status of history cohere with the claims emerging from historical inquiry and how do their assumptions about the past agree or disagree with the presuppositions of historians whose task it is to provide knowledge of that past? Finally, what do those claims emerging from historical inquiry suggest about the adequacy of these theological interpretations of history?

Crossan's Work amid Postmodern Theologies

It is impossible to scan the entire field of historical inquiry in search of answers to these questions. But in this context, I would like to undertake a thought experiment by engaging the work of one historian of Christian origins and interpreter of biblical texts, John Dominic Crossan, with these theological theories concerning the past in order to test the fruitfulness and limits of these theological assumptions when seen in the light of actual historical research. Such an experiment does not presume that the relation of theology to historical studies or textual analysis is one of theory versus indisputable fact. Rather, it presumes that both theology and history are interpretive enterprises whose mutual engagement might clarify each effort, though it will simplify neither.

John Dominic Crossan's work, *The Historical Jesus*, is a profound example of the complexities of historical inquiry in a post-Enlightenment era. It assumes the interpretive and traditioned nature of such inquiry, but refuses both the deconstructionists' contention that past events and texts set no parameters to our understanding and the postliberals' tendency to isolate traditions within narrow historical boundaries. Such assumptions are manifested most clearly in Crossan's method, a method that delimits all that Crossan will claim about the historical Jesus.

Crossan's method entails a threefold approach to the times and person of Jesus of Nazareth with the elements of the method progressively focusing on a narrower range of material. The first methodological approach utilizes the theories and claims of comparative and social anthropology, especially as it has explored Mediterranean culture in general, and specifically peasant culture both in the Mediterranean and elsewhere. On this level, Crossan's method engages the widest range of material, resulting in a sweeping panorama of Mediterranean life not only in Jesus' time in Palestine, but across centuries and geographical locales. It is clear from Crossan's method that he assumes that while human life is always concrete and particular, that such specificity does not rule out comparative analysis, and that interpretive approaches and material claims about widely disparate cultures and societies can fruitfully inform one another. Hence, for Crossan, human historicity does not result in an incommensurability in which traditions or historical periods are either cut off from one another or incomprehensible to one another.

But, if Crossan is convinced of the merits of comparative analysis, he is equally interested in the in-depth explorations of a particular time and place. Thus, the second element of his method is the historical analysis of Greco-Roman history, with focused attention upon Palestine during the period of Roman occupation. Such analysis emphasizes the specificity of historical existence, detailing the intricate relations of political, economic, cultural and religious factors. What Crossan's analysis assumes and reveals is the enormous complexity of human society that cannot be understood in abstraction, but only through the mapping of its particularity. Moreover, his explorations repeatedly point to the importance of the social location of the participants in any particular society, be they oppressed peasants or aristocratic commentators within those societies such as Josephus as well as that of later interpreters of history, such as himself. Social location shapes all levels of experience and thought, infusing experience and knowledge with commitments, values and interests. There is, for Crossan, no neutral or innocent place to stand in history.

Crossan's third methodological approach entails close textual analysis of both canonical and noncanonical material in search of the most accurate portrayal of the historical Jesus that such material can be seen to yield when informed by anthropological and historical insights. On this level, Crossan is particularly clear about the methodological decisions he has made and the repercussions of those choices. Hence, he insists that there can be no privileging of canonical sources and that, for his purposes, only statements that have multiple attestations will count as historically compelling. Moreover, he continually points to the theological, political and social character of the various renderings of Jesus in these sources forcing the reader once more away from abstractions and back to consideration of the social location of their authors and to the nonobjective nature of their depictions of Jesus of Nazareth. Not only is historical material difficult to come by in relation to Jesus, but, Crossan insists, what material we have represents value laden interpretations yielding differing and even contradictory portrayals of Jesus. From the beginning, according to Crossan, the various Christs of faith emerged and the historical Jesus is available to us only within and through those theological portrayals.

Thus, John Dominic Crossan presents an enormously complex picture of historical analysis that continually undermines any easy confidence in its proposals. Texts, persons, and events must always be contextualized, being read both against larger frameworks and within the specificities of localized settings. They must be examined not only for what they seem to say or do but also for what is left out or denied. And they must be scrutinized as well for the role they play in the arrangement of power. Moreover, not only must the object of historical investigation undergo such critical interrogation but so must the inquirer, no longer seen as neutral but also as a bearer of values, commitments and power.

Given all these complexities it is tempting to conclude, as many postmodern thinkers indeed have, that historical inquiry is a form of fiction or poetry yielding creative and innovative visions of reality, but not accurate renderings of the past. Yet John Dominic Crossan does not finally concur with this conclusion, but instead asserts that tentative proposals might be ventured as long as they clearly recognize their interpretive character and always open themselves to the ongoing test of alternative readings and construals. His work, *The Historical Jesus*, offers precisely such a proposal arguing that out of the intersection of cultural, historical and textual analyses emerges a picture of Jesus that, if not definitive, is at least defensible and suggestive of the boundaries within which contemporary understandings of Jesus might negotiate. This portrayal, succinctly stated, is of a Mediterranean peasant living under Roman imperialistic rule who participated in the widespread social unrest of his day. Jesus' particular form of socially, politically and religiously disruptive behavior consisted, in Crossan's scenario, in the declaration of an egalitarian vision of mutuality and commensality and engagement in unconventional forms of social fellowship and interaction that challenged the power arrangements current during that period. Crossan builds his picture of Jesus primarily around his activity as a healer and as one who pronounced what Crossan terms an unbrokered kingdom already present in such unorthodox activities as the sharing of resources and mutual relationships between men and women. Such activities could not but threaten, Crossan notes, the very principles of the standing order.

Crossan, thus, develops out of the intersections of anthropological, historical and textual analyses a portrayal of Jesus of Nazareth that locates him quite thoroughly in his time and place, and that makes him comprehensible in light of the historical realities of Roman occupied Palestine. This picture is, Crossan insists, a reconstruction, a construal built up from historical investigation dependent on particular methodological decisions and fraught with what he terms material investments. Other scholars might venture alternative versions of Jesus, but, Crossan concludes, all such efforts will, always, as is his, be creative reconstructions, never direct, innocent or finally uncontrovertible readings of past reality. Moreover, they will always be built up through engagement with the early Christian interpretations of Jesus—the Christs of faith—not an easily discernable and uninterpreted Jesus of history.

Questions about Crossan's Work

From the perspectives of biblical scholarship and early Christian origins, many questions could no doubt be raised about Crossan's work. Debate could be engaged about Crossan's methodological decisions, about the utilization of work in very different historical locales to illuminate Jesus' period or the move from broad descriptions of an age to claims about a particular person. Or again, many biblical scholars could examine Crossan's claims to multiple attestation, raising doubts about whether, in fact, Crossan asserts too much about Jesus. Or finally, Crossan's reliance on noncanonical material, while uncontroversial for many, would surely prove problematic for those scholars for whom the canon provides the primary field of inquiry.

Theologians, for their part, might also challenge Crossan, raising questions about the adequacy of his method and interpretive theory and the present but not always clearly owned theological commitments that emerge throughout the text. All these concerns are valid and offer legitimate arenas for debate. But, in the present context, this essay wants to raise another question, that is, what does Crossan's work suggest to theology today, especially what does it imply for the three prominent perspectives set forth earlier in this paper?

It is the contention of this paper that Crossan's work both resonates with aspects of these perspectives and, both methodologically and materially, raises important challenges for the ways in which they have framed the relationship of the past and present. Let us examine each in turn.

Postliberalism

In terms of postliberalism, Crossan's proposal, while concurring with the postliberal concern for history, is also suggestive of quite alternative ways of reading how different traditions relate to one another, how historical periods interact and how contemporary persons might view that history.

First, Crossan's very methodology embodies the conviction that traditions, while particular and concrete, are not thereby self-enclosed and insular. Hence, for him, materials from very different locales can illuminate and inform one another. Crossan's material portrayal of Jesus and of his time, moreover, is that of a new vision and movement coming into existence through creative transmutation of the past and transforming interaction among differing traditions in Jesus' own period. Romans and Jews, prophets and Cynics did not exist in isolation from one another but in ongoing interpenetration such that new historical possibilities emerged. To understand the Jesus movement, and by implication subsequent Christianity, requires, in Crossan's scenario, sustained attention to these interactions and to the multiplicity of factors that combined to bring them forth, including economic, political and social ones.

Thus, while the postliberal attention to tradition would cohere well with Crossan's work, the tendency to interpret traditions as self-enclosed entities that subsist over time, continually embodying an unchanging depth grammar, would seem to ignore or render to a secondary status these historical factors and, hence, contrast considerably with Crossan's messier portrayal of traditions.

Finally, Crossan's work raises questions concerning the postliberal claim of a singular-depth grammar that is then endowed with authority. On the one hand, Crossan's continual appeal to the historical Jesus might be read as a similar sort of move, with that historical Jesus functioning as the bedrock for Christian theology. Yet, on the other hand, Crossan's work clearly indicates the complexity of any such appeal. For, while offering a depiction of the historical Jesus, he openly acknowledges its status as a creative reconstruction emergent out of a theory informed process. Moreover, he simultaneously points to the fact that from the outset there were multiple and divergent interpretations of Jesus that are not reducible to one another or to some common experience of Jesus lurking behind them. From the beginning, it would seem, there were many depth grammars and our task, it would appear for Crossan, is to move between the present and a past that was plural, not singular. Hence, from the perspective of Crossan's complex history, the postliberal construal looks very much like an abstraction that claims to take history seriously, but in fact empties it of its richness, ambiguities and possibilities for multiple readings.

Deconstructionist Theology

Crossan's work, as it did with postliberalism, both shares elements in common with deconstructionist approaches as well as challenging them. *The Historical Jesus* employs a number of deconstructionist-like strategies. Crossan repeatedly reads texts against themselves, probing them for what is left unsaid, repressed or present but rendered silent. He assumes always the ambiguity and the indeterminacy of texts eschewing unitary readings. Moreover, he is always clear about the creative role of the interpreter, the play that occurs as text and reader intersect and the impossibility of ever completely separating the two.

Yet, if, from the vantage point of Crossan's insights, the postliberals' position looks too tidy and abstracts too much from the complexities of history, the deconstructionists, despite their affinities with Crossan, seem to wallow too much in its chaos. The deconstructionists' tendency to deny that texts or events or persons place any restraint on how they are understood runs counter to all Crossan attempts to accomplish. While Crossan continually states that his work is interpretive, that it bears the marks of his methodological commitments and ideological values, and that it is therefore neither innocent nor purely objective, he also claims that it seeks to be faithful to a historical reality that puts, if never clearly, certain boundaries on his assertions. Such boundaries are continually negotiated and tested in the community of inquirers and, hence, open to ongoing reconsideration but they are not thereby simply abrogated. In particular, for him, Christian faith is precisely that negotiation between what he terms a historically-read Jesus and a theologically-read Christ. Once more, Crossan's work suggests to theology that the relation of past and present is more complex than it seems.

Revisionist Theology

In many ways, the vision of revisionist theology appears most compatible with the approach articulated by John Dominic Crossan. Theology, in this view, is primarily a hermeneutical enterprise in which the present engages the past for the theological purpose of uncovering insights helpful for today. It does not assume a singular history nor that the proper relation to the history we have inherited be one of acceptance. Moreover, it clearly acknowledges that both the contemporary inquirer and the complex history she or he encounters are fraught with values and assumptions that do not always cohere. Finally, revisionists have, often invoking the work of Hans-Georg Gadamer, insisted nonetheless that the past constrains us in some fashion, requires us to contend with it, not merely endow it with our creative speculations. With all this Crossan might well agree. But if more compatible with revisionist theology than postliberalism and deconstructionism, Crossan's work is also suggestive here.

In particular, Crossan's analysis points to the pluralistic character of the past and to the complex ways in which various construals of Jesus and the Christian vision developed. There were many interpretations and the ways some were designated "classics" had as much to do with political power and the vagaries of history than with their self-evident reliability or theological richness. Crossan's very utilization of noncanonical sources, the versions that lost out in the historical process, argues for a wider appeal than to the classics, not only for the historical purpose of developing as comprehensive a picture of Jesus and his times as possible, but equally important for theological purposes of constructing visions appropriate for today.

Pragmatic Historicism or Constructive Historicism

This paper has argued that in contemporary thought there has emerged a strong sense of human historicity and that contemporary theology, endorsing such sensibilities, has turned its attention once more to how that past should be understood and what role it should have in present-day theological reflection. But when prominent contemporary theological perspectives are analyzed in light of present-day historical research a number of questions can arise that challenge the adequacy of these theological stances. In closing, I would like to offer, in brief, an alternative theological proposal for interpreting theology and in particular its relation to history. This one, like the others, will be seen to resonate at points with Crossan though, as was the case with these other perspectives, places of conflict or divergence will also be clear. I am designating this approach as pragmatic historicism or alternatively constructive historicism.[1]

In this view, the task of theology is to define, critically analyze and reconstruct the interpretive frameworks and symbol systems out of which human beings live in order that we might gain orientation in life and better confront the specific issues, crises and transitions that face our era. Thus, theology's role is neither to reprise the past nor merely to deconstruct it. But it is also not to ignore our history. As historical beings we are dependent upon history for the raw materials out of which we fashion the present. Hence, that history must be engaged. How such engagement is to be understood entails, for theologians of this orientation, several important assumptions.

First, the history we confront is plural, multifaceted and complex. To carry out the historicist mandate means, therefore, that we must engage the complexity of historical reality, not abstract from it. This plural character of the past does not suggest that there are no boundaries but only that they are multileveled, contentious and always requiring new negotiation. Second, our historical legacy is ambiguous, a mixture of good and evil, full of tensions and contradictions. No moment of history, including that which gave birth to Christianity, escapes such a mixed nature. Moreover, visions that in one period provided illumination or liberation, might offer only destruction in another. Hence, our past must be viewed not only for what it positively extends to us but with suspicion concerning its negative effects.

Third, if the past is plural and complex, both life-giving and death-dealing, then the task of contemporary persons is to evaluate and make judgments about that history's utility for the present. In this view, to be historical is surely to be shaped by history and to require it for the present. However, historicity also fundamentally implies that out of engagement with that history, contemporary persons forge visions for today that we are responsible for and whose adequacy is determined not by whether they embody the depth grammar of a past age or the classic answers of a bygone era, but whether they offer a way of interpreting reality and a vision for living that meet our present needs.

Hence, the normative locus for theology is, in this approach, always in the present. History is important, it tells us where we have come from but it does not normatively determine where we should be in the present or go in the future. Those decisions are the inevitable responsibility of every present generation. To assume otherwise is to engage in a deadly illusion.

The approach articulated by John Dominic Crossan and the one labeled here pragmatic historicism might well find fruitful grounds for conversation. Their common commitment to a thick reading of history, their resistance to simplistic construals, their recognition of the multilayered dimensions of every historical occurrence and the internal tensions and conflicting possibilities in every historical moment, and their acknowledgment of the value- and interest-laden role of the interpreter all suggest that theology and historical studies in these modes might inform one another's efforts and support one another's tasks. But, there are other questions, theological in nature, that clearly require further conversation. What weight should be given to continuity and to creativity? What and whose norms inform the theological evaluation of history? Are not Jesus and his vision also open to criticism, and what does that mean for how one understands being a Christian and a theologian? How should one balance the historically-read Jesus and the theologically-read Christ? What should they have in common? For the proponents of constructive historicism these are, finally, all theological questions that require theological debate. So, let that theological conversation begin!

Notes

1. The term *constructive historicism* is borrowed from Delwin Brown's *The Boundaries of Our Habitations* (Brown 1994).

5.

Reconstructing Jesus for a Dysfunctional Church

Crossan's Christology and Contemporary Spirituality

ROBERT A. LUDWIG

The Catholic Church is today fraught with criticism and conflict. The theological revisioning that eventually led to the Second Vatican Council has expanded in the time since the Council, with calls for structural reform becoming increasingly intense, particularly around the requirements for ordination and the manner of decision making at the local, regional, and global levels. (See Bianchi and Ruether 1992.) The forbiddance of women from the clergy and the continuing discipline of mandatory celibacy for priests, the defining of sexual ethic with primary reference to procreative function, the appointment of unqualified loyalists as bishops, and, most important of all, the preoccupation with controlling power and authority — these issues have become rallying points of dissent within the church, leading millions to abandon active attendance and participation in the church's life and others to become more openly critical and more vocal in their protest.[1]

One of the more astute critics, Capuchin Franciscan priest Michael Crosby, applies the insights of psychology and family systems theory to the church. Utilizing the exploding research on shame and addiction, he sees the patterns of "dysfunction" in the Catholic Church. (See Crosby 1991.) The church, he suggests, is involved in denial and cover-up in its addiction to controlling power and authority, and the codependency of the faithful allows the focus on maintenance to dominate and overshadow community, mission, and authentic spirituality. With the language of Twelve-Step recovery programs, Crosby calls for "an intervention" in which the church is confronted with its addiction to preserving the male, celibate-clerical model of the church and Catholics come face-to-face with their patterns of codependency, which reinforce this addiction. Recovery can occur only through spiritual conversion, by turning to "a higher power," looking to God to fill the "hole" in our wholeness and finding support in prophetic small communities modeled on the Twelve Steps.

Ernie Larson and Janee Parnegg echo the same theme in their book *Recovering Catholics: What to Do When Religion Comes Between You and God* (1992). The term "recovering Catholic" refers to the struggle facing many Christians who seek to overcome the shame and pain they feel as a result of their experiences in an authoritarian church of secrets and controlling power, much as adult children of dysfunctional families struggle with issues arising from their family of origin. For many, particularly women, being Catholic has been an experience of shame and silence, learning to distrust feelings and distancing themselves from their own bodies, their sexuality, and their own creativity. Many have not learned self-esteem, an ability to form and sustain intimate relationships, and a healthy sense of their own abilities and limits to contribute to society in generative love and the work of justice. Rather, their god is an exacting judge with rules and an expectation of obedience. "Religious experience," for these, means "shame on you!"

Larson and Parnegg point out that coming to recognize that "God is not religion" is key to the process of healing. When we make religion God, we abandon our own responsibilities, our own freedom, and engage in a kind of idolatry—and we open ourselves to a process of abuse. Overcoming the shame of abuse begins with the insight that religion must answer to "a higher power." One begins to see the institutional church as limited and open to criticism rather than as divine and infallible, above all criticism.

The Church as Broker of Grace and Salvation

The Vatican, in its counterconciliar efforts today, tries to silence its critics (Hans Küng, Charles Curran, Matthew Fox, Leonardo Boff), condemning revisionist theological innovations and asserting its own teachings as "authoritative," even when its research is sketchy and its logic specious. A growing list of issues is declared "nondiscussable" (artificial contraception, the ordination of women, the celibacy requirement, homosexuality).

The church declares itself as a divinely-instituted organization that must be distinguished from the "merely human" institutions and structures all about us. The clergy are seen as "metaphysically elevated" and "ontologically changed" because of their ordination. Their maleness and their vows of celibacy permit their inclusion in the process of "binding and loosing" in the closed decision making of a hierarchically-structured body that claims to speak for God. Their function is seen as brokering grace and salvation to a humanity so wounded by original sin that the church itself is seen as a desperate imperative.

This self-understanding of the church has been radically challenged from within by twentieth-century theology and, particularly, by the spirit and the documents of the Second Vatican Council. A new Christian anthropology and a new theology of grace seeks to overcome the dualisms of Tridentine theology (nature and grace, history and eternity, body and soul, and in christology, humanity and divinity). Grace is not defined as an antidote to original sin, but is given with human existence itself, in our capacity for transcendence, through such natural human activities as knowing, loving, creating and hoping. We are still free, and we are still pulled away from our openness to divine mystery by inherited sin, but God's self-gift to persons is not determined by baptism, church membership, or explicit Christian faith. God is in relationship to persons in their spiritual existence, universally. Explicit faith, then, becomes a process of thematizing the unthematic, naming our diffuse experience and celebrating it as our deepest meaning and purpose.

Being Catholic or Christian is not an imperative; grace is loose in the world! Church is not broker for grace, but support group for transcendent experience, the community that remembers Jesus as both sacrament of God's self-gift and model for human transcendence. More of this later. For now, however, it should be clear that the church's self-understanding is shifting from within—from hierarchical and juridical brokerage to "pilgrim people" who bear the memory of Jesus and celebrate their own existence in communion with his, searching for personal and corporate transcendence within the context of lived existence and historical transformation.

The notion of church as authoritarian grace-broker and sole mediator of salvation has been criticized as well by the behavioral and social sciences and organizational development theory and practice. The principles of personal autonomy, self-esteem, the psycho-spiritual equality of persons, concern for participation and mutuality in the empowerment of people in systems—all of this presents a radical challenge to a dysfunctional church. The church as egalitarian spiritual community, "the people of God," takes actual form in the development of communication skills (active listening and self-disclosure) and participatory democratic processes in setting corporate priorities and making collective decisions. (See O'Brien and Swidler 1988.)

Today the dysfunctional church is becoming unraveled by the praxis of politically-oppressed and economically-exploited peoples in the Third and Fourth (indigenous) Worlds and the therapeutic psychological recovery of adult believers in Europe and North America.

Dysfunctional Christology

The dysfunctional church looks to a dysfunctional christology for its foundational legitimacy. This dysfunctional christology is caught up in the denial of Jesus' humanity and a cover-up of his own radical critique of hierarchy and God-brokering. The post-Constantinian addiction to power is founded on the practical outcomes of the early christological councils: a Gnostic, docetic, and monophysite Jesus—simply God, stripped of any authentic humanity.

Jesus Christ is then seen as "God coming to earth"—mainly to die on the cross. His death is a sacrifice for our sins, redeeming the children of Adam (and Eve) from the consequences of sinful rebellion. His death is "a ransom" for sin, which pays a divine price for our reconciliation with God. His death "makes satisfaction" to an angry God, who now—rather reluctantly—offers forgiveness and salvation through the church and its sacraments.

Crossan's careful reconstruction of the historical Jesus is part of a larger movement within Catholic theology to retrieve the humanity of Jesus and, with it, the specific and concrete experience of the human Jesus and his impact on others within his own historical situation. This can become a credible basis for present-day spiritual meaning. The traditional christology was part of "an imperative theology"—that is, a construct that saw humanity as wounded (Augustine) or inadequate (Aquinas), ontologically in need of supernatural healing (Augustine) and elevation (Aquinas). First, Jesus Christ and, then, the church, are seen as imperatives. Without his sacrificial death and the church's sacraments, there is no hope and no salvation. To retrieve Jesus' humanity is to be reconciled to our own. To perceive Jesus in the limited contexts of a particular history, a particular culture, is to see the church as always limited by history and culture. But in all this, one also begins to see in historically credible terms the dynamics of Christian origins as an authentic basis for spiritual meaning and the praxis of faith in today's world. This is an expression of a larger "grace" at work in humanity and history really reconciling at the personal and at the social level. Crossan's Jesus is helping people take responsibility for their own bodies and live a radical egalitarianism now—that is real reconciliation, even from the shame of dysfunctional religion! Crossan's work is a critical challenge to dysfunctional Catholicism and a vital resource for the reconstruction of authentic and meaningful Christian spirituality.

Crossan's Work as Christology

Crossan's reconstruction of Jesus is a compelling christological portrait, both for its methodological rigor and its radical conclusions. Historians and biblical scholars may want to criticize Crossan's work from within their own disciplinary expertise, but from a *theological* perspective, I find myself affirming this image of Jesus. The humanity of Jesus is fully restored, and his followers' experience of the Sacred in his person, message, program, and performance becomes credible and accessible to contemporary persons. I don't find this portrait to be reductionist, but, in christological language, Jesus' divinity is clearly anchored in his humanity—and in the dynamics of historically credible circumstances and events. Faith in Jesus is not denigrated, but enhanced.

Those committed to church reform will be inspired by this Jesus who challenges religious presumptions and hierarchical structures, proclaiming a God who needs no brokering and orchestrating a movement that is radically egalitarian, healing persons by challenging structural injustice. In a world that is too often religiously cynical, and in which we experience the widespread loss of personal meaning and rampant social injustice, people are hungry for this kind of Jesus.

Returning to the historical Jesus as ground for a contemporary christology has become normative in Catholic circles today, and Crossan's rigorous method, academically correct if anything, is more thorough and comprehensive than others. His use of noncanonical Gospels yields a more extensive pool of Jesus material, and his broad utilization of anthropological research furnishes both a wider context and a more detailed perspective of Jesus' actual historical situation. Insistence on multiple attestations provides a certain journalistic objectivity. Finally, by separating the nonliterate (oral) and literate sources of the Jesus tradition, we get a much more radical portrait, freed even from the limits of scriptural Judaism's interpretive patterns and metaphors.

Crossan admits that his reconstructed Jesus is "a portrait," the result of his own conversation with the past in and through the best triangular methodology he could shape. Whether he is as self-conscious as he might be about how his own roots in a colonized Ireland and his own experience of oppression by the Roman Church have influenced that portrait, is ambiguous. Crossan never spells out explicitly where he is coming from *theologically*, and he seems less aware than he might be about how his own religious/spiritual situation cannot help but shape and influence both how he investigates the truth about Jesus of Nazareth and what his reconstructed portrait actually looks like. The hermeneutical laws seem to apply — even when one is doing "history." Our own self-understanding and our own "geography" (the contexts in which we find ourselves) in the present will always determine and shape what we find in texts from the past, whether canonical or not.

Having said that, and wishing for a more explicitly *theological* rationale from Crossan, his Jesus portrait is, nonetheless, appealing and undoubtedly finding a ready audience that longs for a Jesus this credible. While Crossan's Jesus poses a radical challenge, unquestionably, he also images a contemporary faith. He may be deconstructing a traditional Christ, but his reconstruction of Jesus becomes the historical basis for a truly contemporary Christ. Cardinal Ratzinger and other Vatican loyalists will not take well to this Jesus portrait because of the ecclesiology implied in the absence of hierarchy in the Jesus movement and because this Jesus challenges the brokering function. Any of us not destitute likely will cringe a bit at our situation of comfort and privilege, feeling some sting in the radical demands that this kind of discipleship sets before us. Still, for many Catholic revisionists, this is an exciting Jesus, an inspiring Jesus, a spiritual figure worthy of their religious instincts and sensitivities.

This Jesus, carefully reconstructed with rigorous historical methods from his Mediterranean and Jewish contexts, looks not only pre-Constantinian but also postmodern. He resembles not only a first-century Jewish peasant, but also a twentieth-century Latin American *campesino*. His program of common meals and healing is relevant not only to the destitute in Galilee centuries ago, but also to the marginalized and oppressed in urban slums and third-world villages, people of color, women, gays and lesbians, and all today who suffer illness from the tensions of inequality, poverty, abuse, violence, and discrimination.

Crossan and Contemporary Catholicism

It is noteworthy that Crossan's Jesus appears on the centennial anniversary of *Rerum Novarum*. Clearly, modern Catholic social teaching is not exactly this Jesus' commensality. Nevertheless, the effort in the twentieth century to retrieve the church's mission to the world, to see social justice as "a constitutive dimension of the gospel," to speak openly and forcefully about human dignity and human rights, peacemaking, and a "fundamental option for the poor" — there is in this an unmistakable continuity with Crossan's portrait of Jesus, his message, his program, his performance. One can easily see this historical Jesus, twenty-five years after the Council, as a worthy expression of revisionist and liberationist Vatican II Catholicism! The peasant Cynic Jesus embodies a radical contemporary faith that is witnessed to by Dorothy Day and her Catholic Workers, by the Berrigan brothers and the Plowshares Movement, by Green Christians in Europe, and base communities in Latin America. Oscar Romero and the "kairos" of contemporary Salvadoran faith communities who struggle for dignity and justice against demonic "Death Squads" — this seems remarkably parallel to the Jesus movement in Galilee that Crossan describes so adroitly. However, there are more explicitly christological connections as well.

Developments in Contemporary Christology

In a groundbreaking essay on "The Problems of Christology Today" (1951), Karl Rahner pioneered contemporary Catholic christological developments. He wanted, on the 1500th anniversary of the Council of Chalcedon, to loosen up rigid, dogmatic consciousness with respect to the Chalcedonian christological formula ("truly God and truly man"). The popular Catholic understanding of Christ was basically monophysitic: Jesus was simply God, the Second Person of the Trinity. It was docetic: Jesus only appeared to be a human being. The *practical* results of the early christo-logical councils had been the eclipse of anything resembling genuine humanity in Jesus. Rahner interprets Chalcedon's dogma as a beginning, not as an end, for present-day theology's focus on Christ.

What is needed today, he says, is twofold: (1) a new Christian anthropology that will reinterpret humanity/divinity existentially; and (2) "plain historical testimony about what happened in Jesus ... about what in its unique, irreducible, and historical concreteness forms the basis of the existence and of the event of salvation for a Christian" (Rahner 1978: 176-77). Rahner insists that "the basic and decisive point of departure lies in an encounter with the historical Jesus of Nazareth" (177). Yet this encounter with history itself requires a prior corrective to understanding reality non-historically—that is, dualistically. When Rahner asks why the Christian message has lost its credibility today, very often even for those who affirm it in faith, he inevitably points to a conceptual dualism that has been mistaken as real, historical, existential. In truth, the traditional distinctions (such as Chalcedon's "truly God and truly man" or the Fourth Gospel's "the Word became flesh") are legitimate only conceptually. The ontological reality is a unity in diversity. In retrieving a sense of unity (divinity *in* humanity; incarnation and creation as two phases of a single process in which God gives Godself to what is other than God), the Christian message becomes compelling again and speaks to us where we know ourselves and where we live our lives. The first movement of Rahner's christology, then, is to establish a new credibility for Jesus by discovering an existential meaning in a fundamental unity.

From the Rahnerian emphasis on the "true human being" of the dogmatic formula, contemporary theologians have gone on to "Jesus of Nazareth." "The translation of 'humanity of Christ' into 'Jesus of Nazareth' has rephrased the very significance of the christological task. The concrete content of Jesus of Nazareth, over and above this profession of his 'true humanity,' has forced christology's self-revision" (Sobrino 1982: 56).

Hans Küng and Edward Schillebeeckx, both of whom have developed important christological texts in recent decades (Küng 1976; Schillebeeckx 1979, 1980), are significant players in this self-revision. They, like Rahner, focus on "two poles" (Küng) or "two sources" (Schillebeeckx). Küng, in reviewing his own work together with that of Rahner and Schillebeeckx, refers to "a new fundamental consensus in Catholic (and not only Catholic) theology ... a basic hermeneutical agreement" (1988: 108). The consensus theme is echoed by the International Theological Commission on Special Questions in Christology,[2] which sees "a novel emphasis on Christ's humanity and its salvific character" as central to the enormous body of christological literature produced in the sixties and seventies.

Schillebeeckx describes the two sources from which contemporary theology must draw as "the whole experiential tradition of the great Jewish-Christian movement" and "today's new human experiences shared by both

Christians and non-Christians." Küng speaks of theology's two poles as "the history of Israel and the history of Jesus" and "our own human world of experience." This importance of the historical Jesus has become typical of contemporary Catholic christology. Küng calls reference to the specific experience of the historical Jesus "the source, norm, and criterion for Christian faith." "Historical probing into the Jesus of history is possible and necessary because Christianity is based not on myths, legends, or fairy tales, and not merely on a teaching, but primarily on a historical personality: Jesus of Nazareth" (Küng 1988: 111). Such a history is a source of critiquing deviant christology and the dysfunctional church's self-understanding:

> There must be no contradiction between the Christ of faith and the Jesus of history. The Christ of faith must be able to be identified as the Jesus of history. . . . A theology conscious of its responsibilities has to take seriously the doubts of so many contemporary men and women about the traditional image of Christ. Its job is to defend the Christian faith, not only against the attacks of unbelief but also against distortions and false conclusions on the part of the Church. Projections by belief or unbelief are subject to critical comparison with what the historical Jesus really was. Thus, we have *fides quaerens intellectum historicum* — a faith seeking historical understanding — and at the same time *intellectus historicus quaerens fidem* — historical understanding seeking faith. A believing interpretation of Jesus that has no need at all to hide the interests of faith has to be a historically plausible interpretation (Küng 1988: 111-12).

It is, thus, important that theology look to history "to get a fresh view of the original outlines of his message, his way of life, his fate, and so of his person, which have so often been painted over and concealed in the course of centuries" (111). Crossan's work opens up "a historically plausible" Jesus and provides a much more detailed understanding of his actual historical existence than the Gospels provide. As Crossan himself shows so well, the Gospels clearly are in the tradition of literate Judaism and the stories, images, metaphors from Jewish scriptures. Crossan's portrait opens up the historically plausible Jesus that is a necessary prerequisite to comprehending the metaphorical interpretations from literate Judaism.

Jesus in Latin American Liberation Theology

Latin American liberation theology reflects this important role for historical method and its picture of Jesus, as well. According to Jon Sobrino "Latin American theology has accorded a methodological primacy to the moment of the historical Jesus" and thereby thinks it has found "a better point of departure for the articulation of the totality of Christian faith . . .

and the best route of access today" (1982: 55). Liberation christology likewise begins with a suggestion of Chalcedon's contemporary inadequacy,
suggesting that the dogmatic formula presupposes concepts that simply
cannot be presupposed when it comes to Jesus:

> [It] assumes we know who and what God is and who and what human
> beings are. But we cannot explain the figure of Jesus by presupposing
> such concepts because Jesus himself calls into question people's very
> understanding of God and human beings. We may use "divinity" and
> "humanity" as nominal definitions to somehow break the hermeneu-
> tical circle, but we cannot use them as real definitions, already known,
> in order to understand Jesus. Our approach should start from the
> other end (Sobrino 1982: 82).

Starting from the other end implies as well "the rehabilitation of the
revelatory import of Jesus' earthly existence." Traditional christology has
placed so much emphasis on the Paschal Mystery (Jesus' death-resurrec-
tion) as the salvific moment, that all that went before—his life, his teachings, his program and performance—were revelatorily eclipsed. Crossan
puts the encounter with the Sacred back into Jesus' historical existence and
sees the resurrection narratives as interpreting this theologically. Schillebeeckx does the same thing in his emphasis on the salvific experience of
the encounter with Jesus in history. Only through recourse to Jesus' history
can the content of the formulations about Christ be invested with meaning
and connected to the contemporary quest for meaning. Thus, the hermeneutical focus has shifted "from the understanding of the Christ of faith
and his import for the present, to the understanding of the historical Jesus"
and his meaning, first within his own contexts, then in our own.

Latin American theologians see a real connection between the abstract,
ethereal Christ of traditional christology and the oppressive conditions of
the poor. Retrieving the Jesus of history, especially one like Crossan's peasant Cynic Jesus whose mission is social revolution and radical egalitarianism, withdraws religious legitimacy from the politics of oppression and
indifference. In Europe and North America, our postmodern hunger for
existential wholism summons us beyond dualism to a demythologized
Christ, but in Latin America, what has happened to Jesus through the
centuries is the source of "moral indignation."

J. Comblin describes the traditional Christ as an "iconization" of Jesus'
historical existence: "The life of Jesus is no longer a human life, submerged
in history, but a theological life—an icon. As happens with icons, his actions
lose their human context and are stylized, becoming transformed into signs
of the transcendent and invisible world."[3] Gustavo Gutiérrez points out
that the life of Jesus is, thus, "placed outside history, unrelated to the real
forces at play" (1988: 130). This ahistorical Jesus is seen as problematic by

liberationist theologians precisely because it is so open to "manipulation and connivance with idols":

> The most profound crisis to which Latin American christology must respond lies not along the lines of pure demythologization, but along those of rescue of Christ from appropriation as the alibi for indifference in the face of the misery of reality and especially as an excuse for the religious justification of this misery. . . . What is in crisis is not purely and simply the "name" of Christ, as having lost its meaning and import, but what is actually occurring "in the name of Christ." A post-Enlightenment culture entertains doubts about Christ; Latin American reality produces indignation at what is done in his name (Sobrino 1982: 59).

One experiences indignation, first, because of the tragic repercussions for the poor of Christ's manipulation, and second, because the reality of Christ "has been manipulated, distorted, kidnapped." Behind this second sense of indignation is a sorrow — "not just on account of the oppression of the poor, but also on account of the falsification of the identity of someone of supreme personal significance and meaning." On account of this false presentation of Christ, some have abandoned faith in him (12).

Liberation theology has intuited an image of Jesus from their own historical contexts, their own experience of oppression and poverty. Crossan's image of Jesus, reconstructed through historical research, looks much the same. In fact, the similarities are astonishing, as Sobrino's review of key aspects of the figure of Christ in Latin America shows: (1) Jesus is presented, first of all, in his relationship with the kingdom of God; (2) the practice of Jesus is seen as service to this kingdom of God; (3) this practice is described not only as an historical, observable fact, but as Jesus' response to the will of the God of the kingdom — a God who feels a special preference and tenderness for the poor; (4) Jesus makes real demands on his hearers in the sense of radical conversion and in living the kingdom now; and (5) the historical reasons for Jesus' death are emphasized — the conflict he aroused and his being sentenced to death as a political agitator (13-14).

Latin American christology understands the resurrection as faith's interpretation of Jesus' life and death, a revelation and an inspiration that "the one who was crucified has been raised and the one who has been raised is none other than the one who was crucified." The God of the resurrection, the one who can call nonlife to life, is seen as "love for whoever is small, whoever is crushed and under sentence of death, as hope for whoever is small, crushed, and under sentence of death." Thus, in Jesus, "God's love has been historicized in credible fashion" (15). Crossan, likewise, talks about the resurrection texts as "prophecy historicized" — that is, meaning making in the unpacking of the experience by reference to the literary tradition. The experience being unpacked is the being healed by overcoming controlling power's intimidation. To live in the reign of God is liberation!

Faith in Jesus Christ

For Jon Sobrino and other liberation theologians in Latin America, all of this focus on the historical Jesus ultimately leads to a timely and distinctive faith and spirituality:

> If persons and communities follow Jesus and proclaim the kingdom of God to the poor; if they strive for liberation from every kind of slavery; if they seek, for all human beings, especially for that immense majority of men and women who are crucified persons, a life in conformity with the dignity of daughters and sons of God; if they have the courage and forthrightness to speak the truth . . . if, in the discipleship of Jesus, they effectuate their own conversion from being oppressor to being men and women of service . . . if in doing justice they seek peace and in making peace they seek to base it on justice; and if they do all this in the following and discipleship of Jesus because he did all this himself—then they believe in Jesus. . . . If they abide with God in the cross of Jesus and in the numberless crosses of history; and if in spite of all this their hope is mightier than death— then they believe in the God of Jesus (53-54).

Believing is precisely to the point with Crossan's reconstruction of Jesus—believing that is not intimidated by threats, but overcomes raw power with its own, more numinous power. One moves from the reign of fear to the reign of God, from being controlled by the powers that be to a freedom from such control. In and through Jesus' liberation, one steps over boundaries, taking a place where one "doesn't belong," according to convention. Taking responsibility for one's own body and sitting at the table with whoever is hungry, refusing to honor the proper hierarchies and discriminations, overcoming the polarities that segment and separate—this is the faith of Jesus. It is healing, precisely because one's allegiance and trust is singular, clear. Not Caesar or his procurator, not Herod, not Caiaphas and his sanhedrin—only God reigns! To believe is to be set free from pretentions—to overcome one's codependent status!

Shame, Grace, and Crossan's Jesus

Crossan's reconstruction of Jesus provides a scholarly, historical basis— not just for Latin Americans' intuition of Jesus as liberator, but also for codependent Catholics who have grown up with a shame-based "imperative

theology" and seek an internal liberation from shame and guilt. Gloria
Steinem writes about "a revolution from within" (1992), developing the
thesis that liberation is not only about removing external barriers by chang-
ing social structures, but also about interiority—about how we internalize
those barriers and need to seek internal change. This is the adult work of
self-esteem, reclaiming psychologically an empowered self. John Bradshaw,
a former priest who has published best-selling books on shame, self-esteem,
and Twelve-Step healing, discusses "toxic shame" as "a true sickness of the
soul" that is, in fact, "life-destroying." Toxic shame is experienced as the
all-pervasive sense that one is flawed and defective—precisely as a human
being; a sense of failing and falling short—as a person. When one experiences one's true self as defective and flawed, a "false self" emerges psychologically. This development of a false self is a flight from being an
authentic human being, an effort to be more than human, an abandonment
of one's true humanity. "It takes tons of energy and hard work to live a
false self," he writes, a situation in which we are increasingly disconnected
from our emotions, needs, and drives, and given over to an isolating life of
cover-up. One becomes "an object of contempt to yourself . . . watching
and scrutinizing every minute detail of behavior" (1988: 13). This notion
of the false self seems to be very close to what the Gospels, especially
Matthew, criticize in the Pharisees' spirituality—and what many would criticize today as Catholic spirituality.

Bradshaw's insights about dysfunctional families and the shaming process lead him to identify seven "dysfunctional family rules," which demonstrate the suppression of authentic humanity and the nurturing of false
selves:

> *1) Control*—One must be in control of all interactions, feelings, and
> personal behaviors at all times;
> *2) Perfectionism*—Always be right in everything you do;
> *3) Blame*—Whenever things don't turn out as planned, blame your-
> self or others;
> *4) Denial of the Five Freedoms*—the power to perceive, to think and
> interpret, to feel, to want and to choose, and the power to imagine;
> *5) The No-Talk Rule*—which prohibits the full expression of any
> feeling, need, or want;
> *6) Don't Make Mistakes*—Cover up your own mistakes and, if some-
> one else makes a mistake, shame him;
> *7) Unreliability*—Don't trust anyone and you will never be disap-
> pointed (39-40).

Crosby sees these same rules operating in the Catholic Church, where
the destructive patterns of thinking, feeling, and acting are made normative,
as in dysfunctional families. Control and perfectionism require the denial
of freedoms and the no-talk rule. The definition of infallibility (and its

implied extension to almost everything the magisterium says or does) denies the possibility of mistakes. An anthropology that defines humanity as "sinner" is the source of blame and unreliability. Catholic spirituality, in this dysfunctional scheme, becomes the development and maintenance of a false self.

Christology is implicated in all of this. By denying Jesus' humanity and then making him the model for morality and ethical living, we have created an impossible ideal. By seeing Jesus' salvation as an antidote to our situation of being radically flawed by original sin, natural humanity is seen as defective and worthless. By focusing on Jesus' horrible death as "sacrifice for our sins," we are led to view ourselves contemptuously. By covering up Jesus' critique of hierarchy and his disdain for religious brokerage, especially by seeing Judaism as a religion to be blamed and "replaced" by a better broker, we have founded a church that is all-controlling and that must be obeyed because it speaks for God. Perhaps most damning, however, is the fact that we have covered over and hidden the real Jesus—one who can heal our shame and set us free from the prison of our false selves—with a false Christ.

Crossan's historical Jesus makes that covering over and hiding more difficult. But, in addition, he makes that healing and that being set free more possible. The reconstructed Jesus models courage before external tyranny and thereby issues an invitation to others: be healed, be free, embrace the peasant's dream now! He calls us to take responsibility for our own bodies, for our own lives—to live beyond convention's cool and calculated control, whether from state or church. He calls those of us who are "dead" to life again by retrieving the real self that we allowed to die in giving birth to the false. His "Abba" is a higher power, who empowers us to challenge the church's own claims of divinity. His kingdom is available in small communities of healing and courage, now.

Increasingly, psychotherapy is understanding its work as spiritual healing.[4] A sense of "grace" as the most profound ground for self-esteem and personal empowerment is seen as a prerequisite to any real recovery from shame and addiction. Grace is simultaneously our capacity for transcendent openness and our actually acting on the impulse to go beyond. Grace is available only through irony and paradox, embracing the more in trust not by flight from limits, but precisely in and through accepting them with humility. Empowerment begins by admitting powerlessness; healing begins by admitting illness; liberation begins by admitting that we are bound. This is where a new christology can help—one that dispels any false flights beyond our humanity, one that sees and feels the real pain of suffering in history, one that activates our imagination by listening to our deepest hungers and our most passionate drives, one that tolerates ambiguity and imperfection and shadows, and, finally, one that heals, empowers, and liberates because it is grounded in real healing, empowering, and liberating. Such a christology might be found in a historical reconstruction of Jesus of

Nazareth, Mediterranean Jewish peasant. Crossan's work, to the extent that it provides us access to that Jesus, can help heal the contemporary church and empower it to serve the reign of God in history.

Notes

1. See Hans Küng 1990. In addition to Küng's own reflections on the future of the reform movement and "keeping hope alive," the book contains the 1968 declaration "For the Freedom of Theology" (Küng, Congar, Rahner, and Schille-beeckx); the 1972 declaration "Against Resignation" drawn up at Tubingen and signed by numerous European theologians; the 1989 Cologne Declaration "Against Disenfranchism: For an Open Catholicity"; and the 1990 "Call for Renewal in the Catholic Church" drafted in the United States by the Call to Action.

2. *Gregorianum* 61 (1980): 609-32, quoted by Sobrino (1982: 4).

3. *Theologie de la revolution* (Paris: Editions Universitaires, 1970): 236, quoted by Gutiérrez (1988: 130).

4. See, for example, Gerald G. May 1988, Thomas More 1992, and M. Scott Peck 1978.

6.

The Jesus of History and the Feminism of Theology

CATHERINE KELLER

"Actually, it is primarily the context that has been ignored — vanished, disappeared, buried. . . . In the Keres way, context is female and it is God, because it is the source and generator of meaning."
— Paula Gunn Allen

"Jesus"! The most agonized and trivialized, overused and misused name in history. So, left to my own devices, I might endlessly defer the naming of Jesus. I might even justify this deferral christologically. Therefore, I am ruefully grateful for the opportunity to engage the name, the question, the problem of Jesus — in conversation, precisely, not with a theologian pursuing christological constructions, but with a biblical scholar reconstructing "Jesus." Biblical criticism, even in its tendency to participate in modernist meaning-reduction, has offered a great corrective to the self-sacralizing inflations of theological christology. John Dominic Crossan's *Jesus*, however, manages the deflation without the reduction. But the correction is less a matter of correctness than of the reconstruction of context.

Salvation from a decontextualizing Christ is the prerequisite of any feminist Christian theology. At least this is the case for any feminism that is unwilling to forfeit its own contextual honesty, whether for the sake of legitimation by premodern or modern universalisms or by postmodern deconstructions — all of which end up obscuring the cultural force of gender in the construction of our standpoints (cf. Bordo 1990). The dimension of the women's movement that recognizes its own economic, national and race specificity along with, indeed as integral to, its gender analysis, has increasingly revealed the judgment and the blessing, the complexity and the connectivity, inherent in context. (So, my whiteness, my relatively stable U.S. professional status, can at least be recognized as tending me toward a numbing abstraction — even toward a "white woman's Christ" over "Black woman's Jesus" [Grant] — which will, however, ever again be thankfully disturbed by the bodily misfit of the norms of academic theology and the communal creativity that has rarely failed me among women colleagues.) In this essay I will seek to elicit the contextuality that connects Crossan's reconstruction of Jesus to a feminist reconstruction of theology.

Let me suggest that this connection is to be discerned in an enormous resonance field of time and space, through which certain liberating impulses rehearse the radical connectivity of the *basileia*. To trace the outlines of this context, I read Crossan from the vantage point of a recent journey to El Salvador and, also, of the gender consciousness that has long accompanied me.

Blessed Deferral

While first reading along in Crossan's text, I might have wanted him to draw his inferences right away—from his analyses of honor and patronage, slave, protestor and revolutionary in the ancient world, to Jesus himself. To get to "the point." Yet Crossan is not here to broker Jesus. Somewhere between the brokerage of empire and the breaking of bread, fascinated into accepting my fate with the great volume of a great volume, I noted in myself a slow-dawning relief. Relief at the long (225 pages) textual postponement of Jesus. Now of course this was partly gratitude for the rich offering of original sources and their settings. But something else was at play. By the time we got to Jesus, I was actually excited by the suspense. This is uncharacteristic. I am conditioned to react to discussions of Jesus with some mix of boredom, sadness, embarrassment, anger and defense (of my Jesus against theirs). Even feminist retrievals of Jesus sometimes conjure for me the mustiness of church basements accompanied by an out-of-tune piano.

I began to suspect that Crossan's deferral of Jesus is itself very much to the point—that form, here, embodies content. The postponement, in fact, permits the critical action of recontextualization. What emerges thereby in the text resembles a topological device graphed out by A.N. Whitehead as philosopher of science, which he called "extensive abstraction":

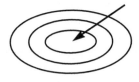

The point of the geometric field theory is that there is no actually perceivable point, or line, to which geometry may refer. There are, however, "perceivable relations" defining points in terms of the "overlapping" between volumes and the "convergent sets" just produced (Whitehead

1917: chapter 7). By analogy, there is no actual spatiotemporal point, or line, which any historical science can perceive as the literal life of Jesus. But a life there was, relative to many other lives, including our own. Crossan's own triadically relativistic methodology purports to bring us close to it, by laying, one on top of the other, the prerequisite anthropological, political, social volumes, and then scrutinizing the regions where they overlap with the earliest texts.

Thus, Crossan's postponement is a work of contextualization, which actually has the effect of foreshortening Jesus *into* his historical particularity, but like all foreshortening, this involves an art of perspective. One theological effect of the foreshortened Jesus of history is a relativist christology—the Christ you get is the Jesus you have constructed. Of course, Crossan is too gracious to invade theological turf head-on, and claims to see no contradiction between historical Jesus and theological Christ—at least not before Constantine. But that is no mean proviso, from the perspective of the late great United States empire, with its still-echoing appeals to the Constantinian Christ in justification of its own expansionism.

By relocating Jesus as this particular Jewish-peasant, male Cynic, with capacities uncharacteristic of the Cynics for collective ritual and mobilization, Crossan gently deflates the Christ-Jesus of theology. That is, he undermines the historical basis for various inflated claims to Jesus' unique ontology. Jesus is, thus, left again to walk his own Galilean roads with his friends, to foment his short-lived social revolution of commensality, to work healing magic, and to die brutally and indecorously, without human trial or divine justification. And theologians are fortunately *not* quite left to do what they want with his afterimage.

In a certain sense, the work of theology can only take up where Crossan's theology leaves off (not that his ever does). When it comes to christology and its largely post-Constantinian tradition, it is difficult to get on with theological construction, given all the deconstruction work to be done. But, in a certain sense, work such as Crossan's accomplishes this deconstruction, for us in advance. Deconstruction here means not destruction, but exposé of the constructions *as* constructions. In this sense deconstruction is disclosure of the layers of supernaturalist, imperial and patriarchal ornamentation of Jesus as the triumphant exception to any human condition he might have illumined. In this work, Crossan is not about exposing the naked, true and essential Jesus—this would be to commit what one might call the fallacy of the historical striptease. His claims are historicist-relativist, not historicist-essentialist. But the relativity designates not mere self-referential projection, but rather a set of relationships in which a visionary practice unfolded, a practice which we—from the vantage point of our relationship to the newly filtered text—might already, and so again, embrace. These relationships express, from a normative theological point of view, an alternative christology—alternative at least to that inflated Christ who has gotten in the way of the local, contextual struggle for just and vital com-

munities—that Christ, or well-brokered Christ-construct, who has sabotaged the spirit of Jesus. The reappearance of a bread- and brokerage-
breaking Jesus, foreshortened into his own scrappy history, well-serves the
radical transformation of Christianity now well underway. The christologically decentered Jesus who steps back into his context and, thus, releases
us into responsibility for our own, inspires us to recenter our theological
practices around what Asian-American feminist theologian Rita Nakashima
Brock and, elsewhere, Native-American Episcopalian theologian Steven
Charleston have called "the New Reformation" (Charleston 1990: 60).

So, what I want to examine now is how this return of Jesus to a hypothetical field of historical particularity forms a "convergent set" with the
two zones of christological work most real, most un-Sunday school, for me
right now: one in the ongoing institutional struggle of feminist theology,
the other in the two-thirds world epitomized by peasant El Salvador. These
zones converge in the New Reformation—a transmutation of Christianity
recognizable in the commitment to postpatriarchal and postcolonial practices, and in loosening the grip of Euroamerican empire and the missionary
Christ which has accompanied that empire since 1492. But its precedents
lie over a millennium earlier, and thus involve us in what Crossan calls a
"basic cost-accounting with Constantine."

The Feminism of Christology

How would we read Crossan through feminist Christian eyes?

Never mind how inutterably counterproductive the notion of a feminist
christology remains for postchristian feminists. What are the analogues in
feminist theology to the foreshortening process observed above? They
would have to be sought, I suspect, amid our ambivalence. Roman Catholic
theologian Elizabeth Johnson puts well the perplexity with which feminists
approach the subject: "Despite the potential benefit devolving from the
history of Jesus the Christ, feminist theology raises a most stringent critique,
pointing out that of all the doctrines of the church Christology is the one
most used to suppress and exclude women" (151). As the church acculturated to the Greco-Roman context, it molded itself to the patriarchal household, with Christ as its head. The high christologies erected in the name of
Jesus' unique, exclusive and final incarnation of God, the Absolute Mas-
culinity, still serve very practical functions. The essential maleness of God
in Jesus is still evoked by the patriarchs of Roman Catholicism to abort
women's sense of vocation to ordination, that is, their humanity. (Sadly,
that gifted denomination is thereby bleeding itself of its own talents and
energy.)

The most obvious implication seems to be that the more inflated the
christology, the more oppressed the women. This inference might prove
simplistic, but it is at least true that when the historical Jesus is identified

with an imperial, centralizing Christ, the divine maleness, raised to the second power, becomes, well, omnipotent. This leaves no breathing room in which the spirit might work publicly, in and through women. It is the perennial challenge of feminist history, seeking our solidarity with women in the past, grasping after hints of the agency, the voice, the resistance of women in Christian history, to read beyond the numbing spectacle of millennia of gifted women endlessly waiting for some male figure—Prince Charming or Lord Jesus—to save them from the ruder patriarchs. And failing that, from life itself. The problem is not solved by the anachronistic proposition that "Jesus is a feminist." Mary Daly answered that two decades ago with a simple "so what?" The last thing we need is a refurbished hero, whether he is called savior, liberator or feminist. Indeed, as Rita Nakashima Brock has assessed it, any version of the myth of Jesus, the heroic individual, "who defies established authority and reveals, through his work and . . . life the liberating will of the deity he worships," tunes in all too readily to the image of the "single conqueror who defeats death, injustice or evil" (Brock 1991: 58).

It would be nice, of course, if there were one, and people of every religion will continue in moments of desperation to wish for such. But the very expectation seems to so sediment the spirit that the sources of action become clogged. Injustice thrives unimpeded when the passivity of a subordinate class, race or gender is thus spiritually reinforced.

Because Crossan offers us a minimally christological Jesus, his work does not give rise to the misdirecting question of whether Jesus "saves" us. Rather, he excavates the traces of a figure at the heart of a popular movement. Its strategies do not so much aim at stabilizing belief in its leader, but at "building or rebuilding peasant community on radically different principles from those of honor and shame, patronage and clientage."

Having earlier marked the peculiarity of Mediterranean understandings of honor as defined by male control of female bodies as primary, Crossan's analysis coincides warmly with women's concerns. His work seems to intersect meaningfully that of Elisabeth Schüssler Fiorenza, especially concerning the criteria of inclusive, communal and commensal mutuality enacted in the early Jesus movement. Given that Crossan's text overflows with quotations, it is disappointing to find virtually no engagement—but for the honorific flourish of his allusion to "in memory of her" in his book's final paragraph—with Schüssler Fiorenza's own reconstruction of the same movement. Indeed, for all its satisfying grimaces at chauvinism, there is virtually no dialogue with feminist sources.

The Christology of Context

Perhaps, Crossan wanted to avoid being sucked into the vortex of transparent ideological commitments, preferring that his historical arguments speak for themselves. Nor does he perform any ritual of social location. Yet, he admirably eschews the quest for an "unattainable objectivity," preferring instead "an attainable honesty." But at least in feminist theory, such honesty is only believed attainable by textually situating oneself-in-context in relation to context and text. This matter of self-contextualization still strikes me as elusive, indeed as less concretizing than we like to imagine, given the vast generic emptiness of categories such as "race," "class," and "gender" until they are painstakingly filled, and as sometimes provocative of mere confession. But there is theological, let us say christological, depth in the intuition that our *logos*, our *logoi*, reveal themselves only by incarnation into our scandalous particularities—even that of white males. Making this a conscious dimension of academic truth-telling has become an exercise in de-objectification, encouraging the expansionism characteristic of both theology and science to collapse into a more accountable particularity. Nonetheless, situating oneself becomes meaningful only as a manifestation of the practice activating the theory—that is, what Schüssler Fiorenza more recently names a "critical feminist rhetorical model," which in its reading of the Bible "seeks to articulate feminist interpretation both as a complex process of reading and reconstruction and as a cultural-theological practice of resistance and transformation" (Schüssler Fiorenza 1992).

Like the Christian trinity in relation to the world, Crossan's own methodological triplet of triplets accomplishes its triangulation at a distance from himself and his own social, political, economic positions and passions. Does this mean he is less than fully honest? Well, we all are that in the academy—feminists and social self-locators included. I do not fantasize that the call to an accountable and contextualized practice of theory somehow cleanses us of the ambiguous privileges of the university. It may inoculate rather than authenticate. But at least it "outs" the hidden politics of scholarship. One might wish for more contextual self-implicature on Crossan's part. Yet his authorial invisibility strikes me as more modest than arrogant, and as strategically effective in his "outing" of Jesus' context. It helps to sustain the suspenseful deferral of Jesus himself within the text. Perhaps Crossan's discretion is no more the evasiveness of some pale male, hidden in a veil of transcendent neutrality, than it is the dark interval of parabolic indirection.

From my rough-grained perspective on New Testament studies, preoccupied with what I can "use" rhetorically, the overlap with feminist liberationist concern appears impressive. The focus on the eschatological Jesus movement as grassroots strategy of protest and mutuality works against the high patriarchal constructions of Jesus the savior and hero—and, therefore, for the release of the aims those constructions expeditiously sabotaged.

There is another point of convergence in and with the growing feminist christological literature. That is Wisdom. Like feminist scholarship, Crossan brings into relief the role of the sapiential tradition in forming both Jesus' self-interpretation and his interpretation by the early community. Schüssler Fiorenza, drawing on the work of Burton Mack and others close to Crossan's project, has described Jesus as "prophet and incarnation of Sophia" (Schüssler Fiorenza 1983). Johnson writes as constructive theologian:

> Jesus is Sophia incarnate, the Wisdom of God . . . Not only does the gender symbolism cast Jesus into an inclusive framework with regard to his relationships with human beings and with God, removing the male emphasis that so quickly turns to androcentrism. But, the symbol giving rise to thought, it also evokes Sophia's characteristic gracious goodness, life-giving creativity, and passion for justice as key hermeneutical elements in speaking about the mission of Jesus (Johnson 1992: 157).

The flourishing—and persecution—of the Sophia spirituality as part of the new reformation, particularly in its liturgical self-expression, suggests the attractive luminosity still conveyed by this metaphor. Like "Spirit," Wisdom imagery feels remarkably free of the chauvinizing and canonizing tendencies of those early Christian trajectories that lent themselves to the Constantinian order. Of course, if she steps out naively as a scriptural panacea for patriarchy, her marginality becomes a problem rather than a promise. Crossan's work helps refocus her dissident historical power in its early Christian context and thus lends a hedge against her literalization today.

Postheroic Jesus

Finally, does Crossan's Mediterranean peasant Cynic, even with his pointedly noncynical communalism, evade the heroic individualism which, according to Brock, can take even the low—prophetic and liberationist—christological forms? In many ways it does. We are left with no need of a sacrificial atonement or other heroic myths of sacrifice. The soteriological implications of what he calls "shared miracle and shared meal" unfold in the interstices of relationship. Yet the events upon which Crossan focuses our attention seem to flow unilaterally from Jesus' own extraordinary, if not ontologically unique, set of talents and projects. He is the one who models and generates mutuality. Jesus himself *does* the sharing. Brock, by contrast, reads in Mark evidence of a more foundational mutuality—that is, she points to several instances in which Jesus *learns from* and is *empowered by* the women who risk relationship with him. He is, thus, dependent upon—and only thus truly part of—the mutuality he seeks. Hence, she is able to "redeem" christology, wide rather than high or low, by relocating the christic reality in the relationships themselves. The Christ becomes Christa-community. This christology of erotic power generates excitement, even love, among many of its readers—precisely because of its capacity to release connective and healing energy long held frozen in precisely the sort of Christ that Crossan, in his more scholarly manner, deconstructs. Though Crossan fails to interrogate the text from the vantage point of Jesus' own dependency upon the interdependence he models, nonetheless the foreshortened figure emerging from his de- and reconstruction poses no threat to a radicalization of the theology of justice in mutuality.

This is all to say I am cautiously grateful for this book on feminist grounds—it advances the christological forcefield of a wisdom-grounded mutuality—one that I suspect must reveal itself finally as a soteriology without savior, male or otherwise.

Presence Not Promise

What is there, then? Something less like a messiah and more like a messianic field of relations. This is traditionally named—unfortunately for its hegemonious class and gender resonances—"kingdom." Crossan remains faithful to the language of "kingdom," seeking to return its dissident usage within a pre-Constantinian context. But he does not do this through the normal justice-Christian evocation of the hoped-for *future* of shalom. Crossan's kingdom is "at hand or near in the sense not of promise but of presence."

Indeed, it is in part by locating the efficacy of the *basileia* in the present, rather than in an endlessly deferred future, that Crossan accomplishes his foreshortening of Jesus. For only through the old apocalyptic deferral, which endlessly promises what century after century does not deliver, can the patriarchal cult of the outsized hero be sustained. Is this paradoxical to my own initial experience of gratitude for deferral in reading Jesus? The contextualizing deferral of Jesus in Crossan's text rewards one, ironically, with release from the endless eschatological deferral. The critical deferral backward into history frees us from the apocalypticizing deferral forward. Is this a liberation—to be delivered from deliverance? Orbis-style Christians have, of course, gotten the message, through some mix of a Blochian-Moltmannian eschatologism, and first-generation, U.S.-filtered liberation theology, oddly enforced among intellectuals more recently by the Derridian dismissal of "the metaphysics of presence," that "the present" is a trope for the status quo. The eschatological privilege of the future represents the present as the site of mere brokerage—"the world." I suppose Crossan strengthens my own suspicion—that deferral of salvation forward into worldly or otherworldly futurity has been read backward into the Gospels; and that such futurism in fact allows *certain* present forces to use past vision to broker our futures—to control the outcome of the unknown.

Salvadoran Presences

Like a flash of unaccustomed vividness, my recent brief experience in Central America illumined the matter of *basileic* presence. There the present is more charged with grief and horror than anything I have encountered before. Hope is the hard-won essence of survival. Yet strikingly, the extraordinary Christians who guided or shared our *conviencia* do not privilege the future. They are too fully committed to Life—the life of the people now, and of the land, and of the spirit felt in love—as it constantly seeds the future. Having survived every mode of terror, of loss and torture, so many of these figures walk with feet more firmly in the present than, again, anything I have encountered in North America, where, by contrast, life always seems to be wafting off into obsessions with past and future. I suppose I want to admit that for the first time in my life the early Christian story became real for me. My Christianity graduated from Sunday school (from which it had in any event long been playing hookey). In the *presence* of so many dead martyrs and living saints, full-blooded human beings who live(d) for their people, but in so doing participate in an extraordinary quality of life for themselves. They live with next to nothing—as our guide Marta put it, quoting a favorite poem, "to get to heaven you only need a stone and the tip of your shoe"—by choice as well as by necessity, cycling all resources into their projects with the people. Projects that revolve, one notes, around activities of eating and healing—a healing of abysmally deep wounds to bodies and souls, to society and to the earth. But the healing and eating unfolds, in precise analogy to Crossan's account of the Jesus movement, as a political grassroots strategy.

I think, for instance, of Blanca Mama—with enormous eyes, luminous with excess love, who runs the little food service for students at the National University, which is the blood-sanctified center of free thinking and political resistance in El Salvador, as in other Central American states. Her sons had been students there, and both were killed while demonstrating. Rather than collapsing in on herself in grief, she began at great risk to organize feeding expeditions to students and faculty held in prison (the government does not provide food to prisoners). We heard that many of the students who would otherwise go hungry at the university have "accounts" with Blanca. Instead, they sit here in this shack surrounded by lush tropical foliage, nourished and talking, planning, organizing.

Or I think of Marta Benevides, who facilitated our expedition, and the compost heap we helped to create one sun-drenched day on the edge of jungle, in a largely indigenous village in the mountains, dancing on it with children to mash together its elements—a bit of a project that models ways of recycling, growing, preparing food and herbs for greater independence from external supplies of food and medicine, ways that, at the same time, teach an alternative ecological and economic polity, one grounded in and requiring community collaboration, one once known to these peasant people but lost, like the taste for the vegetables and fruit that they can so easily grow for themselves, through too much genocide and exploitation. After hard work, we all sat, laughing and exhausted, eating soup out of local pottery bowls, the soup itself a teaching device.

What imagery surrounds the work of these women in the two-thirds world — if not that so clearly etched into Crossan's Jesus, that of commensality and miracles, feeding and healing, martyrdom and community?

Decolonizing Jesus

However, what does all this christic presence have to do with the decentralization of Christ and the foreshortening of Jesus?

Quite simply, in another paradox: everyone we encountered was quite seriously Christian. Also, I believe we heard not one explicit reference to Jesus. Often there was biblical allusion (of the sort Jesus himself might make). But often that allusion was iconoclastic. In its most "protestant" or at least protesting form, for instance, Marta, in a theological discussion with two other Salvadoran intellectuals, noted to us: "When we get together, we three theologians, we try to discern not the Word of God but the needs of the people. Then we realize — *that* is biblical!" Marta, herself ordained, even expressed annoyance at a progressive Christian poster of Jesus surrounded by mostly indigenous folk, simply because Jesus stood there in the midst of them. "The people themselves are Christ," she whispered. This is no antagonism against Jesus. Rather this is iconoclasm raised to high heat in a situation in which the image of Jesus has so often been used to eclipse the calling of the people. Crossan's historically-based foreshortening of Jesus into context meshes with the christological rhythm of this praxis of faith in context.

The maximum Christic figure in El Salvador is the resurrected Romero, who appears on murals everywhere, indeed right in the heart of guerilla (FMLN) headquarters in Perquin, never superseding, but rather updating the story of Jesus. But then he appears on a continuum with all the other people's martyrs, male and female, who "gave their life for the people" — precisely *not* in any grotesque attempt to satisfy God through an atoning sacrifice, but by sharing their lives so fully that the death forces could not tolerate them.

My experience was of an entire loose-knit network of Christs — some sisters and catechists in the Church of the Poor, some in high places in the Roman Catholic structure, many working deliberately outside of church (including B.C.C.) structures. Why call it a Christ-network, however?

What was extraordinary to me was the combination of life and death — or rather life in the face of death. For all the fear and grief, there remains in many leaders a zest and high good humor, a delight in the sensuality of terrestrial life, an iridescent hope (not optimism), combining itself with clear critical analysis of history and global politics. Something about the epistemological tone of our conversations with Salvadorans and, finally, even a bit among ourselves, in the setting, seemed striking. Not only were these voices less depressed but strikingly more clear, indeed contextually well-informed and articulate, than any groups even of progressive church leaders and intellectuals I encounter here. We found no cynicism outside of our own, but over and over the quality of (not promise for) hope is not in a guaranteed outcome, but presence. The presence-to-the-future known as *basileia* made *sense* to me for the first time—that is, it presented itself to the senses, incarnate as a particular frequency of life force. And the way of knowing voicing it—embodied and never overgeneralized, grounded in orthopraxis not orthodoxy. Isn't this the sound of Wisdom?

Therefore, it was most illumining to return from the trip and enter into Crossan's work, only to find the situation of El Salvador so precisely anticipated in that of Judaea: there they were, those peasant protestors wanting not vengeance but justice, wanting not riches but simple fullness of life. And the configuration of ancient colonial dominance, with the collusion of the upper class and its religious support system, homologizes the neocolonial scene, with only subtle distinctions (unlike Rome, the United States did not provide the soldiers for repression, only their training and funding; also, unlike the Jewish, the Salvadoran oligarchy is of the stock of colonialists). Striking also, given Crossan's exposition of the peasant context as intrinsically dissident, that the two-thirds world situation is largely one of the wholesale exploitation of peasants (always a difficulty in translation for the Marxist proletarian assumption). Like Crossan's peasant Nazarene, Salvadoran peasants experience their destiny as controlled by urban centers of power. Crossan follows Horsely's "spiral of violence," according to which "injustice" is followed by "protest and resistance"—Jesus' phase. Yet at the point of Jesus' death, the situation had not yet advanced to that of the full-fledged repression and revolt, as it did soon after with the Zealots. And as it has in El Salvador, where the revolt was not successfully defeated.

While Crossan's life of Jesus minimizes the importance of crucifixion and resurrection in the earliest accounts, priorities operate differently in El Salvador. Again, it is not so much Jesus' own historical death and resurrection that seems centrally important there anymore, so much as the crucifixion and resurrection of the people. But the faith that a new life can arise out of the blood and filth of systematic injustice does not emerge *ex nihilo*; its historical precedent is self-evident. Of course, Crossan's foreshortened Jesus allows space for precisely this sort of mythic christological transformation—such as the one depicted on a cross I brought back from the trip. While its form is crucifixion, its content, like most Salvadoran crosses, is riotous with joyful peasant life and color, animals, villages, sun and fields. This is resurrected life indeed, and nothing short of the *basileia* unimpeded. The peculiarity of my particular kind of cross is that all the figures are peasant women, schoolteachers, breast-feeders, farmers, cate-chists—with the image of a thin woman with arms uplifted and patches on her dress, precisely there at the intersection of the bars. A resurrected peasant Christ, indeed—or rather, "Christa-community"?

Cross Purposes

So, if feminist christology would lift up the egalitarian movement of mutuality and the Sophia who grounds it—the experience of El Salvador brings, also, a woman-identifiable crucifixion and resurrection into focus. Not the exclusion of man but of machismo. These four elements—egali-tarian protest movement rather than heroic individualism, Sophia versus logocentric orthodoxy, *basileia* as presence rather than promise, colonial cross versus cross of sacrificial atonement—suggest dimensions of agree-ment between the Crossan scholarship here discussed, feminist christology and postcolonial Christianity. Or, at least, they stand all three at cross-purposes with the same crucifying force of expansionism that Constantinian Christianity inherited from the Roman Empire. This constitutes a shared context for the work of a decolonizing theological imagination.

Together they yearn toward resurrection—not as the once for all certi-fied miracle that never happened, which therefore has demanded a once for all *eschato* that just as surely will not happen. Another kind not only might but does happen, a resurrection of the flesh of the people, a resur-rection in the spirit of life itself. Nancy, daughter of Maria Christian Gomez, a feminist martyr of El Salvador, defined this inadvertently. Her mother had emerged too visibly, too bountifully full of vitality and inspi-ration, when having accepted the agony of divorce, loss of daily contact with her children, and therefore rejection by the Baptist church that had been her base, in order to give her life fully to her commitment—to wom-en's groups, teachers' organizing, demonstrations for justice. One day she was predictably abducted, gang raped ("pierced" indeed), stripped, tor-tured, beaten, murdered by death squad. Nancy did not mean to be pious when she named three things that kept hope alive in her mother's legacy. First, she said, because she was a woman. Also, because she worked so much through the churches, and because "the evil forces were not able to stop what for her had meant life."

7.

The Quest of the Historical Jesus

Origins, Achievements, and the Specter of Diminishing Returns

FRANS JOZEF VAN BEECK, S.J.

John Dominic Crossan's *The Historical Jesus* is a remarkable, stimulating book, and (unlike some recent books on the subject of Jesus) a significant scholarly accomplishment as well. Its author is not only a seasoned New Testament critic but also an imaginative thinker with a bold vision. The present essay will not come close to doing justice, either to the ingenuity and exceptional grasp of detail displayed throughout the book, or to the insightfulness that characterizes, in my view, much of the exegetical analysis, especially in chapters 11–13, which paint a picture of Jesus' ministry in function of its socio-political-religious context.[1] The book bristles, not only with wide and deep learning, but also with the confident claim that there are ways to retrieve a picture of the historical Jesus that are (a) reliable by *historical-critical* norms and (b) capable of shedding light, at least indirectly, on the exorbitant *theological* affirmations made by the Christian Tradition on Jesus' behalf.

1. Historical-Critical Method and Theology

The claim that we have this kind of access to the Jesus of history was first successfully made three or four decades ago, by the exegetical movement known in the English-speaking world as the New Hermeneutic. Crossan is implicitly critical of that movement, yet his book is unthinkable without it. So, incidentally, is another, much shorter, no less insightful book, equally critical of the New Hermeneutic. Crossan's book bears an uncanny resemblance to it in regard to both atmosphere and intent. But, curiously, it differs from Crossan's scholarly book in that it is fictional (at least ostensibly) as well as genuinely funny. I am referring to Gerd Theissen's *The Shadow of the Galilean*. Read it.

Now let us be more specific.

First, in regard to *historical criticism*, *The Historical Jesus* not only represents the newer developments in method, it also takes (if I am not mistaken) significant steps in the direction of further refinement, especially in its consistent use of the criterion of *multiple attestation*. In this regard, the dazzling Appendix 1, "An Inventory of the Jesus Tradition by Chronological Stratification and Independent Attestation," is an immensely useful tool, though not invulnerable to criticism, especially in the area of the *dating*; I seem to detect a tendency to assign relatively late dates (and hence, limited authority) to canonical documents, and relatively early dates (and substantial authority) to extracanonical ones. I wonder if this reflects a bias in favor of the underdog. If it should, that would be an anachronism; by and large, all of first-century and most of second-century Christianity was still a "Little Tradition" sorting itself out; as yet, there was no "Great Tradition"—only scattered claims to it, and these gathered momentum only in the latter part of the second century, when the New Testament canon, too, was taking shape.[2] To treat any New Testament writing as the product of a victorious mainstream Christian establishment controlled by authorities capable of forcing writings *we* now know as extracanonical into oblivion is to forget that there existed, as yet, no established, authoritative consensus capable of asserting itself at the expense of any presumed (and oppressed) Little Tradition. With this qualification, I suggest that the appendix, a product of painstaking research, could very profitably be published in computerized form.

Crossan's book also exemplifies how the quest of the historical Jesus, in recent decades, has abandoned its narrow focus on Jesus as an individual. That focus was often inspired by christological worries;[3] accordingly, one of the New Hermeneutic's favorite criteria—that of dissimilarity—gets very short shrift in *The Historical Jesus*. Accordingly, and in my view unnecessarily, the picture of Jesus that emerges lacks some of the striking features persuasively identified as historical by the New Hermeneutic—those recently surveyed and evaluated in Ben Witherington's *The Christology of Jesus*.

Instead (and this is a positive thing again), Crossan places Jesus—his person and his historic impact—firmly in the context of Judaism, but even more of the wider Greco-Roman culture, and beyond that, of the world of the Mediterranean. To achieve this evocation of Jesus' world, Crossan brings into play, especially in Parts I and II of his book, an impressive, detailed familiarity with both ancient history and worthwhile cultural-anthropological theory (as well as a shrewd sense of humor). To mention one instance, the book paints a pertinent picture of the oppressed, largely landless peasantry around the Eastern Mediterranean. This gives a fresh profile to Jesus' association with the discontented, restive, and religiously active rural and small-town poor. It should also dispel forever the rosy hues with which biblical theology has sometimes invested the *'anawîm*.[4]

The application of sociological and anthropological theory is relatively new in New Testament studies, and I wish to raise one methodological issue in its regard. Social-scientific theories often interpret social phenomena by means of ideal types. Examples are such broad typifications as "ruling class," "retainer class," and "peasantry." Ideal types are products of the perceptive scholarly imagination; they are enlightening because they can assist in discerning order in the seemingly random facts of society and culture-at-large. However, being quite general, they work best when applied to the social systems that inspired them in the first place, and they work better as the social systems to which they are applied are more homogeneous; besides, since they usually imply value judgments, they lend themselves to the promotion of hidden agendas. Ideal types, therefore, have potential, not only for enlightenment, but also for projection, special pleading, and prejudice. To give an example of the latter, observing that exploitation and oppression are systemic in a strongly stratified society is not the same as claiming that they are universal. No theory can explain the occurrence of prominent families with a tradition of benevolence and even beneficence, or of approachable and just landlords and even kings—of the kind that peasants, no matter how aware of their position of subjection, will rightly like and even admire. Crossan, I suggest, is right, as well as frequently successful, in putting ideal types to the task of illuminating the world of which Jesus is part. Still, he seems insufficiently aware that the application of ideal types is very different from the use of the technical, much more impartial tools of analysis scripture scholars have been developing for over a century to get behind the surface meaning of texts, nor does he always appear to appreciate the fact that the enormous cultural complexity of first-century Palestine counsels extreme caution. Sometimes, it would appear, *interpretation of data* in light of ideal-typical distinctions and classifications almost imperceptibly turns into the *postulating of facts*; put differently, *reconstruction*—the stated purpose of the book—turns into *construction* on the basis of preconceived theory.

Here we must recall, perhaps, that even scholarship has limits; that, as the data get dimmer and scarcer, it is more imperative to discern among imagination, fancy, and fantasy; that to decide that the data are too slender to support firm conclusions is a genuine (if largely unsung) form of understanding.

Second, in the *theological* area, Crossan's work, first of all, invites comparisons with another recent book, volume I of John Meier's *A Marginal Jew*. Meier programmatically brackets any and all theological and doctrinal concerns in order to do history and history alone. He considers this a matter (not of principle, but) of *method*. If we *initially* establish what we can know historically, Meier thinks, we will *eventually* be able to tell just what we believe, *both* theologically *and* historically, and on what grounds. I appreciate Meier's intentions and have great respect for his first volume, but I must point out that the methodical separation of history from theology is easiest in the case of the infancy narratives and the other preliminary matters covered in volume I; thus the remaining two volumes will have to tell the story. Frankly, past experience is not on Meier's side; doing history without bias (or at least without a viewpoint) has turned out, time and again, to be an elusive pursuit.

Unlike Meier, Crossan appears to accept implicitly that the retrieval (the "reconstruction") of the historical Jesus is, from the outset, a theological venture.[5] It is concern with *theology* that animates the search of a picture of Jesus' historic person and significance—one that is as imaginative theologically as it is insistent on historical-critical method. Thus, it comes as no surprise that theology boldly surfaces at the end:

> But how . . . can one ever reconcile speaking of a brokerless Kingdom [of God], of Jesus proclaiming the unmediated presence of God, with . . . Christian interpretations . . . ? Christianity . . . when it attempted to define as clearly as it could the meaning of Jesus, insisted that he was "wholly God" and "wholly man," . . . the unmediated presence of the divine to the human. I find, therefore, no contradiction between the historical Jesus and the defined Christ, no betrayal whatsoever in the move from Jesus to Christ (Crossan 1991: 423-24).[6]

Thus, Crossan refuses to draw, from the requirements of historical-critical method, a warrant for the separation of history from theology; after all, what is at stake is the *credibility* of Christianity. It makes no sense for Christian theologians (and for the countless Christians for whom the problem of the historical Jesus is no longer academic) to profess faith in the Word made flesh without insisting that at least some of the flesh be made visible and credible in its historical particularity. No wonder it is, again, *theology* that governs the book's parting shot:

> This book, then, is a scholarly reconstruction of the historical Jesus. . . . [O]ne could . . . offer divergent interpretative conclusions . . . But one cannot dismiss it . . . Because there is *only* reconstruction. *If you cannot believe in something produced by reconstruction, you may have nothing left to believe in* (426; italics added).

2. The Historical Jesus: The Original Agenda

In opting for this fundamentally theological approach, Crossan has taken an enormous risk. To appreciate this, we must notice the affinity between his approach and that taken by Gotthold Ephraim Lessing (1729–1781), one of the first thinkers—if not the first—to set the agenda of the quest of the historical Jesus. Let me briefly review Lessing's thinking on the subject, with the suggestion that this can shed light on Crossan's book.

In Lessing's view, if Christians wish to define Christianity at all, they must do so in roundly *theological* terms: "The Christian religion must be understood in terms of the doctrines contained in the *symbola* of the Church of the first four centuries" (Lessing 1957: 62). However, Lessing feels, *this* Christianity is no longer a live option in eighteenth-century Europe. First, and most importantly, *it no longer exists*. Such Christians as still exist are fanatics, obsessively professing a positive religion by crusading on behalf of either the Bible's authority or the pope's. Christians now wholly fail to understand the spiritual import of what they profess; they misconstrue even the letter of the profession of faith, by interpreting it in a crudely super-naturalist fashion, unacceptable to any thinking person. For, second, even if historic Christianity were still to exist, *it would fail to convince* a century in which "the proof of the spirit and of power" is no longer available. In the eighteenth century, miracles no longer happen (Lessing 1957: 52).

But how about a sensible, rational, moderate Christianity? For this option, proposed by the Neologians and other residually Christian Deists, Lessing has nothing but scorn. Why trade in a coherent type of credulity — and one with an established intellectual tradition — for one that is incoherent?[7] Thus, in the final analysis, for those who wish to believe with integrity, Lessing sees only the straight dilemma between honest, historic Christianity (now extinct and in any case no longer convincing) and Reason.

This, however, is not the end of the theological story; one bridge between Reason and Christianity remains. Lessing may not *accept* Christianity as a system of *theological beliefs*, he can *understand* it as *true religion*. Christianity can be appreciated and even followed, provided it is interpreted as a work of genius; like any work of art, the Christian religion delivers up its true secret only to those who allow themselves to be drawn into the central experience it embodies. That experience is twofold: toward God, it consists in an upright life, lived in abandon to divine providence; toward humanity and the world it consists in loving all that is truly good. This is both the essence of Christianity and the perfection of humanity. Admittedly, it is a far cry from the Christian religion represented by the churches. In fact, it is entirely different from it. It is the religion of Christ himself (Lessing 1957: 106).

Thus Lessing's aesthetic, imaginative reconstruction of Christianity turns out to be *both theological and historical*: true Christian existence is the shape of the most authentically human existence before God, in imitation of the historical Jesus; somewhat surprisingly, Lessing the agnostic turns out to have been, all along, the advocate of the purest, most original Christianity.

In this way, Lessing has helped inaugurate the modern discussion on the essence of the Christian faith. The pale, rational Christianity of the Christian Deists had succeeded only in reducing Christian doctrine to a set of universal truths. But true Christianity does not depend on that kind of bloodless teaching for its identity; it has *historical* claims to make — *claims of universal appeal.* The true essence of Christianity, Lessing suggests, can be understood only on the basis of the *historical* Jesus, but this Jesus exemplifies what is timeless and most universal (and hence, by implication, most theological) about humanity. No wonder Lessing took an interest in Reimarus' *Fragments.* No wonder, either, that he became one of the first articulate representatives of the proposition that the Christian religion must be completely reconstructed. That is to say: Scripture must be interpreted afresh, in its historical purity, apart from any particular doctrinal commitments.

This, of course, opens a chasm between Reason and traditional Christian faith. The historical, exemplary Jesus worships and proclaims God as only a truly human being can; the transcendent, divinized Christ is worshiped and proclaimed as God by those who are less human according as they are more emphatically Christian. The former has a universal appeal and belongs to all of aspiring humanity; the latter is the property of the established churches, dying in their narrow dogmatism.

Lessing's program became the impetus of an impressive series of critical reconstructions of the life of Jesus sceptical of Christian doctrine and intended as imaginative, liberating, provocative clarion-calls for *human and theological renewal.* Names like Friedrich Schleiermacher, David Strauss and Ernest Renan, Albrecht Ritschl and Johannes Weiss, and of course Albert Schweitzer, come to mind. They all attempt to render Jesus historically real by being meticulously biblical; but all of them also try to make him theologically appealing by cultivating universalism — that is, by casting him as the historic proponent of the most attractive humanism imaginable: authentic and thus universally appealing. Crossan's book, both painstaking and imaginative, places itself in this company. Strategically placed quotations from Renan and Schweitzer confirm this judgment. So does one from Joseph Klausner's *Jesus of Nazareth,* the first important twentieth-century, consistently universalist Jewish interpretation of Jesus. Crossan, too, ends up associating Jesus and the primitive Jesus tradition with universalism — of a Jewish type this time. Curiously, however, in a book so insistent on history, this presumably first-century Jewish universalism is left nondescript, which raises the suspicion that we are dealing with a theoretical projection reminiscent of the Enlightenment rather than with historical fact (418-21).

Now the risk involved in Crossan's enterprise is becoming clearer as well. The just-mentioned retrievals of the historical Jesus have largely turned out to be, in George Tyrrell's famous phrase, reflections of liberal theologians' faces, seen at the bottoms of deep wells.[8] Is Crossan's picture of Jesus yet another mirrored face — an exercise in projection proposed under cover of claims to historical reconstruction?

Crossan's book is too complex to admit of a simple answer to this question, which I wish to explore under two headings. The first and lengthier exploration will start with a question of method and move on to both history and theology; it centers on Crossan's data base — its validity and appropriate use. The second is crisper as well as more directly theological; it will test the reconstruction proposed by Crossan on its theological merit.

3. Orality, Textuality, Suspicion, Reconstruction

I have long wondered why the historical-critical approach to the Scriptures has largely kept its distance from the systematic study of *oral performance*, Werner Kelber's effort (Kelber 1983) being a rare exception.[9] Unlike the writings of, say, an individual apologist with an agenda like Flavius Josephus (as well as utterly unlike modern printed texts) the vast majority of the writings that embody the Jesus tradition — the extracanonical as much as canonical — are inseparable from *oral performance in a community setting*. In fact, their purpose in being written down is precisely that they should sustain and guarantee reliable oral performance. Thus, they resemble scores for musical performance rather than manuscripts or books designed to lead an independent, written life, and geared to visual, often private, often silent, and sometimes downright critical perusal and even study. That is, the documents of the Jesus tradition are essentially tied in with living oral/acoustical community cultures.

Oral performance differs from the "literal/literate" reading of texts in that its dynamics tend to encourage freedom and spontaneity of expression, while at the same time ensuring that both stay within the bounds of accepted structure. Thus, oral performance helps keep communities on course without rigidity. The idiomatic, formulary lore, which is the staple of oral performance, helps uphold traditions that are *fairly conservative, yet flexible*; formulary stability helps insure continuity, formulary flexibility much-needed adaptation. Oral performance and the texts associated with it are also designed to further *loyalty* rather than *the knowledge of objective truth*. This means: the point of community writings, even of *logia*-collections like *Q* and the *Gospel of Thomas*, is invariably to keep a community and its tradition (not so much mindful of facts or truths but) *true to itself as the privileged (and hence, appreciative) trustee of facts and truths recalled and treasured in the act of rehearsal*.

Thus oral rehearsal creates room for the active cherishing of tradition and for active efforts to ensure its continued significance and impact. Not surprisingly, therefore, texts rooted in oral performance will show, over time, two features: creative *expansion* and quiet, subtle *modification* (which, incidentally, may include loss). Expansions reflect that the tradition is being cherished; modifications bear out that it is being accommodated to suit new situations. But in an oral/acoustical environment, too much adaptation or manipulation raises suspicions of disloyalty, and novelty is not ordinarily accepted; originality is largely unknown, and if it should be attempted, it is usually anathema. For in oral cultures, immemorial custom is the surest guarantee of truth. "I have nothing new to say, but only ancient doctrines," Celsus can boast (Origen, *Contra Celsum*, IV, 14).

Let me now, on the basis of these brief characteristics, make some suggestions regarding the interpretation of the written records of oral performance. My eventual conclusion will be that the hermeneutics of suspicion are far less appropriately applied to documents written down, *for community use*, to support oral performance than to documents intentionally composed for purposes of persuasion or propaganda, to promote a point of view among outsiders; concretely, it is far more appropriate, when trying to tease out underlying history, "to read Josephus against himself" (or, for that matter, Professor Crossan) than to do so with the documents of the Jesus tradition.

The reason is that *the redactional forms of oral-performance documents reflect community process*; that is, they are as much the carriers of continuity as the specific, "hard" data they incorporate. Thus, in the case of the Jesus tradition, I think it is a mistake (as well as a misreading of Crossan's database) to think that the "real" tradition is in the discrete data, and that the redactional forms and contexts from which they can be (and have been) disengaged are secondary—a matter of arrangement or invention, if not downright manipulation or even distortion, and in any case, obstacles to historical truth. It is clear, of course, that Mark, Matthew, and Luke as we have them, and even *Q* and the *Gospel of Thomas*, reflect redaction and, hence, community agendas; but it is mistaken to picture redactors as operating at will, turning (as it were, with scissors and paste) discrete textual elements into new, historically misleading constructs.[10] Any redactor's liberty would be kept in check by community traditions—that is, *living faith-traditions of relatively long standing*—enforced by oral performance.

Not surprisingly, given this background, if we are too eager to disengage the "hard" data from the fairly flexible contexts that hold them in place, they tend to disintegrate on us; the deeper we move into the subatomic recesses of the texts, testing the data as if they were particles (Attridge's metaphor; Attridge 1992: 223) the more conjectural and unstable the data become and the more polyvalent their reference. This void of cohesion will cry out for consistency; the data beg to be recombined. The problem is that the further the data have drifted apart, the more we have become dependent on *ingenuity* to put them back together. But now the problem becomes one of *control*. Set in their original contexts, the data reflect early Christian faith-traditions supported by oral-acoustical habits and thus, subject to at least a reasonable amount of *conservative community control*. But what will guide ingenuity going it alone? In the best case, a blend of learning, imagination, and discretion in suggesting conclusions. But when one or more of these fail, what will keep unacknowledged preconceptions from sneaking in by scholarly ingenuity's back door? What will prevent prejudice from rushing in to take charge of the reconstruction, under cover of acumen?[11]

This is where the specter of diminishing returns begins to loom on the horizon of our intelligence. Is there not a point where reconstruction ceases to shed light on the history underlying the text, and becomes self-referential instead? That is, is there not a point where reconstruction begins to guarantee that we *lose* sight of the history and the tradition behind the text altogether? There is little doubt that the earliest Christian communities witnessed a remarkable level of creative expressiveness,[12] but does this mean that we must picture the development of the Jesus tradition between, say, 30 A.D. and 50 A.D., as a process of hectic production and manipulation of discrete texts and factoids to cover up a fundamental void of recollection and information? And, in thus construing the Jesus tradition, do we not sound (if I may borrow Crossan's terminology) like the theater critic who commends the first performance no one remembers by damning all subsequent performances with faint praise? And in doing so, are we not once again making the historical *and theological* mistake of separating Jesus completely from the community he gave rise to? That is, are we not cutting ourselves off from the original "performance" (Crossan 1991: xi, xxvi) by discrediting the part of the performance that is the life of the early Christian communities — the bit actors who remain our only historical and theological clue to the Performer? And in doing so, could we be giving in, way out of season, to the Romantic fallacy, which insists that truth can be found only in the unattainable, lost original?

Let me illustrate my general contention with a few examples. I am choosing them from chapters 14 and 15. These two chapters stand somewhat off by themselves, away from the rest of the book: they make relatively little use of the materials developed in Parts I and II; they deal with the reconstruction, not so much of a *picture* of Jesus in the context of his world, as of *facts* — Jesus' death and burial, and the factual ingredients of what we call his resurrection; there is a hurried, breathless quality about them; the author, often at his most ingenious, also appears more fiercely determined to come up with a reconstruction, at the expense of any discussion of alternative interpretations.

To take a first instance, I agree that the absence of passion and resurrection narratives in *Q* and the *Gospel of Thomas* warrants radical hypotheses. So does the fact that the passion narratives are so clearly dependent on identifiable scriptural and apocryphal materials. This suggests that the narratives of the last supper and the passion are prophetic (and, I would add, liturgical) narratives; they would seem to substantially reflect, not known facts first of all, but processes of interpretation and assimilation (and, I would add, celebration) on the part of the earliest Christian communities, trying to come to grips with Jesus' last days, his execution, and his burial. There is something deeply inspiring about this hypothesis of Crossan's, much of which I share (van Beeck 1989: 178-95, 198-202).[13]

Still, as a comprehensive interpretation it fails to convince. Let me explain. One conspicuous feature of oral performance is *the absence of dissociation*. Live formulary speech is precritical: it has no interest in differentiating between prophecy (or its equivalent), realistic narrative, and historical fact. Crossan's hypothesis, therefore, does not permit the insinuation that the traditions behind the passion narratives were perfectly well aware of the differences, but proceeded anyway, *deceptively*, to turn prophecy into narrative and narrative into fact. Yet Crossan can write—in what must have been a moment of inattention to the demands of both critical scholarship and sensitivity—that the prescription behind these narratives is precisely, "Hide the prophecy, tell the narrative, and invent the history" (372). This slogan begs for disagreement, because it marks the end of careful historical scholarship. Here the hermeneutic of suspicion has turned into an open charge of fraudulence. Instead of befriending the texts, which are his allies, the critic has turned against them. If the sole function of prophetic narrative about the last supper, the passion, and the burial is to fill a gulf of ignorance about the facts, it begins to sound hollow. And even if it were granted that the narrative *is* predicated on such total ignorance, this would logically entail the conclusion that reconstruction—*any* reconstruction—is impossible. To argue from *postulated* silence about the facts, on the sole authority of one passage in Philo's writings (390-91), that those who executed Jesus must have buried him in an unidentified grave is not reconstruction but learned fantasy. Does a less sweeping, more conscientious reading of the data not cast substantial doubts on this construal?

Similar points could be made in regard to Crossan's highly selective and rather narrowly focused treatment of the accounts of the risen Jesus' appearances. Is it likely that their only (or even main) function is the assertion of the authority of a few insolent apostolic eyewitnesses, who have taken charge and succeeded in foisting faith in Jesus' resurrection upon a docile community of "ordinary" people, by obliterating, *in less than two decades*, a much less striking belief, which (allegedly) that same community originally held—namely, that the significance Jesus had in life continues even after his embarrassing death, in anticipation of an eventual *parousia*? Such a construal of the sources strains the limits of credibility, if only because it treats as sheepish the very community it pretends to extol in disparagement of the apostolic authorities.

One more instance. To appreciate it, we must recall that oral performance is quite tolerant of mixed metaphor and logical inconsistency; this is connected with its flair for the dramatic, which encourages unresolved tension as a favorite ingredient. The sweep of oral performance appeals to the synthetic ear, which hears and understands and holds together particulars that, *in textual form*, strike the observer's analytic eye as *disiecta membra*, incoherent and incompatible.[14] Texts for oral performance rely on acoustical synthesis; we need not take them apart to determine their meaning.

Now for the instance at hand. Crossan suspects an inconsistency between Jesus' resurrection and his descent into Hell. He is not the first one to do so. He may, however, be the first one to connect this problem with an alleged inconsistency between Jesus' death and his resurrection on the third day;

what (so he has Jesus' earliest followers asking themselves) is the sense of Jesus dying at all if he was going to be back so soon? The only meaning of the three days, he submits, is that room had to be created to accommodate the (Jewish) notion of Jesus descending into the Nether World. This was needed for Jesus to liberate the dead, before he could become available on earth (at least for a short period) as the risen One, for the (sole?) purpose of giving the disciples their official mandate and apostolic authority (388, 395-96). But surely analysis has here turned into caricature? A passage like 1 Peter 3: 18-22; 4: 6 precisely shows the capacity of oral-performance texts to hold logically incongruent elements together. Jesus, dead in the flesh and made alive (in the Spirit), descends into Hell (in the Spirit), where he evangelizes the long-imprisoned dead, who have been waiting since the Deluge and now find themselves both judged (according to their humanity, in the flesh) and made alive (according to God, in the Spirit). For those alive, members of the Christian community, the equivalent of Jesus' visit to the dead is his resurrection and ascension, actualized in baptism (i.e., being cleansed *in* water and saved), which in turn actualizes the salvation that occurred by Noah's Ark (i.e., being saved *from* the waters of the Deluge). Taken as a whole, the passage conveys what Paul conveys by saying that Jesus Christ risen is Lord of both the dead and the living, to the equal advantage of both (Rom 14: 7-9; cf. 1 Thess 4: 15). Put differently, the text intimates that there is *harmony*, not conflict, between Jesus' resurrection and his descent; there is, I submit, no reason to suppose that the earliest traditions felt otherwise.[15]

4. Egalitarian, Magician, Cynic?

It is time to move on to our second exploration. To do this, we must turn to the three engrossing chapters 11–13, in which Crossan lays out the features of Jesus' program and person under the rubric of "Brokerless Kingdom." Crossan here cashes in on the vivid *collage* that conveys, in Part II, the complex socio-political-religious situation in mid first-century Palestine — the one that was to result, in 70 A.D., in the disaster of the Jewish War. In this setting, in which the alternatives for action range from opportunistic collaboration (Josephus) to outright urban guerilla warfare (the *sicarii*), Crossan casts Jesus in the role of an unlikely, but enchanting, and probably quite infuriating presence. At first a follower of the Baptist's apocalypticism, he becomes a radical exponent of "the Little Tradition": he becomes the agent of God's Kingdom by adopting a countercultural, wholly egalitarian type of cynicism of part apocalyptic, part sapiential inspiration, and not so much taught as *enacted* ("performed"). That performance consists in healing and exorcism and open-table fellowship, practiced, both by Jesus and by such disciples as he sends out, in a consistently itinerant lifestyle.

In the course of these chapters, a pattern of interpretation emerges. In Part II, Crossan has construed the contemporary situation as one in which all that is original and authentic is stifled by forces of brokerage jockeying for ascendancy: Josephus is a conniver, the priestly aristocracy is in collusion with the Romans, the rabbinate is ready to doctor the record in order to turn honest magicians like Honi the Circle-Drawer into one of their own (by ascribing to him prayer, of all things!), and promising bandits disappointingly aspire to be self-serving kings. Consequently, the destitute, landless peasantry is outside all available structures of influence, belonging, and intimacy (or, in good nineteenth-century language, their identity is in alienation alone). Crossan, then, allows this pattern of social typology to dictate the features of Jesus, to the point where his individuality is absorbed by his social-political-religious *persona* as the critic of "the system" and the champion of (in Shakespeare's phrase[16]) "unaccommodated man": the destitute, the oppressed.

This has two consequences. First, Jesus' identification with the resourceless poor (supported by the Jesus tradition) becomes, not only an unsettling warning to the established rich (also supported by the tradition), but also an attitude of positive disdain in the latter's regard (the tradition suggests a different story). Second, his advocacy of an unbrokered Kingdom of God (supported by the tradition) becomes, not only a challenge to the religious establishments (supported), but also a cause positively contemptuous of them (unsupported). As a result, the picture of Jesus has gotten encrusted by a reconstruction of his socio-political-religious significance, and a biased one at that. Jesus, nicely characterized by Eduard Schweizer as "The Man Who Fits No Formula" (1971: 13-51) is obscured by being made to fit yet another formula.[17]

Obscured, and unnecessarily so. By both historical and theological standards, Crossan's reconstruction *could* have accommodated the New-Hermeneutic picture of Jesus, which (in fact) it significantly enriches, by placing it in a historical context. It is the picture of Jesus, now risen, who went about enacting rather than teaching (but also teaching) a new, unprecedented, urgent divine offer of salvation, calling for total abandon to the living God, and defeating the power of real, historical evil; the Jesus who set aside accepted forms of socio-religious discrimination so as to encounter all comers, regardless of allegiance; who challenged allegiances and establishments by assaying them all in the light of God's Kingdom and by declining to associate unconditionally with any of them; yet who did associate with every kind of people, in word and deed, in an itinerant ministry of compassion; who defied the sole authority of the Law, especially in matters of ritual purity; who confronted the Temple establishment by challenging the commerce connected with it; who did all of this with unprecedented, authoritative freedom—evidence of an original sense of mission. Most importantly, his style implicitly laid claim to an unparalleled intimacy with God, in which he invited his followers to share. His person and ministry elicited bursts of faith, healing, and new life, even among non-Jews, but not universally or for long. Miserably, he turned out to be altogether too much to take; he met with misunderstanding and rebuff; in the end, a disciple betrayed him; sentenced as a criminal blasphemer, abandoned, desolate, and executed by crucifixion, he accepted what was inflicted on him, and entrusted himself and his mission wholly to his Father's saving will.

This raises a delicate issue of interpretation. What, if anything, is the agenda behind Crossan's decision to have Jesus' person absorbed by his provocative social *persona* — by his casting Jesus as a magician, a Cynic, and an egalitarian? Let me reflect on all three and venture a suggestion.

In regard to *magic*, Crossan wisely (if in somewhat too slapdash a manner) avails himself of Murdock's insights: there is a difference between disease and illness; illness and demonic possession are a function of the conflicted experience of the powerless; the scientific medical model is not the only valid approach to suffering. This move deserves a cordial welcome; it creates room for the unabashed acceptance of Jesus' activity as a miracle worker (310-32).[18] But Crossan's agitated descriptions of magicians and magic (138, 156-58, 304-10) contain more caveats, pleas for correct understanding, and disclaimers than quiet affirmations; his explanations teem with the kind of nervousness that suggests fast footwork and special pleading. Just why, in the teeth of much contrary anthropological evidence, distinguish thaumaturgic magic so peremptorily from "communal ritual?" Why, if faith-healing is endemic and irrepressible in nonrationalist religious cultures, call it "religious banditry?" Why balk at the idea of associating magic with holiness? Why insist that it is strictly individual and that prayer is alien to it?

In regard to *Cynicism* (76-88, 421-22), made much of by Gerd Theissen, too, why suggest that it is a form of "introversionism," if its social-critical agenda is so obvious? And why note the parallel between the Cynic's standard outfit and the Jesus tradition's itinerant evangelists', proceed to mention Jesus' prohibition of the wallet (that symbol of the Cynic's aggressive posture of self-reliance) and explain that it is connected with itinerancy and open-table fellowship, only to conclude, in the most theoretical of ways, that "it must be explained in terms of the *functional symbolism* of *the social movement [Jesus] was establishing*" (338-39; italics added)? Why fail to note that the absence of the wallet may have been more than symbolic? And even more, that it may have had a theological symbolism, to convey the exact opposite of *self*-reliance?

Finally, in regard to *egalitarianism*, most dramatically conveyed by the practice of open-table fellowship, why fail to note that guests, whoever they are, are always *particular* guests? In other words, that egalitarianism *in performance* deals with neighbors, not with a disincarnate idealist conception? It is clear that, in a social environment acutely aware of differences and incompatibilities, Jesus had infuriating habits of association, but these habits *challenged* social distinctions — they did not abolish them in favor of radical universalism. It is also clear that, in Jesus' view of the Kingdom, sexual and social, political and religious distinctions come under unsettling criticism, as all the New Testament epistles show, in one way or another. But why write that such distinctions have been rendered "completely irrelevant and anachronistic?" If this means anything at all, it is reminiscent, not of openness and universalism, but of the gnosticizing, elitist, *factionalist* claims heard among Christians in Corinth, in the mid fifties of the first-century A.D.

The common theme is now hard to miss. The pictures of Jesus the egalitarian, the magician, and the Cynic share three features: Jesus' significance to the socio-political-religious world he is part of is strictly a matter of immanent caliber — not of personal relatedness freely lived out, whether to God or to particular others; Jesus' striking intimacy with God and his prayer are overlooked, or perhaps excluded, while his openness to others becomes a matter of universal principle, not daily (that is, limited but actual) practice; and all institutionality is implicitly disparaged as humanly and religiously misleading. It is hard not to conclude that what we have here is a twentieth-century version of a Romantic preconception: true religiosity is a matter of the *inner* experience of human authenticity alone; articulate worship of a transcendent God and positive engagement in socio-political structures are inauthentic and alienating. No wonder Crossan's work is reminiscent of Strauss, Renan, Schweitzer.

5. Envoi

Blood is thicker than water. Pedigrees persist. The search for the historical Jesus is a child of the Enlightenment and Romanticism, and it continues to bear the family features. It does so in Crossan's book, too. Of those features, some are positive, some negative.

Among the positive is the demand for human integrity in believing. The profession of faith in the Word Made Flesh requires of theologians that they make an effort to test the written record, which only reluctantly lends itself to historical-critical study, for such vestiges of the Word Made Flesh in its historical particularity as appeal to the religious imagination. Those vestiges may be few and far between, but to give up the search is to settle for discontinuity between the historical Jesus and the faith of the Christian tradition, and to embrace a form of pious docetism.

Among the negative features is a degree of rationalism. In his tract "On the Introduction of Rationalistic Principles into Revealed Religion," John Newman wrote of the rationalist, "He professes to *believe* in that which he *opines*" (1877: I, 35). Rationalism is the reduction of the faith-abandon to the affirmation of theological opinion. Crossan's book, I think, shows evidence of such reduction, even if it correctly insists that faith be appropriately *informed* and *tested* by reasoned opinion. In regard to history, it claims that its far-flung historical reconstruction of Jesus' person and program qualifies as reasoned opinion, and thus, as an enrichment and a test of Christian faith today. In regard to theology, it suggests that Jesus' aggressive practice of radical equality, healing liberation, and fellowship without discrimination meets the universal human thirst for God and thus can be interpreted as the very shape of God's Kingdom.

But there are problems. The historical reconstruction, I have argued, while ingenious, does strain the bounds of reasoned interpretation, while at the same time isolating Jesus from the very tradition he called forth. And while the theological construction does justice to some pertinent modern conceptions of the living God, it offers an abridged (and in some respects a distorted) version of Jesus' person, ministry, and presence.

Is Crossan's book, then, another case of the face of Jesus being seen at the bottom of a deep well, showing so many features of the face of a modern thinker as to cause problems of recognition? Not the face of a nineteenth-century liberal Protestant this time, but of a late twentieth-century critic — an irritable observer suspicious of even the semblance of establishment? A belated Romantic utopian perhaps, of the unflattering variety? A hippie, inoffensive but infuriating? *A CYNIC?* Not likely. More probably a capable, quite original, rather skeptical New Testament professor with the soul of a leprechaun.

Notes

1. Still, I do find myself demurring at the section entitled "A Kingdom of Undesirables" (276-82). Crossan explains, rightly, that the parables treated here have provocative features: the deliberate planting of an obnoxious shrub and of ubiquitous weeds; leaven, associated with corruption and ritual impurity; the widely scorned merchant profession; and the suggestion of impious fraud. But the contention that the parables do not *compare* the Kingdom with the *story as a whole*, but *specifically identify* it with the *undesirable features in it* (the offensive properties of mustard trees, the darnel not the wheat, the unpalatable features of leaven, the shady deal, etc.) strains the texts, and seems designed to *épater le bourgeois*. And in the process, it revives the old Protestant habit of viewing God's activity in terms of action *against* a self-righteous world rather than a loving (if demanding) engagement *with* it.

2. "Christianity" must be used with caution. In modern usage, the word implies that one can be a Christian without belonging to a tangible Christian community. But this meaning did not arise till the seventeenth century, when the Christian commonwealth had definitively come apart (Bossy 1987). It is anachronistic to think that there was, in the first two centuries C.E., a "Little Tradition" of free Christians with no ties to any community.

3. These worries are legitimate, if sometimes pressed in misguided ways. This explains the widespread animus against the criterion of dissimilarity; cf. Theissen 1987: 141 for an example.

4. Still, a book like Norbert Lohfink's *Lobgesänge der Armen* reminds us that oppression and destitution did generate a genuine spirituality of the poor, witness the Qumrân *hōdayōth*.

5. But cf. Luke Timothy Johnson (1992: 26), comparing Meier and Crossan: "Is not both authors' hope for a historical foil to theology or faith still fundamentally a *theological* rather than a historical project?" It is, of course.

6. Crossan adds, pertinently, "Whether there were ultimate betrayals in the move from Christ to Constantine is another question," and quotes Eusebius' embarrassing account of the bishops' presence at the imperial banquet at the end of the Council of Nicaea. Yet this move is also disingenuous. First, it suggests, wrongly, that the incident typifies the relationships between the fourth-century church and imperial power. Second, in the context of the book as a whole one wonders if we are to understand that the New Testament affirmations of apostolic authority are a prelude to the ambitions of power-hungry ecclesiastics of all times.

7. Thus Lessing can write, on February 2, 1774, to his brother Karl that the attempt to blend the Bible with rationality is futile. The nonrevelatory, residually Christian theology produced by the Christian rationalists is nothing but "a patchwork of bunglers and half-philosophers" (Lessing 1968: 597).

8. "The Christ that Harnack sees, looking back through nineteen centuries of Catholic darkness, is only the reflection of a Liberal Protestant face, seen at the bottom of a deep well" (Tyrrell 1909: 44).

9. Still, Kelber is doctrinaire in that he tends to separate orality from literacy. My own access route to this body of knowledge has been mainly the work of Walter J. Ong, who has relied on, and significantly developed, the work of Milman Parry, Albert B. Lord, Marshall McLuhan, and Eric A. Havelock. For a summary of Ong's views, cf. Ong 1970, 1982.

10. In view of this, I distrust Crossan's otherwise ingenious proposal that canonical Mark "dismembered" *Secret Mark*'s "offensive" account of Jesus raising a young man from the dead and initiating him by nude baptism, and then "scattered parts of it" throughout his Gospel (1991: 329-32, 411-16).

11. In that sense, we must be wary when Crossan writes: "If you cannot believe in something produced by reconstruction, you may have nothing left to believe in" (426). We do have access to the *community* that developed *the original construction* prompted by Jesus risen. This gave rise to the faith-tradition, which received, cherished, expanded, and modified the data of the Jesus tradition, and which we are now trying to order and reconstruct. But in doing so, we willy-nilly place ourselves in that continuing tradition.

12. But this is quite responsibly interpreted, not as an attempt to cover up the ugly truth, but as a sign of a vivid sense of a new truth (cf. Wilder 1964). Cf. Attridge 1992: 223: "the complexity of early Christian literary activity . . . the originating impulse(s) of the whole Christian movement."

13. Still, in my construction *faith in Jesus risen* is the energy that inspires prophetic narratives, whose original, properly theological function is *cultic*; they then proceed to serve as the vehicle for the community's commitment to the imitation of Christ.

14. Metaphysical Poetry provides a parallel. Where the analytic critic sees only "the most heterogeneous ideas . . . yoked by violence together" (Johnson 1905: 20), the listener/speaker, aware of the dramatic qualities of the poetry, experiences, *in the act of performance*, that they are held together, and how.

15. Nor did the later tradition. The marginalization of the Descent into Hell in

favor of the Resurrection that Crossan sees is not evident in the Greek Fathers. A quick reading of Hans Urs von Balthasar's *Mysterium Paschale* (1990: 148-88) will confirm this.

16. Cf. Lear, accompanied by Kent and the Fool, encountering Edgar on the heath: "Is man no more than this? Consider him well. Thou owest the worm no silk, the beast no hide, the sheep no wool, the cat no perfume. Ha! here's three on's are sophisticated; thou art the thing itself; unaccommodated man is no more but such a poor, bare, forked animal as thou art" (*King Lear*, III, iv, 103-11).

17. Cf. Attridge's observation that Jesus was probably quite a bit more complex a character than recent analysis of *Q* has allowed him to be (1992: 234).

18. This is where Crossan most decisively parts company with Lessing. Incidentally, Lessing could have noticed the need for healing miracles as well as their occurrence right in his own milieu. The early eighteenth century gave us the first descriptions of a new class of diseases: the "lowness of spirits" and other "nervous distempers" among "people of the better Sort"—phenomena a later age would recognize as neuroses. But within fifty years, a wave of magnetizers, hypnotizers, and other wonder-workers like Franz Anton Mesmer (hence "mesmerizing") were healing these sufferers by spectacular means that strike us as wholly irrational (van den Berg 1974: 88ff.).

8.

The Brokerless Kingdom and the Other Kingdom

Reflections on Auschwitz, Jesus and
the Jewish-Christian Establishment

MARC H. ELLIS

In the spring of 1992, I was invited by Jonathan Weber and the Oxford Centre for Post-Graduate Hebrew Studies to participate in a symposium with other Jewish intellectuals and scholars at Auschwitz. After spending a week at Auschwitz in dialogue with my Jewish colleagues, the experience weighed heavily on all of us. There was an anger in the air throughout our time there, a justifiable anger in light of the Holocaust. And yet there was as well another level of introspection and self-absorption that sought to freeze history in the frame of Holocaust. We pointed the accusatory finger, never expecting one in return. It seemed that the Holocaust was being used as a way of refusing to examine our present life, the life of Israel to be sure, but also our lives as Jews within Britain and the United States. Could Auschwitz be used as a way of avoiding our accountability, even as we demanded it for ourselves over and over again from those who persecuted us? Could Auschwitz be used — in a perverse way to be sure — to claim an inherent and eternal superiority?

Ending Auschwitz

The phrase "ending Auschwitz," which came to me after leaving Poland, was, at least initially, difficult to decipher. Surely it means "never again" an Auschwitz for the Jewish people, a common Jewish understanding, and "never again" anything that approximates this for other peoples as well, the latter being a less-emphasized understanding proposed in early Holocaust theology. For me "ending Auschwitz" carries both of these understandings as a given, with the present as central as the past. Yet something remains to be articulated; by "ending Auschwitz" I mean that this episode of our history is creating such anger, isolation and a pretense of unaccountability that it is eroding the basic sensibilities and foundational ethics of our existence. *That is, Auschwitz has become a burden to the Jewish future that we as a people now further.* If the burden was thrust upon us, unexpected and unwanted, in a sense we now assume and expand it in a way unforeseen by the victims of the Holocaust. The point is less the historical fact of our suffering; rather it is how we use this suffering in the present. The choice is clear and in the main already decided: Do we use our past suffering as a way of understanding and entering into the suffering of others? Or do we use it as a blunt instrument against others, protecting our suffering as unique and incomparable to the suffering of others?[1]

At Auschwitz I witnessed the Jewish dilemma of how to view Christians and how to view ourselves. Two moments come to mind. The first occurred in the discussion of what to do with Birkenau, the extermination arm of Auschwitz where over a million Jews were killed and where, unlike Auschwitz, few of the original buildings are left standing. Should, for instance, a place of Jewish prayer (or indeed a place of prayer for anyone so inclined) be provided within one of those buildings at Birkenau? There was much to be said on this point and as the discussion continued, one member of our group suggested that a place of meditation, sparse and open, be our recommendation. To this another member angrily pounded the table, shouting, "Jews pray. Jews do not meditate." The second moment involved a group of French Jewish survivors who were returning to Auschwitz at the same time our group was there. They paused at certain places on the grounds to read Jewish prayers and recall histories of their travails. Another colleague derisively labeled their trip a "pilgrimage to Auschwitz" and likened it to the Christian custom of the stations of the cross. These French-Jewish survivors represented to him something antithetical to Jewish life and, indeed, something of an abomination. Though we ultimately acceded to the meditation place and discussed the fact that Jewish survivors could commemorate their travails in ways they themselves determined, the desire to root out any "Christian" influence was apparent. The lesson of Auschwitz, at least to some, was a complete separation of Judaism and Christianity—and we would define the parameters of both—and perforce a separation of Jew and Christian.

Yet the anger could hardly hide the profound historical experiences that Christians and Jews share, not only the bond that oppressor and oppressed forge, but the bond of joint suffering under a common oppressor. This latter bond crystallized as I left the Maryknoll classroom, where I was teaching a course titled "The Future of Religious Resistance and Affirmation," for the trip to Auschwitz. The class began with an analysis of Columbus' voyage to the Americas in 1492 and its ramifications for Europe, European Christianity and, in counterpoint, for the rest of the world. As I worked through the horrendous reality of 1492 and its continuation in 1992 in European (now American) hegemony, expansionism, militarism, imperialism and slavery, something crystallized that I had experienced, but had yet to articulate over my years of traveling and teaching at Maryknoll. That is, the experience of indigenous peoples and the Jewish people vis-à-vis dominant Western Christianity is essentially the same. And that what dominant Christians did inside of Europe to Jews, they did outside of Europe to others. For example, the consolidation of the Spanish state and Catholicism, which saw the Inquisition and resulting expulsion of Jews and Muslims, was visited even more brutally upon the indigenous people of the Americas and Africa. What I had experienced came into focus: there was a continuity between 1492 and Auschwitz, and there was a history to be traced from the Spanish, British, Portuguese and French conquest of the Americas and Africa to the gas chambers of Auschwitz. If it is true that Europe, then poor, became wealthy and the majority of the world, settled and cultured, became poor in the event of 1492, large parts of the world and nature also were on their way to becoming disappeared and dead as well, including, ultimately, the disappearance and death of millions of Jews.[2]

To analyze Jewish suffering within the perspective of 1492 is hardly to minimize the effects of Christendom on the Jewish people or to generalize away the particularity of Auschwitz. Rather it seeks to broaden our sense of the world, our suffering within it, and our possible future with other peoples. Can we recognize that the decimation of the native peoples of the Americas, the kidnapping, death and enslavement of millions of Africans in the European slave trade, are not ancillary to our experience, but central to it? Can we begin to understand that the majority of Christians in the world have been conquered by Christianity and have suffered under it in ways similar to how Jews have suffered? These Christians of color and non-European culture have lived under the same gospels under which we have lived, though less the Gospels of Christian liturgy, Matthew, Mark, Luke and John, which have served as a cover of the gospels dominant European Christians have embodied. Rather, I speak of the historical and living "gospels" of Constantine, of Columbus, of Luther, of Auschwitz, and of apartheid that have oriented the mainstream of European Christian life over the centuries. With this understanding in mind perhaps it is easier to recognize the common origins of Holocaust theology and liberation theology emanating from third-world Christians—the suffering of peoples at the hands of European Christendom. The goal of liberation theology is similar to the goal as defined by the early Holocaust theology phrase, "never again": end the physical and psychological oppression of 1492 and Auschwitz.[3]

The recognition of a common oppressor and a common experience of European Jews and Christians of color and non-European culture vis-à-vis European empire and European Christianity is difficult for many Jews to assimilate. To see that many Christians in Europe and America are also reevaluating their Christianity in light of 1492 and Auschwitz is, on the one hand, comforting (we should be safer) and, on the other hand, disorienting. Disorienting because this poses a possible reconciliation with our major historical enemy, Western Christianity, and raises again the question of our future. If we are not eternally embattled in Palestine (by understanding the binational reality of Israel/Palestine) or among European- and American-Christians (their opposition to 1492 and Christendom) — two major points of our contemporary identity — who are we?

The Christian struggle to "end 1492" is a struggle within the mainstream of Christianity, i.e., theological triumphalism and the violence of empire, and against many of the symbols and dogmas that characterize that mainstream. If it is true that we as Jews must now jettison our sense of Jewish innocence and redemption through Israel, dominant European and North American Christians must also leave behind their sense of innocence as well as their belief that to affirm Jesus Christ as the savior of all is somehow redemptive for the world. In actual fact, this "redemption" is covered with the blood of many peoples, including the majority of the world's Christians. Of course it is possible to be a Christian, conquered and oppressed by the Gospels, and still hold fast to the innocence and redemption, thus a triumphalism for the left as well as the right. Increasingly, however, Christians outside of Europe and America, and Christians within the empire are waking up to the fact that redemption played out in the world for one person or people is a disaster for the other.[4]

Interestingly enough, those Christians who seek to move beyond innocence and redemption, like many Jews, find themselves in an awkward and ambivalent place. If Christian history is not innocent and the Christian sense of redemption is covered with blood, what does it mean to be a Christian? The Christian establishment, like its Jewish counterpart, trots out various orthodoxies, enlarging or trimming them when necessary. But they are being undermined by history and critical thought. To many third-world Christians their overriding existential and even philosophical concern is simply ending 1492, or at least mitigating its effects. Could it be that the essential task of both Jew and Christian is "ending Auschwitz" (in the sense of "never again") and ending 1492 (with the critical understanding of Jew and Christian in Europe and America that we are now participating together in the continuation of 1492)? And could it be that the essential division between Jew and Christian, the figure of Jesus, was and is today a false dividing point, one that covers over the contemporary essential solidarity of dominant European and American Christians and Jews over against much of the world? This is one way of defining the ecumenical dialogue, which I have characterized elsewhere as the "ecumenical deal": the discussion of the Jewish-Christian establishment on how to keep intact their own self-definition and institutional arrangement against the onslaught of history and critical thought coming from dissenters outside and within the empire. Do Jewish and Christian participants agree to the old intratribal warfare — are there one or two covenants, did Jesus come for the

Jews or the Gentiles—so that both can survive the new challenge of ending Auschwitz and 1492, which they recognize to have profound political, cultural *and* religious ramifications?[5]

One might say that despite the attempts to resurrect it today, Christian orthodoxy planted the seeds of its own destruction in its complicity in the formative event of 1492. The victory proclaimed and seemingly achieved, at least to some extent, that every head should bow before Christ, is achieved but in name only. In many areas of the West, the churches are relatively empty memorials to church and empire. And those Christians who take the religious search seriously are often "lost in America and Europe," traveling to the Third World to be with those who have been conquered by the Gospel. However these travels are more complex than a desire to work for the uplift of the downtrodden or even a solidarity with fellow Christians. Rather, it is an attempt to find a foundation of faith and identity that is missing and has been destroyed in the victory. This is why their return to Europe and America is so disorienting; what these traveling Christians left is what remains upon their return. They look inside and around and find nothing.

The great crime of 1492 in the religious sense—and exemplified at Auschwitz—is the massive uprooting that Christianity has promulgated. In the destruction of culture and indigenous religiosity, Christian belief has spread a thin, covering layer over the deepest connections and longings of many peoples. When that layer is challenged or stripped away ancient deposits resurface. But what happens when the Christian layer is so powerful and persuasive—though still superficial—that the ancient becomes inaccessible, lost forever? This I believe is the fascinating dynamic of third-world/first-world Christians: the former uprooted by Christianity, but as yet tied to tribe and geography; the latter completely uprooted without hope of return. Thus 1492 and Christianity introduce a cycle of uprootedness that is difficult to escape, echoing the words of Simone Weil, the French-Jewish philosopher, when she wrote in 1943, "Whoever is uprooted himself uproots others." Could not this cycle be seen in the faces of the conquistadors, the SS, and the architects of the British, French and American colonial empires? And is not this cycle carried to the world today in the guise of modern life and the reason that Christian renewal, while beautiful and to be applauded, is destined to fail (Weil 1952: 45)?

Jesus and the Jewish-Christian Establishment

With the failure of Judaism and Christianity in our time, the task before us can be seen either as a need to resurrect the moral foundations that are failing, or an opportunity to raise foundational questions as to the viability and importance of both traditions. Would a full commitment to "ending Auschwitz" and "ending 1492" bring us closer to the traditions we inherit, or distance us further from them? In the final analysis, should our commitment be to rescuing or abandoning the traditions? Is it possible that Judaism and Christianity, whatever their rhetoric, need to continue these events of Auschwitz and 1492 to survive? What comes to mind in considering these questions is the desire of the institutional churches to speak of justice, even to renounce their previous methods of missionary work while they continue to evangelize, with new methods and renewed energy, the peoples of Latin America, Africa and Asia. As in 1492, the internal decay of Christianity in Europe, rather than evoking fundamental discussions about the Christian enterprise itself, increases evangelization outside of Europe. Christianity within the empire diminishes at the same time that it uses empire to expand outside those boundaries. On this, as on the issue of Israel, the ecumenical deal holds: Jews force Christians to renounce their desire to convert Jews as we remain silent, even at times give permission for Christians to continue to evangelize the world.[6]

Despite these contemporary issues, one cannot help but feel that a series of tragic errors were made centuries ago that either intentionally or inadvertently lend to the present impasse. From the Christian side, the most obvious error was the movement from the canonical Gospels to the gospels of Constantine and Columbus. Yet, perhaps, this error came from an even more fundamental mistake: the movement from the Jesus of history to Jesus the Christ. In the beginning this shift was internal and therefore one of perspective and choice. It represented a choice of direction rather than the founding of an institutional religion. However, the internal choice of direction, that is following the way of Jesus, soon was projected onto the world, thereby becoming one of objectives and demands. The internal understanding of redemption that an outsider could find compelling, provocative, indifferent or repulsive, was replaced by the "fact" of redemption that people had to affirm under penalty of exile or death.

The separation of the canonical Gospels and the gospels Christians subsequently lived out are difficult enough to disentangle. The most obvious example is a contemporary Catholic parish built and staffed in the way of empire (the architecture, the separation of cleric and lay person, the substitution of the communion wafer for a substantive meal, the formal codified liturgy rather than the informal recollection of stories related to Jesus). The parish may still discuss how the gathered community should oppose a particular aspect of empire—which the church originally blessed and from which it still benefits. More difficult is the separation of the canonical Gospels, which in Christian renewal are seen as wholly good and function to avoid the history of the gospels within which Christians have lived, from the life, background and teachings of Jesus. For the most part, the canonical Gospels are seen as representing the life of Jesus and the variance from the historical to the interpretive stories is ignored. But what would Christian renewal look like if the historical Jesus essentially undermines much of the canonical literature, indeed is at odds with it, and thus undermines the foundations of Christian religion as it was and is communicated?[7]

On the Jewish side the questions are somewhat different in history and scope, though no less challenging. By the end of the first century, Judaism was a defeated, if not decimated, religious movement. Though Judaism had before the first century demonstrated at times its propensity toward empire and conversion, the rise of the Roman and then Christian empires ended these possibilities until the birth of the state of Israel in 1948. Thus with very few exceptions, the Jewish internal discussion of religiosity was played out in the confines of a small, defeated and persecuted community. Outsiders were spared any evangelization by Judaism, only to face a powerful and relentless Christian evangelism.

The Jewish discussion was heated both because of the external pressure of the Roman and Christian empires and the internal pressure of conforming to an emerging orthodoxy that we now know as Rabbinic Judaism. It is important to note that just as Christians pursue renewal through an attempt to jettison the historical for the canonical Gospels—presuming that the more basic question of Jesus is thus answered—so, too, Jewish renewal is often pursued by returning to the rabbinic sources. In doing so, Jews bypass a critical engagement with our own current history of displacing another people in Palestine while ignoring our role in the present empires. Returning to rabbinic sources functions in an ahistorical way and also closes off more radical questioning of the rabbinic system itself. An example is the congregation in a plush synagogue whose rabbi emphasizes Jewish suffering, pledges unequivocal support for Israel and proceeds to read from a portion of Isaiah. All is safe.[8]

Crucial to understanding the synagogue setting is the fact that few Jews live within the rabbinic framework other than the rabbi, whom one might call a professional Jew, trained and paid to live within that system. How the rabbinic system and the combination of rabbinical and Jewish particularism came into being is unasked, and, out of ignorance, is almost impossible to ask. What is before and behind this system that is promulgated as Judaism and that most Jews in their everyday life essentially reject? Like the question of Christian renewal, Jewish renewal is haunted by its prehistory, interestingly enough the same prehistory that haunts Christianity, that is, the time preceding and including the era of Jesus. It is here that the fundamentals of Christian and Jewish life as we know them today begin to take shape and the fundamental separation of both faiths becomes definitive.

So often the essential division of Judaism and Christianity is assumed to revolve around Jesus. Yet this separation is simplistic, for some Jews rejected Jesus as messiah while other Jews accepted Jesus as the Christ. Still others lived and worked with Jesus as a fellow Jew, or met him in his travels and no doubt admired his insights and methods as a Jewish thinker and actor. To most Jews, Jesus was simply unknown. After the tumult of the first century, Judaism and Christianity went their separate ways. But the question of Jesus seen in his historical setting actually subverts the rejection/acceptance model of Judaism and Christianity and subverts both of these religions in the forms that they assumed historically. Could the renewed discussion of Jesus function to subvert the Jewish-Christian establishment and promote the end of Auschwitz and 1492?

The suggestion of a revived discussion of Jesus—discussion of an historical Jesus which subverts the Jewish-Christian establishment—is fraught with dangers. The first danger is the probability of offending Christian *and* Jewish sensibilities: the former by seeming to suggest that Jesus is not the messiah for Jews *or* Christians; the latter by suggesting that Jesus is somehow important for both Jews *and* Christians. At the same time, by challenging the prevailing orthodoxy put forth by the ecumenical deal, one is in danger of being disciplined simultaneously by the guardians of both traditions. The ecumenical deal states its orthodoxy boldly, for each tradition defines itself and each is accorded its own beliefs and structures. Outside of these parameters no critical thought is allowed. And after the Holocaust, who would dare raise the question of Jesus to Jews who have suffered so much in his name? Yet is it not true that hundreds of millions of others, many of them Christians, have likewise suffered in his name, once again linking Auschwitz and 1492? Perhaps the deeper question is whether it should be prohibited even to raise again the question of Jesus to Jews (or Christians for that matter), again because of what has been done in his name.[9]

This is not to say that Jesus has gone unmentioned in the ecumenical dialogue. Some of the great Jewish theologians of the twentieth century have carried on a friendly, if spirited, dialogue with Christianity. These include, among others, Leo Baeck (1873–1956), Martin Buber (1878–1965), Franz Rosenzweig (1886–1929), Will Herberg (1901–1977) and Abraham Heschel (1907–1972). As Fritz Rothschild points out, the central themes of these authors revolve around four topics: the person and significance of Jesus; the polarity of law and gospel; the place of the Hebrew Bible in Christianity; the role of the church as the New Israel, pointedly characterizing the Jews as the Old Israel.

As anyone who has followed the ecumenical discussion over the years knows, Jewish participants essentially attempt to link the witness of Jews and Christians. That is, both traditions, while clearly distinct, share foundational principles and aspirations, including that Christianity should not and really cannot fulfill its mission without its Judaic heritage and a living vibrant Jewish community. How could a Christian understand Jesus without understanding him first and foremost as a Jew? Instead of fighting with one another, the recognition of a common heritage presupposes the real fight in the modern world against which Jew and Christian can join forces: secular pagan influences that deny the transcendent and the inherent dignity of humankind. At certain moments the recognition of a common heritage can jointly boost the theological work or the renewal movement in each community. Heschel's essays, "A Hebrew Evaluation of Reinhold Niebuhr" (1956) and "The Jewish Notion of God and Christian Renewal" (1967), are two examples that come to mind. Another example is found in Will Herberg's essay, "A Jew Looks at Jesus" (1966), in which Jesus is hailed as a great moral teacher and a prophet in Israel, and the church and synagogue are coworkers in the vineyard of the Lord.[10]

What is important here is the Jewish desire to join itself with the dominant Christian ethos and, hence, stand indispensable to the mission of Christianity in the modern world. Clearly the agenda of Jews in this dialogue is more than simple survival, for it is also an avenue to status and identity in a Christian culture. Since 1967 it also lends itself to the creation of a united front on the question of Israel. At the same time, the pairing of Judaism and Christianity after the Holocaust attempts to forge an establishment that once and for all banishes the questions Christians ask of Jews and Jews ask of Christians. In the moral warfare against paganism, it is the good Jew and Christian battling the bad pagans. Of course, in the 1950s and early 1960s neither the Christian nor Jewish establishment anticipated the outbreak of radical Jewish and Christian theologies, theologies of the death of God and theologies of liberation against which they would later effectively unite. Suffice it to say that the union of the Jewish establishment with the Christian establishment, *to become one establishment*, makes it even more difficult from both sides to explore in a radical way the issues before us. By burying the differences of Judaism and Christianity as they have been lived out, the foundational questions are declared closed. Of course, it goes almost without saying that a Christian critique of Judaism is now impossible, at least in the public discourse of the religious establishment. A Jewish critique of Christian history vis-à-vis the Jews is allowed so long as the messiah question is left alone and contemporary Christianity is affirmed. And we should also note that this establishment, far from conservative, is filled with liberal Jews and Christians who actually set the limits of public discourse and, indeed, as Noam Chomsky has pointed out, "the limits of thinkable thought."

John Dominic Crossan's book, *The Historical Jesus: The Life of a Mediterranean Jewish Peasant*, undermines the foundations of the Jewish-Christian establishment by analyzing the identity and historical milieu of Jesus. As the title indicates, there are two foci of Jesus' identity: Jew and Mediterranean peasant. Unlike other authors who have recovered the Jewishness of Jesus in relation to the varieties of Jewish belief and groupings, Crossan, by emphasizing the locality and social class of Jesus, sees him in a broader context. Crossan's Jesus emphasizes less his dialogue with Jewish authorities than his assimilation and confrontation with Mediterranean peasant culture and Hellenistic ideas, both of which permeate the world Jesus was born into and acted within. For Crossan, Jesus is a peasant Jewish Cynic whose practice includes a "combination of free healing and common eating, a religious and economic egalitarianism that negated alike and at once the hierarchical and patronal normalcies of Jewish religion and Roman power." Thus Jesus never settles down or forms a group that sees him as a broker or mediator of God. Rather he sees himself as an announcer proclaiming that neither a brokered nor mediated relationship should exist "between humanity and divinity or between humanity and itself. Miracle and parable, healing and eating were calculated to force individuals into immediate physical and spiritual contact with one another." This is why, according to Crossan, Jesus announces the "brokerless kingdom of God" (Crossan 1991: 421-22).

In this announcement, Crossan's Jesus opts for an inclusive Judaism over against an exclusive Judaism. That is, Jesus was close to a form of Hellenistic Judaism that Crossan defines as Judaism "responding with all its antiquity and tradition to a Greco-Roman culture undergirded by both armed power and imperial ambition." The point that Crossan is making here is critical: with other Jews Jesus rejects an exclusive Judaism that seeks only to distance itself from Hellenistic culture. Instead Jesus seeks to adapt his ancient tradition as liberally as possible to aspects of Hellenism that he, along with other Jews, finds intriguing and beneficial. Thus Jesus is seen within a dialectical relationship—approving and critical—with his own inheritance, which was Jewish *and* Hellenistic, Mediterranean *and* peasant. However, this dialectical reality that Jesus embodies and struggles within is soon obscured by the events of 70 to 135 C.E., when Judaism rises against Rome and is systematically defeated. According to Crossan, the war saw two results: the destruction of the temple and Jewish exclusion from Judea, and the destruction of Egyptian Judaism, which "facilitated the move from levitical to rabbinical Judaism and also the ascendancy of exclusive over inclusive Judaism." This meant that both Jesus and the Jewish-Hellenistic dialectic, and later the emerging Christian movement, would be judged in Jewish circles by those who emerged as leaders of the new Jewish rabbinic framework—that is, by the rabbis. On the Christian side, Jesus was interpreted by a Constantinian Christianity that likewise placed its own interpretation on a Jewish Mediterranean peasant it was incapable of understanding. The Christian church, then, early in its history, could not or did not wish to understand that the early followers of Jesus inherited an inclusive Judaism that the church, beginning with Constantine, systematically betrayed. Thus considered historically, the religious disputes of the last 1500 years have been between a rabbinic exclusive Judaism with internal power only, and an inclusive Judaism, now Christian and exclusive, and carried by the likes of Constantine and Columbus (Crossan 1991: 420-21).

The point here is that as they became institutionalized, both the rabbinic and Christian movements distorted their prehistory as a way of legitimizing their ascendancy. Early on Jesus and the Judaism of his day, as well as his cultural and social base, are lost to a Judaism and Christianity operating in a new social, political, cultural and religious world. The rise of imperial Christianity profoundly impacts the Christian understanding of Jews and

Judaism as it reshapes its own identity. The rise of the rabbis also has a profound effect on Judaism and the identity of the Jewish people. As important as the distortion and rejection of Jesus by the Jewish establishment is the consolidation of the exclusive tradition. Because of this, much of Jewish history comes to be interpreted as a defiance of outside influences, as if "the other" threatened self-definition, rather than enhanced it, and an understanding that the world is intrinsically dangerous to physical survival as well. No doubt the rise of the Roman and Christian empire did much to reinforce or even create this understanding, for it stifled what seems to be a dialectic in Jewish history represented by the Jesus whom Crossan presents: on the one hand, a people profoundly conservative and tribal; on the other, liberal and subversive.

To fix attention solely on Jesus was probably the first mistake of the early Christian movement, for by the time of Constantine it had become a form of idolatry. At this moment in history, it would likewise be a monumental mistake to suggest that Jews should take the life of Jesus as central. Crossan avoids this partly because so little can be attributed to Jesus directly and partly because the overall sensibility exhibited by Jesus and other Jews in this peasant Mediterranean culture seems to be the message. The drama being played out is less one against others, or even one as unique. Rather, at a particular moment in history, at the intersection of empire and community, a small group of people explored a different path. By focusing on the path taken, rather than simply on Jesus, ancient Palestine is opened again to Christian and Jew without either needing to be for or against. In doing so, a deep history is revealed that takes us beyond the ahistorical canonical Gospels and rabbinic framework.[11]

A deep history most often proffers subversion of accepted religious dogma and practice. As a Jewish Mediterranean peasant, Jesus and those around him seem concerned to give all to the present and invite all to share in that present — hence, the centrality of the shared table with commensality, as Crossan interprets it. Jesus' sense of the kingdom as one filled with "nobodies and undesirables" subverts a variety of distinctions — sexual and social, political and religious — and this, too, seems to be central to Jesus' understanding of what Crossan names as the brokerless kingdom. Or perhaps it is better stated that Jesus and those around him felt that the brokerless kingdom arrived in the shared meal and subversion of political, social, cultural and religious hierarchy. Pursuing this brokerless kingdom by acting to bring it about, Crossan's Jesus reflects little about what religious authorities see as the important questions: whether one is acting within the tradition or transgressing the tradition's boundaries; on what basis is one acting and what are the consequences for those whose function it is to carry forth the tradition; whether the thought and action further advance or at least safeguard the place of the tradition in society. Instead, Jesus and his followers seem to delight in simply moving in history — radicalizing the teachings, taking the opening to cross boundaries and through expressive activities forcing the questions to new levels (Crossan 1991: 341).

That these understandings can be considered a "break with the Law" or an "adversarial position" with regard to Jesus' own people is pure retrospection from the Jewish-Christian establishment. Crossan's Jesus is simply acting to do what needs to be done. In an era that speaks of the confines of tradition, this may be the central message of Crossan's book: Jesus and his followers were of a Jewish Mediterranean peasant culture; they did what they felt needed to be done. They acted the way they traveled, as themselves, without guards or luggage, nor were they defending, exhorting or expanding. They were neither brokers nor builders. But they breached all sorts of deals, including the ancient ecumenical, social, political and cultural deals. In short, as Crossan analyzes it, Jesus and his followers were simply being faithful within their history as they saw it. That they would be caught up in a two-thousand-year debate, used as ideological instruments to prove or disprove salvation, and most horribly to legitimate Auschwitz and 1492, is to understate the obvious quite beyond what they could have imagined. Within a short time every deal that Jesus and his followers broke was literally resurrected, and done so in his name.

Crossan's Jesus as Corrective

How did the brokerless kingdom of Jesus become the Other Kingdom of Auschwitz? How did those who suffered the Other Kingdom come to legitimate the expansive policies of the state of Israel? How did the peasant ministry of Jesus come to be housed in imperial churches and those who rejected those imperial churches come to worship in plush suburban synagogues? How did the religious leaders of both traditions become so smug, so filled with illusion that their brokering has become *the* brokering?

What was missing at Auschwitz was Crossan's Jesus and those with him who simply gave all to the present without rejecting or being burdened by the past. There seemed to be little or no ulterior motives in this Jesus movement, certainly not fame, wealth nor a religion to be pursued in one's name. The method — the shared meal, egalitarian living — represented also a vision: the brokerless kingdom subverting the powers who, then and now, pursue the Other Kingdom, realized in 1492 and Auschwitz. As Crossan analyzes it, the Jesus movement centering on the shared table with commensality *is* the healing: the missionaries "share a miracle and a Kingdom, and they receive in return a table and a house," thus initiating a shared egalitarianism of spiritual and material resources. "I emphasize this as strongly as possible, and I insist that its materiality and spirituality, its facticity and symbolism cannot be separated. The mission we are talking about is not, like Paul's, a dramatic thrust along major trade routes to urban centers hundreds of miles apart. Yet it concerns the longest journey in the Greco-Roman world, maybe in any world, the step across the threshold of a peasant stranger's home." Interestingly, at Auschwitz all our meals were kosher, flown in from Switzerland at an exorbitant price, precisely to draw in public the boundary of a meal that in our own private lives we seldom draw. It was a symbolic gesture to say that we had survived, but it also symbolized a brokenness and lack of vision. Our summons was remembrance rather than a future (Crossan 1991: 341).

What was this longest journey in the Jewish and Greco-Roman world, then, and what is it in the Jewish-Christian-secular world today? Does this journey speak to Auschwitz and 1492? It seems that in the final analysis, crossing the threshold of a stranger's home was for Jesus and his followers a discipline wrought from their Jewish inheritance and culture in contact with Hellenism and the Greco-Roman empire. It was a discipline which constantly clarified the social, political, cultural and religious differences as it confronted the injustices of the Jewish and Greco-Roman establishment. This discipline was based neither on rejection nor acceptance. In itself it established a freedom of movement and invitation. That is, the discipline *is* the freedom and the healing, one at the same time. It is born in the "broken middle"; that is, the discipline is forged in the mix of history, at the depth of a historical moment, rather than transcending history by pretending to go backward to a golden past or forward to a glorious future. Crossan's Jesus is neither a romantic nor a utopian. Rather, the longest journey is a practice that opens the person and the community to the world in all its dimensions.

At Auschwitz both Jew and Christian inherited a discipline as well — the discipline framed by the rabbis and by the triumphal church which, while not completely estranged from that of Jesus and his followers, significantly distorts it. These disciplines form the backdrop for life in the world: something to be measured against but no longer lived out. For are we not governed more by the discipline of the modern world than these Jewish and Christian disciplines about which we speak so piously? And had not the discipline of the modern world overwhelmed the ancient disciplines in Auschwitz and 1492?

We cling to these disciplines as the important measures of our lives, as if they are significant in and of themselves and to preserve them is fidelity while to leave them is betrayal. Is this because we are trapped in a self-definition of Jew and Christian through the synagogue and the church that is increasingly irrelevant in the world? Or is it because we are trapped in a time-framed definition of Jew and Christian which has come to an end?

As I left Auschwitz the answers were less than clear. What I saw before me, however, was the need for a discipline similar to the one lived by a band of Jews before the rabbis and the church. To some Jews this will be seen as a betrayal, a sacrilege to mention Jesus after Auschwitz. Some Christians will raise their hands in triumph as another religious thinker — and a Jew no less — explores the path of Jesus. Can one keep silent in the face of such distortion when the "betrayed" and the "victor" have strayed so far as to miss the point completely? It is a history so confused, so tangled, so bloody and, yes, so smug that only the Jewish-Christian establishment in service to modern empires can make the same mistake as the Jewish and Greco-Roman establishments before them. But before us is a much larger task than to name who is victor and who has been betrayed. Rather, it is the fashioning of a discipline requisite to the crisis which confronts us: ending Auschwitz and 1492.

Notes

1. For the theme of unaccountability, see the Israeli author Boas Evron (Evron 1981).

2. For a fascinating discussion of 1492 see Sale 1991.

3. It is important to emphasize that for liberation theologians the crisis is now. Thus the Peruvian theologian Gustavo Gutiérrez writes that for Latin Americans the question is not, "How are we to do theology after Auschwitz? The reason is that in Latin America we are still experiencing every day the violation of human rights, murder, and the torture that we find so blameworthy in the Jewish Holocaust of World War II. Our task here is to find the words with which to talk about God in the midst of the starvation of millions, the humiliation of races regarded as inferior, discrimination against women, especially women who are poor, systematic social injustice, a persistent high rate of infant mortality, those who simply 'disappear' or are deprived of their freedom, the sufferings of peoples who are struggling for their right to live, the exiles and the refugees, terrorism of every kind, and the corpse-filled common graves of *Ayacucho*. What we must deal with is not the past but, unfortunately, a cruel present and a dark tunnel with no apparent end." See Gutiérrez 1987: 93.

4. While it is true that much of the writing of liberation theology is somewhat triumphal, i.e., the absolute sense of Christ among the poor, personal conversation with many of these authors reveal a much more nuanced sense of the problematic of God within suffering. The problem is that they are competing for space in a tradition which allows only certainty with relation to God. For a fascinating Christian discussion of the problematic of God in the face of suffering see Casanas 1983.

5. For my discussion of the ecumenical deal see Ellis 1991: 47-64.

6. The relationship of the decay and expansion of Christianity in 1492 is a powerful subtheme of Sale 1991.

7. Liberation theology attempts to understand the historical Jesus before the church and even to some extent the historical Jesus before the canonical Gospels. Unfortunately, though understandably, their argument seeks mostly a radicalization of the church, i.e., a confrontation with gospels of Constantine and Columbus. Thus the turf has already been defined, as the argument is blunted within that definition.

8. Some forms of Jewish renewal attempt to return to rabbinic interpretation with a critique of contemporary politics and culture. My own sense is that the possibility of such a return is, for the most part, limited to the enhancement of Jewish identity. For an example of such renewal see Waskow 1978.

9. For a succinct statement of the "rules" of the ecumenical dialogue, see Swidler 1983.

10. For Heschel's essays see Rothschild: 283-300, 325-40. For Herberg's essay see Rothschild: 256-66. As Rothschild points out, not all of the public affirmation of Christianity made by these authors reflected their private opinions. See Rothschild: 10-11.

11. Crossan walks a fine line with reference to Jesus and the church. He points out that the ultimate betrayal of Jesus was the movement from "Christ to Constantine," but finds "no contradiction between the historical Jesus and the defined Christ, no betrayal whatsoever in the move from Jesus to Christ" (Crossan 1991: 424). To me, Crossan's entire book undermines the movement toward both Christ and Constantine.

9.

Sapiential Eschatology and Social Transformation

Crossan's Jesus, Socially Engaged Buddhism, and Liberation Theology

CHARLES R. STRAIN

Crossan's Jesus is disconcerting to a theologian. Theologies traditionally thrive within institutions whose boundaries they define and, in part, create. Jesus, we are told, transgresses all boundaries, creates community apart from the oppressive weight of institutions. Theologies mediate; Jesus proclaims and performs the unmediated availability of divine power. Theologies discourse about the routes and pitfalls of salvation; Jesus heals. If Crossan's Jesus does not disconcert, a theologian must be seriously self-deluded.

Sensing that our work might ineluctably further the kind of political, cultural and economic systems that Jesus renounced, we theologians wriggle. Like sensitive lawyers or dentists, we trip over our professional persona as we take sides with "the other." Socially engaged theologians say that theology is critical reflection on the praxis of base communities, that it is the voice of the oppressed. Others adopt narrative voices seeking to attune themselves to the immediacy of transformative experience. Courageous thinkers, like Gustavo Gutiérrez, do so at some risk and with rare authenticity; most of us do so while remaining safely inside the institutions of university or seminary.

Fleeing self-delusion, I confess to being disconcerted. I accept the role as mediator of theory and practice, of religious experience and vision with cultural interpretations. I am not only part of institutions, I believe in them, see them as essential to levering real social change. Structures matter. Without them far fewer of the sick would be healed, naked clothed or hungry fed than the inadequate number we actually serve. Yet, like other Christian theologians, I know that apart from magic and meal, apart from the sort of radical experience of community performed by Jesus, mediation is for naught and institutions have no soul.

Yet theologians too can transgress boundaries. I have written in areas of political theology and social ethics because of my commitment to human liberation. And yet I have come to think that our Western paradigm of liberation is deeply flawed. So I have turned to what is called "socially engaged Buddhism" as a possible source for the transformation of Christian models of liberation. Crossan's work provides the opportunity to challenge myself from inside as well as from outside my own tradition. To limit this discussion, I will focus on two issues: (a) Jesus' and Buddhists' "sapiential eschatologies" as transformative of the theory and practice of liberation, and (b) the idea of a radically egalitarian community in Jesus' and Zen Buddhists' visions and its relationship to social structures.

Sapiential Eschatology and Liberation

Albert Schweitzer announced an apocalyptic Jesus and generations of theologians developed the contrast between eschatological thinking and the bourgeois myth of progress. Moltmann's theology of hope, Metz's eschatological proviso, and Gutiérrez's utopian thinking became critical elements in the development of political theologies. Now, Crossan announces that the apocalyptic Jesus changed his mind. "John's vision of awaiting the apocalyptic God, the Coming One, as a repentant sinner, which Jesus had originally accepted and even defended in the crisis of John's death, was no longer deemed adequate. It was now a question of being in the Kingdom" (Crossan 1991: 237-38). Subordinating the greatest to the least, Jesus overturns apocalyptic eschatology:

> Among those born of women, from Adam until John the Baptist, there is no one superior to John. . . . Yet I have said, whichever one of you comes to be a child will be acquainted with the Kingdom and will become superior to John (*Gospel of Thomas* 46 as cited in Crossan 1991: 237).

So far it seems as if apocalyptic and eschatological modes of vision and action are interchangeable. But Crossan moves beyond conventional theological distinctions to redefine the relationship. "I need the term *eschatology* as the wider and generic term for world-negation extending from apocalyptic eschatology . . . through mystical or utopian modes, and on to ascetical, libertarian or anarchistic possibilities" (238).

The term "world-negation" is problematic at least with regards to the Buddhist texts that I will examine shortly. Crossan, however, interprets the term with reference to peasant experience. The world is all that weighs upon, that crushes peasants and "peasant culture and religion is actually an anticulture, qualifying alike both the religious and the political elites that oppress it" (264). In a peasant context eschatology is the language of resistance. Distinguishing between the apocalyptic and the sapiential poles of eschatology on the one hand, and scribal proclamations and peasant performances of the kingdom on the other, Crossan suggests that Jesus with his free healing and open commensality was a sapiential performer of the kingdom (291-92). The kingdom of undesirables proclaimed in parables is immediately available to anyone. There is no need for recourse to an individual or institutional go-between. This kingdom is purely and simply present "for those who have eyes to see," for those who ask (294-95). A future kingdom of any sort would require some line of connection, some futures market to make available and secure that which, precisely as future, remains radically insecure.

Liberation: The Limits of a Paradigm

It is this sapiential eschatology that I wish to juxtapose against what I take to be the guiding assumptions of liberation theology. In many ways "liberation" is the root metaphor defining the aspirations of our times. Conceptually formulated in a modern, historicist context, it fully translates itself, adapting skillfully to the shifting forms of "postmodern" ideology. Liberation theologians have acculturated traditional Christianity to this new context. Phillip Berryman may have overstated the accomplishments of liberation movements within Christianity when he calls them a new Reformation but I do not believe that he has misstated their promise (Berryman: 6). Christian theologians engaged in interreligious dialogue, recognizing the virtually unanimous concern of all traditions today with issues of poverty, injustice, and oppression, argue that the metaphor of liberation may offer the common language through which we might negotiate religious conflicts and ease human suffering (Knitter).

As with any root metaphor, constantly shifting meanings imperil the original insight. Better to focus on the structural elements of the paradigm, the cognitive DNA that determines it. Like any paradigm, that cognitive coding prescribes a limited field of vision and action. More importantly, we may be able to discover genetic flaws within this coding that can help us to forestall pathologies of practice in religious movements guided by the hope for liberation.[1] To suggest that *any* paradigm is limited and prone to unique pathologies, I insist, is not to dismiss it but to take it with the seriousness required of a world-transforming vision.

Crossan's striking contrast between Jesus the apocalyptic follower of the prophet John and Jesus the sapiential healer, who makes divine power utterly available in open community, leads me to highlight two structural elements of the liberation paradigm that I have struggled with for years. First, the paradigm of liberation in both its secular and religious formulations is radically oriented to the future as the locus of redemption. At best, the future is anticipated in the parabolic experiences of community in the present. Most frequently, the stress is placed upon the present experience of systemic oppression that stands in sharp contrast to the hoped-for future. In secular and religious theodicies which count on the victory of some future generation, those who do not live to experience this future, those whose lives are cut short by political assassins and death squads, and those who lived diminished lives when even the hope for liberation was not available to redefine one's identity, stand mute before a walled kingdom. We need a theory of liberation that recognizes that each person, however diminished in thought and action by systemic oppression, has utter access to the utterly available Kingdom of God.

Second, when liberation is paired with the concept of alienation, it fosters a dialectical understanding of social transformation. Each person simultaneously is alienated by the constraining structures of social life, participates to some degree in their creation, and, hopefully, struggles to transform them. Liberation, however, more frequently is paired with the concept of oppression. Here a dualistic chasm is created with victims on one side and oppressors on the other. What then occurs is what I have come to call "ethical cleansing" as all of us strive to identify ourselves as or, at least, with the victims while simultaneously pinpointing some other as oppressor. Ethical cleansing, like its ethnic counterpart, is always violent. The important point to note is that this is not merely a social-psychological process rooted in the rhetoric of liberation/oppression. Very early in the formation of the liberation paradigm a shift was made from Hegel's clearly dialectical conception to what some scholars have called a "revolutionary antithetic" (Stuke: 141). In contrast to a dialectic in which all historical agents, worlds and worldviews are mutually transformed, an antithetic seeks apocalyptic confrontation. Polarization not mutual transformation becomes the inner thrust. Marx's thought represents a subterranean clash between dialectical conceptions inherited from Hegel and the concept of a revolutionary antithetic set within an apocalyptic eschatology taken over from Young Hegelians like Bruno Bauer. We need not trace this historical shift further here. A simple rereading of the *Communist Manifesto* with an eye on its apocalyptic rhetoric, however, can uncover this San Andreas fault running through the liberation paradigm.[2]

Learning My True Name from Engaged Buddhists

My own efforts to deal with these two structural deficiencies have entailed crossing a religious divide to learn from socially engaged Buddhism.[3] I had not thought until listening to Dominic Crossan and watching his book take shape to find a sapiential Jesus as a resource for reflection on praxis. Now my own interreligious dialogue has become more of a conversation on an extended party line. As the conversation has proceeded, other voices, to be honest voices that represent other versions of myself, have intervened. They ask questions and raise objections in their defense of the liberation paradigm: Doesn't any shift of the future focus of liberation sap the will to struggle? Would not any concept of utter access to an utterly available kingdom of God overturn God's own solidarity with the poor? Doesn't any rejection of a revolutionary antithetic blur the line separating justice and injustice? Would not any dialectical concept of alienation/liberation entail "blaming the victim" or "letting oppressors off the hook?"

Turning to engaged Buddhism has yielded no easy answers. Thích Nhât Hanh is a Vietnamese monk who was the soul of the Buddhist peace movement during the Vietnam War. He lives in exile in France where he works on behalf of Vietnamese refugees and international peace. He is one of the architects of an engaged Buddhism that presents a stark contrast to liberation theology. Thích Nhât Hanh's words and work are important to consider because in his own life he performs the shift of Buddhism from an Asian to a Western context.

Because it relieves the hardship of the present moment, Thích Nhât Hanh suggests, hope is important but it is spiritually inadequate. Western civilization has so fixated itself upon a hoped-for future that it and we need the shock therapy of "refraining from hope."

> When I think deeply about the nature of hope, I see something tragic. Since we cling to our hope in the future, we do not focus our energies and capabilities on the present moment. We use hope to believe something better will happen in the future, that we will arrive at peace, or the Kingdom of God. Hope becomes a kind of obstacle. ... The well is within us, and if we dig deeply in the present moment the water will spring forth. ... This means that we can realize peace right in the present moment with our look, our smile, our words, and our actions. ... Each step we make should be peace (Thích Nhât Hanh 1991: 41-42).

To my Western mind, Thích Nhât Hanh's injunction to refrain from hope does appear to drain the sap of world-transforming struggle. His belief that "peace is every step" seems unbearably sweet and mortally dangerous to the "sacred discontent" underlying prophetic resistance.

But Thích Nhât Hanh has his own parabolic way of creating an alternative community of resistance, a community that is aware of the full horror of our times. His most powerful parable is a poem entitled "Please Call Me By My True Names." The poem has appeared in a number of contexts, perhaps because it represents for this committed Vietnamese Buddhist an unavoidable koan. I found it in a series of talks given to American Buddhists and peace activists in a meditation entitled "Working for Peace" (Thích Nhât Hanh 1987: 62-64).

This poem begins sweetly enough with a Buddhist's identification of "I" with the dependent co-arising and ceasing of all beings.[4] "Do not say that I'll depart tomorrow because even today I still arrive. Look deeply: I arrive in every second to be a bud on a spring branch. . . ." Sweetness ends when the "I" announces that she is a mayfly and the bird that consumes the mayfly, a frog, and the grass-snake "approaching in silence." Such alternations of birth and death are bearable. I can even call them "the rhythm of my heart." But in three stanzas Thích Nhât Hanh plunges that heart into darkness. "I am," the narrator continues, a child in Uganda starving to death and the arms merchant whose deadly trade consumes the wealth of Uganda. "I am" an inmate in a labor camp and the politburo leader who sentences the inmate for crimes against the state. In between these familiar images of the macrosuffering of our times, at the very heart of the poem, is an image of arresting singularity.

> I am the 12-year-old girl, refugee on a
>   small boat,
> Who throws herself into the ocean after being
>   raped by a sea pirate,
> and I am the pirate, my heart not yet capable
>   of seeing and loving.

Can I integrate this concrete horror with the rhythms of my heart, Thích Nhât Hanh seems to ask? Can I say "I am that" without choking and drowning myself? To do less, he tells the Buddhist activists, is to deny the meaning of dependent co-arising. Painstakingly he shows how the young girl's despair and the sea pirate's violence against her "inter-are" with all that I am, all that I have failed to do. To become aware that I dependently co-arise with all beings is to destroy any ready identification with the victim (read: solidarity with the oppressed) that cleanses me of my complicity with her rapist. I can speak in ethical abstractness of degrees of moral complicity and responsibility or I can take a stand in righteous anger against oppressors, but in either case what I can be absolutely sure of is this: If I remain as I am with my lifestyle and patterns of consumption, new generations of sea pirates will follow old. "Please call me by my true names, / so I can wake up . . ." the poem ends. Only an awareness capable of integrating the full horror of the web of violence etched on the face of the world can ground responsible action—"and so the door of my heart can be left open, / the door of compassion." I transmute the horror of self-knowledge, of knowing my true names, by going through that door.

But the door appears to be locked. Dependent co-arising may be a spiritually sublime teaching but it seems, to my Western mind, to undercut a just allocation of moral responsibility and moral culpability. If I dependently co-arise with the sea pirate, does not the twelve-year-old girl also? And if she does, aren't we "blaming the victim?" If the door of hope in a future kingdom of God reached through liberating struggle is slammed shut and the door of compassionate action grounded in the awareness of dependent co-arising is locked, where am I?

Antithetical Bonding and a Revolutionary Antithetic

As Dominic Crossan has taught us, a parable can only be understood in light of its intended audience. To those who are "working for peace" it seems self-evident that others are not. Such simple dualisms, argues Ken Jones, a British engaged Buddhist, generate a destructive spiral. Dualism first becomes a "weighted polarization." Again, it seems self-evident that it is better to work for than against peace, to liberate rather than to oppress. A weighted polarization, in turn, generates "antithetical bonding . . . where the common belongingness identity is more deeply established and exalted by the subordination of another group in competition with it" (Jones: 44-45, 90-92). *We* who work for peace or liberation versus *they* who oppress. If I might add one more turn to the spiral, antithetical bonding in the context of a struggle for peace or justice does tend to generate the revolutionary antithetic that I spoke of earlier. What begins with a simple dualism becomes a world-transforming ideology.

Thích Nhât Hanh's parable aborts this destructive spiral. Antithetical bonding does not allow me to know my true names. Weighted polarizations obscure my true place in the web of violence. From the engaged Buddhist standpoint, authentic practice begins with mindfulness. The parable centers squarely upon the "I" who, like the pirate, is not yet mindful. It discourages any abstract (read: pornographic) speculation about victims' complicity in their victimization. Abstract reasoning is not mindful.

Likewise, mindfulness resists the secretion of calcifying ideas by those who have antithetically bonded. Training in mindfulness removes the cataracts that obscure our awareness of the limitations of any perspective, cataracts that inevitably form when ideologies harden. "All systems of thought are guiding means; they are not absolute truth," Thích Nhât Hanh counsels. "Avoid being . . . bound to present views. . . . Be ready to learn . . ." (1987: 89-91). What applies to thought, applies to practice as well. "In Buddhism it is said that there are 84,000 Dharma doors for you to enter reality. Dharma doors are means of practice, ways of practice" (1987: 110). Neither orthodoxy nor orthopraxis is rightly mindful. Both calcify. Presumably, they are not included among the 84,000 possibilities. 84,000 is not an infinite number. Criteria for practice, including the criterion of mindfulness that we have focused upon, mark out a broad field for authentic engagement. Engaged commitment to liberation neither walks a narrow tightrope nor wanders aimlessly in an infinite space. It chooses its doors with mindful care.

Mindfulness applies, finally, to the core spiritual consciousness out of which we act. Thích Nhât Hanh's dharma talks to peace activists, as we have seen, do not focus so much on working for peace as upon "being peace." But dualistic understandings of being and doing, of inner and outer, even of working on one oneself versus working on the world are false conceptualizations. Our distinction between the spiritual and the political is an offshoot of these false conceptualizations. At the very end of his dharma talks to engaged Buddhists, Thích Nhât Hanh encourages them to sit or walk quietly with their children each morning and evening and to focus on their breathing. "These things are important," he concludes. "They can change our civilization" (1987: 115).

Refraining from Hope

In this discussion of what might be called a sapiential practice of liberation we have come some distance from Crossan's focus on sapiential eschatology. I want to return to it and to Thích Nhât Hanh's discussion of hope as an obstacle. Toward the end of his compelling meditation on Job, Gustavo Gutiérrez argues that Job, having dispatched the cramped theologies of his friends, transcended a final idolatry, "the temptation of imprisoning God in a narrow concept of justice" (1987: 91). Prophetic discourse grounded in sacred discontent fuses with a transforming awareness of God's presence. Gutiérrez speaks of that presence as a hand guiding us along a marked route. He quotes the words of Luis Espinal, a Bolivian priest murdered in the midst of his struggle for justice.

> Train us, Lord to fling ourselves upon the impossible, for behind the impossible is your grace and your presence; we cannot fall into emptiness. The future is an enigma, our road is covered by mist, but we want to go on giving ourselves, because you continue hoping amid the night and weeping tears through a thousand human eyes (cited in Gutiérrez 1987: 91-92).

To open one's mouth in the presence of the martyred Espinal and the endless ranks of those who suffer unjustly is to risk the fate of being one of Job's "friends." I simply want to juxtapose an alternative parable of liberation, one that has taught me to question theological categories that separate emptiness and grace, the suffering present and the enigmatic future. The "Ten Oxherding Pictures" with their accompanying verses and commentaries are a classic Buddhist narrative of the quest for liberation (Kapleau: 313-25). In them an Oxherder searches for a lost Ox. But we are put on notice by the first line of commentary on the very first picture that liberation is not to be understood in terms of a journey along a road, nor in terms of a quest and triumph. "The Ox has never really gone astray, so why search for it?" Irony dogs the Oxherder who, through several pictures, dogs the Ox, follows its tracks, receives a glimpse and finally catches the Ox. "A nightingale warbles on a twig, / the sun shines on undulating willows. / There stands the Ox, where could he hide?" The Ox is not elsewhere; the reign of God is here and now. In the sixth picture the Oxherder rides home on the tamed Ox, but in the seventh picture the Ox disappears. If the Ox is not elsewhere, the Ox is also no other than who we are. In the eighth picture the self too disappears leaving an empty circle. "Ox and man alike belong to Emptiness. / So vast and infinite the azure sky." No future kingdom, here or hereafter, could or should assuage Job. Always, so much is already lost and being lost. A grace *behind* the emptiness would still leave a negative emptiness. Father Espinal echoes Dietrich Bonhoeffer's insight: "Only a suffering God can help." But the Oxherding pictures go further. Nirvana *is* samsara[5]—for those who have eyes to see. This world of injustice and suffering is the Kingdom of God—for those who have eyes to see.

In their original composition the Oxherding Pictures ended with the eighth picture. But a twelfth-century monk rejected the static contemplation of the eighth picture and pushed awareness more deeply into the realm of liberating practice. In the ninth picture we are thrust into the wild profusion of natural reality: "Streams meander on of themselves / Red flowers naturally bloom red." Emptiness like the sapiential kingdom of God is not something that lurks behind or waits ahead. Liberation, like peace, is every step. In the tenth picture entitled "Entering the Marketplace with Helping Hands," a realized Bodhisattva appears as a village drunk. No stink of holiness clings to this individual. Nothing to separate this drunk from the innkeepers and fishmongers. Yet "withered trees he swiftly brings to bloom."

The kingdom of God has ceased to be a goal which, as a goal, remains imprisoned in an enigmatic future. Practice becomes what I would call "eschatological peripeteia."[6] The Bodhisattva, like Jesus, wanders and heals. Neither goes anywhere. No utopia awaits. Wandering or peripeteia becomes the appropriate spatial metaphor for an eschatology of impermanence. It is also appropriate for a form of eschatology that transcends the dualism of world-negation and world-affirmation. This suffering, this agency is the Kingdom of God. "This very place is the Lotus Land," proclaims the Japanese Zen master Hakuin. "This very body the Buddha" (as cited in Aitken: 162). Hope as a form of clinging is doubly delusive. It turns us away from the present and, precisely because it clings, it reifies the future. Genuine practice is not endless as Sisyphus' struggle is endless. Realized with each step on the way, it is, however, unending. Unending struggle is expressed with equanimity in the First Vow of a Bodhisattva: Though sentient beings are innumerable, I vow to save them all.

Surely, all of this Father Espinal knew and lived. Theological contortions that try to usher those whose lives, like Father Espinal's, were brutally cut short into the absent kingdom border on the obscene. My point is a simple one: Present and future in the eschatological categories of the Christian tradition fall prey to the same dualism that infects other theological relationships (God and world, salvation and liberation. ... I could go on).

Buddhism detects the spot on our lungs. We do not breathe the Spirit as we could. Engaged Buddhism, I suggest, is a most delicate chemotherapy for Christians struggling to liberate. I could say the same about Crossan's Jesus:

> His disciples said to him, "When will the kingdom come?" <Jesus said,> "It will not come by waiting for it. It will not be a matter of saying 'Here it is' or 'There it is.' Rather the kingdom of the father is spread out upon the earth, and men do not see it" (*Gospel of Thomas* 113 as cited in Crossan 1991: 282-83).

As in the case of the wandering Bodhisattva, the kingdom is not the object of endless longing, in its very absence the token of our unrequited misery. Jesus, like the Bodhisattva, does not explain away our discomfort. He acts. "What was described by his parables and aphorisms as a here and now Kingdom of the nobodies and the destitute . . . is precisely a Kingdom performed rather than just proclaimed" (Crossan 1991: 292). In a world where the random violence of sea pirates pales before the global piracy of organized economic exploitation, an utterly present and available kingdom may seem an affront. We find it easier to *work* for an unattainable peace than to be peace. The present kingdom confronts us as a koan in a way that parallels our recognition of the dependent co-arising of evil.

Egalitarian Community and Social Transformation

Near the end of *The Historical Jesus*, Crossan states unequivocally the social message conveyed in Jesus' actions.

> His strategy, implicitly for himself and explicitly for his followers, was the combination of *free healing and common eating*, a religious and economic egalitarianism that negated alike and at once the hierarchical and patronal normalcies of Jewish religion and Roman power. . . . He was neither broker nor mediator but, somewhat paradoxically, the announcer that neither should exist between humanity and divinity or between humanity and itself. Miracle and parable, healing and eating were calculated to force individuals into unmediated physical and spiritual contact with one another. He announced, in other words, the brokerless kingdom of God (422).

A brokerless kingdom is a religiously compelling paradox, unless, of course, it is a deceptively compelling oxymoron. For a political theologian to ask which this vision of radical egalitarianism really is verges precariously toward the cliff edge of an unforgivable sin. Let me shift to the second issue that gives focus to this discussion with Crossan and engaged Buddhism by recapitulating the first issue from a very different angle of perception. In *Life is Elsewhere* the Czech novelist, Milan Kundera dissects the "eschatologic faith in an absolutely new world," which has driven European cultures mad (Kundera: vi). For Kundera the poet, however, it is not the liberation theologian but the lyric poet who gives voice to this faith. "[R]evolutions are lyrical and in need of lyricism," he insists (193). In the streets of Paris in 1968 lyrical vision became revolutionary slogan: *Life is elsewhere . . . Dream is Reality . . . Power to the Imagination . . . Poetry is in the streets.* But also: *No freedom for the enemies of freedom . . . Death to the lukewarm!* (173-74). Fueled by a common "passionate monism," poets and revolutionaries alike hurled their *"all or nothing* in the face of history" (220).

All too happily, eschatological absolutism embraces revolutionary "cleansing." Earlier in the "pseudorevolutions" following World War II, Kundera had witnessed beloved poets in their eschatological blindness join hands with Stalinist executioners to betray other poets. The event was shattering. "When an executioner kills, that is after all normal; but when a poet . . . sings in accompaniment, the whole system of values we considered sacrosanct has suddenly been shaken apart" (v).

If the argument of the first section of this chapter makes sense, neither the Oxherder nor Jesus would proclaim, *Life is elsewhere.* Their realized eschatology—itself a religiously compelling paradox—negates a revolutionary nihilism where, in Marx's penetrating phrase, "all that is solid melts into air." But might they not have said in Paris in 1968 or during the recent revolutions in Eastern Europe itself, *Poetry is in the streets?* And if they would have said the former, would the words *Death to the lukewarm* have followed in lockstep? Free healing and common eating *are* lyrical as well as parabolic acts. Do they succumb to the disease of lyricism? Is the absolute of absolute egalitarianism as corrosive of genuine community as any other absolute?

The Ideology of Immediacy

Let me up the ante by turning again to the Buddhist context. In the tradition of D. T. Suzuki, books in the West on Zen Buddhism stress the spontaneous, unmediated character of the enlightenment experience and Zen's subversive, iconoclastic character as a movement within Buddhism. How often have we heard the Zen aphorism, "Meeting the Buddha, killing the Buddha. Meeting the patriarchs, killing the patriarchs?" How frequently have we heard *satori* described as "the simple realization of the intrinsic purity of beings . . . " (Faure: 34-35)? This portrayal of Zen in the West corresponds dramatically with the image of Jesus' brokerless kingdom described by Crossan. Zen's "Man of no Rank" is the kind of person who might inhabit that kingdom.

A new and difficult work by Bernard Faure on the Chan tradition in China and the Zen tradition in Japan overturns this portrayal. "[T]he Chan tradition," he argues, "is a fictional remembering of origins, that is, an active forgetting of the fact that there never was any pure origin" (28). Amnesia set in when some practitioners singled out one pole of a magnetic field and conceived the tradition not as the permanent oscillation between contrasting poles but as the triumphant establishment of a single center. So in Chan/Zen ideological rectitude was created by affirming the icono-clastic over the traditional, nonconformist behavior over routinization of behavior, community over structure, the person of no rank over all hier-archies (Faure: 14-17, 26). The Chan/Zen equivalent to mediated versus unmediated access to the kingdom of God became the dichotomy between gradual and sudden awakening.

The concept of a sudden, i.e. unmediated, awakening in Chan/Zen, Faure argues, is the ideological construct of some branches of the tradition that was created by hypostatizing permanent tensions *within all branches* into a dichotomy that pitted one pure path against a compromised position. This "scapegoating of gradualism" systematically distorted the interweaving of sudden and gradual elements of Zen practice in *all* branches of the tradition. Ironically the "rhetoric of immediacy" became an ideological wedge polarizing branches of the tradition whose practices did not diverge so dramatically (39-45, 48-49).

At the level of social reality the "weighted polarizations" of immediate versus mediated experience, and sudden versus gradual realization, corre-late with the polarity of community versus social structure. We have learned from Victor Turner that the experience of unfettered community always exists in some relationship with social structure. History itself is the working out of the tension between these two poles of a "charged field" in ways that intimate some underlying form (Turner: 274). Recurrent oscillation, conflicting juxtaposition, and dialectical transformation are some of the ways in which this relationship can unfold. But to project social reality as either unfettered community or social structure alone is to conceive of a fabric as a warp with no woof. The threads do not bind.

Faure shows how a dimension of spiritual practice, which stresses imme-diacy and which is deeply transformative in itself, can be rigidified into an ideology of immediacy, how Chan/Zen's commitment to an unfettered com-munity of "mind directly transmitting to mind" is transformed into an ide-ology that fetters. Such an ideological interpretation of the Chan/Zen lineage obscures the ways in which this most subversive of traditions (Hyers: 55) is, after all, a tradition with manifold structures, routinized practices and paradoxical doctrines.

One final example; this one much closer to home. I sit down to write after a meeting in the Dorothy Day room of our new library. In a wood-paneled room with a panoramic view of the campus, this subversive model of egalitarian Christianity has become an institutionalized icon. As you enter the room, a gold-leafed portrait of Dorothy as a Byzantine saint glows on your left. Each time I hear Dominic Crossan speak wistfully and ironically of the transformation of the peasant Jesus into the church's Christ, I think of Dorothy. The ritualized process by which institutions capture and contain subversive models is hardly foreign to our own experience.

Kundera, Faure, and DePaul's Dorothy Day Room represent three ways in which the vision of a brokerless kingdom is falsely brokered. In a distorted, religious version of the Heisenberg principle, each time we lay hands upon the vision and experience of unfettered community we warp it, distort it. And it is a measure, perhaps, of our religious longing that we cannot keep our hands off of it.

Working the Linkages

What, then, do we do with this vision of the brokerless kingdom? Perhaps the wisest advice would be to meditate on the aphorism: Don't just do something; stand there. Allow the vision to do something to you. Like Sisyphus, however, political theologians cannot stand still. They must wrestle their way up a mountain of suffering that, growing relentlessly, shames the inactive.

So far we have only examples of pathological relationship of community and social structure. Are there other, nonpathological types? In recent theological literature it is the *comunidades de base*, the basic Christian communities of Latin America that are trumpeted as the incarnations of Jesus' egalitarian vision. In these communities, we are told, nothing less than a rebirth of Christianity is occurring. Peasants reading the scriptures together—and learning to read in the process—creating their own interpretations and applying them to structures that impose suffering are those who experience the immediately available kingdom. In their common discussions and common meals the free healing of oppressive suffering begins (Berryman: 57-60).

Two statements, the first by a Colombian woman, the second by a Venezuelan man both active in basic Christian communities, dramatize the egalitarian power of common discussions and common meals:

Well, it's like this. . . . We all work to understand better, even me. . . . We read the Gospels and we study every little bit, and here we have people who have never known anything. . . . But here we try to explain things ourselves. We don't have them explained to us, but ourselves we draw it out, we discover what we think (Levine: 137).

Jesus was the first, he joined with people to see how they could get out from under. . . . Jesus came and celebrated, he got involved with people's problems. It's the same with us; a day's work always ends with a celebration. The two things. So you see, Jesus is here with us, doing the same work (Levine: 140).

Liberation theology arises from the voices of peasants like these. It arises from the voices of "history's nameless ones" (Gutiérrez 1983: 204).

> All these experiences in the life of the popular masses . . . have been the hot bed of intense life in Christian communities of a popular makeup and involvement. The attempt to reflect on these experiences in the light of faith is what we call the theology of liberation. . . . The theology of liberation is radiated in this historical, popular process. . . . This is [its] turf and terrain. . . (Gutiérrez 1983: 79).

We immediately associate this terrain with embattled El Salvador. We see liberation theology and the basic Christian communities embodied in Archbishop Romero and other witnesses for peace and justice martyred by El Salvador's brutal civil war. Here, threatened by death squads, Jesus' community has been reborn. Yet even in El Salvador, war has given way to a brokered peace, a peace that, unfortunately, is only the kind that the world gives. Even in El Salvador egalitarian community and social structure must be woven together in ways that transform.

In other parts of Latin America the relationship of basic Christian communities to the surrounding social structure is still more complex. Daniel Levine's study of basic Christian communities in Venezuela and Colombia is one of a growing number of works that go beyond the idealized myth of radical Christian communities as prophetic agents of social change to combine empirical analysis of the organization and workings of these groups with sophisticated political theory and theories of religion's role in promoting social change. Levine insists upon the centrality of basic Christian communities in promoting democratic participation and creating networks of associations—a civil society—that mediate between the individual and the state. Yet he also empirically refutes the idea that these groups arise spontaneously, miraculously. Mediators—priests, nuns, and pastoral agents—play an indispensable role in instigating these communities by overcoming the suspicions and sense of isolation of peasants that Crossan knows well. "Mediators provide access to resources, valued alliances, and a sense of legitimacy" (Levine: 335). For these new forms of associational life to survive, ordinary people and elite mediators must "work the linkages" between these communities and the enveloping social structures. Linkages between communities and powerful institutions, like churches, are necessary to leverage social change. Ordinary peasants work with an acute understanding of their marginality within the institutional church ("[W]hat good is that kind of church, what use is it for the poor? Just to tell us we are going to hell? We live through hell everyday . . . "), but also with a newly won autonomous sense of Christian identity. ("[Y]ou are church and I am church. Doing your work you are making the church" [Levine: 143, 286, 319-20]). But Levine's point is that they continue to *work* the linkages. Despite the structured inequalities of the institutional church, ordinary people respect it and value it as a possible lever. Paradoxically, it was the Colombian and Venezuelan Christian communities—which espoused the radical egalitarian ideal in its purest form, which slipped from prophetic marginality into isolation—that were the least transformative in the long run. Lacking protective cover and institutional alliances, religious and lay leaders risked exposing ordinary people within their communities to intensified oppression (Levine: 116-20).

"[T]he need for change," Levine concludes, must "be rooted in points of convergence between everyday life and big structures."

> If ideas are to change behavior over the long term, they must be built into the routine expectations and operating procedures of groups and institutions. This involves both change and continuity, risky innovation and networks of legitimate structures, words, symbols, and ideas. . . . Religions make for linkages by placing proximate acts in ultimate contexts as a matter of routine, giving public social meaning to personal acts like prayer, gathering believers together repeatedly and binding very different kinds of people in shared identities, however minimal (334).

Institutional change is central to the liberating transformation of underlying social structures. Without this working of the linkages, egalitarian communities generate a sublime experience that, politically considered, is but a frisson of rebellion, a rocket's red glare bursting and disappearing in the darkness. I can put this point more positively with the aid of the Buddhist distinction of *dharma* (truth) and *upaya* (skillful means). In these terms "working the linkages" is *upaya*. Buddhism stresses the interdependence of *dharma* and *upaya* (cf. Pye 1978). The truth that we experience, the sapiential eschatology of an open, healing community, is not held in idealized contrast to daily work within and over against the institutions that structure our lives.

A Disconcerting Jesus and the Task of Theological Meditation

Crossan ends his book with another in a long line of disturbing images, this one of bishops reclining alone with the Emperor Constantine to share a common meal, tended by servants, at the end of the Council of Nicea. "Maybe, Christianity is an inevitable and absolutely necessary 'betrayal' of Jesus . . ." Crossan concludes. "But did that 'betrayal' have to happen so swiftly, succeed so fully, and be enjoyed so thoroughly? Might not a more even dialectic have been maintained between Jesus and Christ in Jesus Christ" (Crossan 1991: 424)?

If truth be told, dialectics are rarely even. Yet Levine's discussion gives reason for cautious optimism. Just as basic Christian communities can learn to work the linkages, institutionalized structures can allow the enclaves of community within themselves to serve as paradigms of social learning. Unlike their Nicean predecessors, the American Catholic bishops writing in the midst of Ronald Reagan's renewal of the arms race sought to place the nonviolent tradition of Thomas Merton, Daniel Berrigan, and Dorothy Day in dialectical contrast to their inherited just war theory (*The Challenge of Peace*, 111-21 as cited in Murnion: 283-85). The recognition of another polarity within the Catholic tradition, of internal tension, was the means by which the leadership of this American institution shook off two centuries of loyal support of America's wars and warmaking power and abandoned the patriotic submissiveness of the outsider who wants to be taken in. To be sure, what the bishops stated as a new, tougher version of just war theory had been preceded by decades of nonviolent practice of Catholic communities inspired by the Catholic Worker movement. But, in this instance, the legacy of Dorothy Day was not rendered a harmless icon, the living, continuing reality transmuted into lifeless gold. I do not wish to overstate the case: Institutions find it virtually impossible to sustain an engagement with those in their midst who create radically egalitarian communities. All too quickly, the disconcerting, disruptive power of Jesus, Dorothy, and Thích Nhât Hanh is captured and contained. The U.S. Catholic bishops remained content simply to proclaim their vision rather than, as Crossan's Jesus would have us do, perform it.

Kundera and Faure make us painfully aware of what can happen when we make a fetish of immediate experience or an ideology of egalitarian community. Over against the model of a brokered society Levine presents "working the linkages" as an alternative model for the liberating transformation of institutions by communities and of social structures by institutions. Perhaps there is a role here for the engaged theologian not as a broker of what necessarily remains disruptive and unbrokered, but as one who transmutes living witness into generative thoughts, ideas that both lever the institution and bond it to those who enact the present kingdom. Working these linkages, however, means eschewing both utopian expectation and apocalyptic eschatology. Performing this task entails entering a world of ambiguity, a samsaric world where oppressive evil dependently co-arises *and* co-ceases within the institutional web. A sapiential eschatology, paradoxically, allows religious activists and engaged theologians alike to carry the experience of unmediated access to a brokerless kingdom into this samsaric realm.[7] The sapiential practice of Jesus and engaged Buddhism can transform our understanding of liberation. We need levers and this transformed concept may be one.

Notes

1. Elsewhere I have tried to lay out this DNA coding of the concept of liberation and its paired concept of alienation and to discuss more broadly the limits and

pathological proclivities of the concept. See Strain 1977 and Strain 1992. Dennis McCann and I tried to situate this discussion of limits and proclivities within the underlying patterns of any practical or political theology (McCann 1985).

2. Many liberation theologians have recognized and sought to correct these flaws. But patching plaster will not do the trick. I believe that only Rosemary Ruether with her concepts of the interstructuring of alienation and God as Shalom systematically goes about repairing the flawed DNA coding of the liberation paradigm. Interesting enough, she does so by turning from an apocalyptic eschatology towards a sapiential eschatology. See Ruether 1975: 116, 132, and Ruether 1983: 71, 235-58.

3. Socially engaged Buddhism is a global phenomenon akin to the worldwide spread of Christian liberation movements. For an introduction to socially engaged Buddhism, see Jones.

4. The doctrine of dependent co-arising (*pratitya samutpada*) is central to the theory and praxis of engaged Buddhism. The concept expresses the emptiness of all phenomena; nothing subsists in and of itself; everything depends upon everything else. In the most ancient Pali texts the concept is formulated in these simple terms: "This being, that becomes; from the arising of this, that occurs; this not being, that becomes not; from the ceasing of this, that ceases" (as cited in Macy: 39-40). In the writings of engaged Buddhists, the idea of dependent co-arising not only serves to deconstruct all forms of substantialist thinking but to ground an ethic of responsible relationality (Cf. ibid.).

5. Zen Buddhism's teaching that nirvana is samsara was mediated from China by the thirteenth-century Zen master Dogen. It is the most powerful way of affirming the nonduality of time and eternity. Functioning as a koan, it overthrows not only most Western notions of eschatology, but of teleology as well (Cf. Abe: 48-55.)

6. On the ironic role of peripeteia in narrative as it transforms our expectations of the end, see Kermode: 17-19.

7. I wish to be clear that I do not understand the experience of egalitarian community nor the disruptive power of Jesus, Dorothy Day, and Thích Nhât Hanh in a way that is similar to Reinhold Niebuhr's sense of the love commandment as an "impossible ethical ideal" grounded in an underlying religious sense of the "paradoxical relation of the eternal to history." While it is clear that I share Niebuhr's realism and his sense that this experience of community is not a "simple possibility," I do not share his conclusion that it is an "impossible possibility" (Niebuhr: 72-73). To work the linkages in the samsaric realm joyfully and mindfully is to experience a dialectic not a confounding paradox. Dorothy Day remains a transformative, sapiential presence in me as I go about my work within and over against an institution that has coopted her into sainthood.

10.

Doing Business with the Historical Jesus

DENNIS P. McCANN

Among the portraits of the historical Jesus developed under the sway of liberal Protestantism, Bruce Barton's *The Man Nobody Knows* (1925), has often been dismissed as an embarrassment. Barton's Jesus is a man few serious Christians wished to know, inasmuch as Barton meant to praise his Lord for being "the founder of modern business." The son of a preacher, Barton is remembered as a pioneer businessman in the field of modern advertising. But none of his campaigns ever equaled the impact of his attempt to overcome the "sissified" Jesus foisted upon him in Sunday school. Remade in Barton's own ideal self-image, Jesus is presented as an "outdoor man," a " 'sociable man' whose friendships transcended 'social boundaries,' " just the sort of go-getter who is destined for success in business (Ribuffo 1981: 218). Indeed, his parables demonstrate " 'all the principles' contained in advertising manuals: brevity, simplicity of expression, repetition, and 'deep sincerity.' " In contrast to Judas Iscariot, whom Barton characterized as a " 'small bore' businessman who still 'looked out for Number One,' " Jesus embodied the "law of service" that was the key to both business success and corporate responsibility (Ribuffo 1981: 219-20).

It may seem quirky to mention *The Man Nobody Knows* in the same breath with John Dominic Crossan's study of *The Historical Jesus: The Life of a Mediterranean Jewish Peasant* (1991). At first glance, they seem to have little in common besides their success in attracting a popular audience. But in what follows, I hope to use this comparison to suggest that Crossan's Jesus is far less hostile to modern business than the partisans of one or another form of the Social Gospel have presumed him to be. My thesis is that Christianity's perennial bias against moneymaking in general and modern business in particular rests less on the teachings of Crossan's Mediterranean Jewish peasant and more on the aristocratic prejudices of Plato and Aristotle.

To the extent that Crossan's reconstruction of the historical Jesus helps to clarify the social content of Jesus' message and mission, Christian theologians and ethicists have an opportunity to liberate themselves from these prejudices. Liberation need not entail a full rehabilitation for Barton's business Man, but it does suggest that solidarity with the oppressed, undertaken in the name of the historical Jesus, may require an openness to forms of economic empowerment that Plato and Aristotle would never have approved of.

Don't get me wrong. The point of this essay is not to substitute a pro-business bias for Christianity's traditional prejudice against business. If I understand Crossan correctly, Jesus' perspective on the Kingdom of God, or better, the Reign of God, challenges the conventions of all brokered forms of human interaction. The Reign of God, therefore, is no more pro-business than it is antibusiness. Nevertheless, thanks to Crossan's reconstruction of the social world confronting a first-century Mediterranean Jewish peasant, it is possible to get beyond a generalized "eschatological proviso" that relativizes all social and political institutions, in order to see that some brokerages are more problematic than others from this peasant's perspective.

Crossan suggests that because routine business practice is marginal in the social world of the ancient Mediterranean peasantry, it is comparatively neutral with reference to the structures of domination that govern their lives. Those who gain their livelihood from buying and selling are neither singled out nor exempt from criticism within the Reign of God. It is anachronistic to assume that economics plays as central a role in explaining social relations in the ancient Mediterranean as it apparently does in our own society. The authentic sayings of the historical Jesus seem to confirm the marginality of routine business practice, for though such transactions often serve as stage props for his parables, they are never condemned as such.

Jesus' indifference to business ethics—which is strange only if one assumes that economics must play a strategic role in the oppression of the ancient Mediterranean peasantry—is evident as soon as one compares his perspective with that of Plato, and particularly, Aristotle. Here it is clear that a life devoted to the cultivation of leisured virtue cannot be reconciled with gaining one's livelihood from buying and selling. The Hellenistic philosophers' condemnation of business, I believe, is not explained by a grasp of economics that somehow eluded Jesus, let alone a superior moral sense. Rather, it is a reflection of the class interests of a landed, mostly hereditary aristocracy, whose control of the existing system of clientage and patronage could well be threatened, as in early modern European history indeed it was, by the development of uninhibited market activity.

For all its seeming progressivism, and its vaunted allegiance to the historical Jesus' own program for the Reign of God, the modern Social Gospel's antibusiness bias is an unacknowledged residue of the aristocratic philosophers' ethic. If this bias were subject to revision, what lessons might Crossan's Jesus teach contemporary theologians and ethicists about business and economic institutions in our own society? Just as Crossan himself pointedly denies any affinity linking Jesus' "radical egalitarianism" with contemporary democracy, I would deny any similar identification of the Reign of God with either capitalism or socialism. The challenge of Jesus' "radical egalitarianism" simply cannot be attenuated by opting for any existing social and economic program; for ultimately, and perplexingly, the challenge transcends the boundaries of human society and politics. Crossan's Jesus, in short, is not good news for any theologian who assumes that making a "decision for socialism" is the crucial litmus test of Christian faithfulness.

Crossan's Jesus and the Economics of Patronal Society

Crossan's most important contribution to our understanding of the social world of the ancient Mediterranean peasantry is his insight into the significance of patronage, a system that emphasizes "informal personal power rather than formal institutions" (1991: 7). In a patronal society, power is brokered through vast networks based on personal favoritism, in complex transactions of "friendship" or mutual indebtedness. One is simultaneously a client relative to those whose superior standing allows them to do you a favor, and a patron relative to those who need a favor from you. Indeed, patronage is one of "the three main forms of stratification which have been observed in the mediterranean" (1991:11) and as such is distinguished from systems based on either citizens' rights or class struggle. Like all such systems, patronage is the bearer of social values, the Mediterranean's distinctive hierarchy of honor and shame. Wealth and poverty may reflect one's standing in the brokered hierarchy of honor and shame; but not vice-versa. Economic status—which is constitutive in a system based on class struggle—here is of merely marginal importance.

Gerhard Lenski's model of an agrarian society helps Crossan understand the logic of the Mediterranean patronal system of stratification. According to Lenski, there are nine classes in an agrarian society: five upper, and four abysmally lower. At the top of the pyramid there is the ruler's immediate household, followed by the governing class, the retainer class, merchants, and finally the priestly class. Of these five, the merchants are an anomaly in that they alone do not necessarily derive their power from the established networks of reciprocal favoritism: "They probably evolved upward from the lower classes, but 'in virtually every mature agrarian society merchants managed to acquire a considerable portion of the wealth, and in a few instances a measure of political power as well' " (Crossan 1991: 45).

The vast majority of the population, however, consists of the peasant class, who carry "the burden of supporting the state and the privileged classes," followed by an *"Artisan Class* ... recruited from the ranks of the dispossessed peasantry,"* the *"Unclean and Degraded Classes* ... whose origins or occupations separated them downward from the great mass of peasants and artisans," and finally, those outside the patronage system, the *"Expendable Class* . . . [which] included a variety of types, ranging from petty criminals and outlaws to beggars and underemployed itinerant workers, and numbered all those forced to live by their wits or by charity" (Crossan 1991: 46). No doubt, merchants had succeeded spectacularly in raising themselves above their station in life. But track down a successful merchant's pedigree and one was likely to discover something shameful, a humble artisan's family, perhaps, or worse, much worse.

Crossan underscores the marginality of economics in a patronal society with this observation taken from Thomas Carney:

> Authoritarian thought-ways were pervasive in this hierarchically ordered and power-ridden society, especially among the military elite. So was an anti-economic ethos: large estates, conferring a gentleman's existence, were the one form of wealth accepted as socially desirable. . . . The life style of The Great called for landlordism at its base. This life style produced a set of values—such as conspicuous consumption—which . . . involved devaluing entrepreneurial and innovative activity in general. . . . Wealth was just as avariciously sought as in any capitalist society, but on a 'seize or squeeze' principle, not by generating it through increased production. Capital was formed in antiquity by taking it from someone else, either as booty in war or as taxes squeezed out of a toiling peasant population. . . . The case for entrepreneurialism was . . . never articulated in antiquity. . . . Preindustrial society did not in fact produce a body of economic thought (Carney cited in Crossan 1991: 51).

Given modernity's historic obsession with economic questions, the ideology of such a society is very difficult to characterize. Certainly, it is neither capitalist nor socialist; but somehow that still misses the point. Crossan refuses to minimize the difficulty, simply leaving it as an "anti-economic" ideology. Personal connections, normally, were the only negotiable asset.

To describe the historical Jesus as a Mediterranean Jewish peasant is to interpret his message announcing the Reign of God in the context of the oppression experienced by such peasants in a patronal society. What peasants generally thought about such a society is not directly available to us. But the stubbornness of their passive and sometimes active resistance is clear from the variety of evasions and disruptions recorded and analyzed, as Crossan notes, by historians like James C. Scott. When Jesus' words and deeds—once Crossan has sorted them for relative degrees of authenticity, using the method of multiple attestation—are interpreted against this background, they do yield a pattern of dissent that is astonishingly thorough in its radicalism. What Crossan calls "the ancient and universal peasant dream of a just and equal world," in Jesus' imagining, is transformed into an open, unbrokered world without patronage of any kind. But such a world, precisely because it is not built upon the intricate reciprocities of familial and political relationships, is just as much a challenge to the modest dreams of the peasants as it is to any other group within the agrarian society of the Mediterranean.

Crossan vividly conveys the uncompromising nature of Jesus' radicalism in his discussion of open commensality and open healing. These two characteristic signs of the advent of the Reign of God are challenging precisely because of their startlingly promiscuous openness. Peasants are as likely to hesitate before sharing a meal with perfect strangers as are their betters. The opportunity to exploit the power of a local wonder-worker to advance the village's overall fortunes is just as tempting for peasants as it is for any other social group. If these are the signs of the Reign of God — as Crossan sees them characteristically presented, among other places, in the tenth chapter of Luke — their intent is not to reinforce any previously existing forms of human solidarity, not even those that have provided a base for peasant resistance. The egalitarianism that Jesus envisions as the Reign of God is simply out of this world.

However utopian, the signs of the Reign of God, as interpreted by the teachings of the historical Jesus, do suggest a social program that challenges all existing social relationships. This, in Crossan's view, is the significance of Jesus' provocative attack on the "family values" (1993: 6-7). The patronage system based upon kinship structures cherished by both Mediterranean peasants and their oppressors is not to be reformed, but repudiated altogether. The Reign of God is not to be confused with some Nietzschean reversal of the structures of domination, as if a peasant takeover of the existing patronage system more closely approximated Divine justice. The historical Jesus may be proposing a social program, but it is not realized through any conventional form of power politics, including those options exercised in peasant resistance movements.

Within the generalized radicalism of Jesus' social program, it is not easy to determine precisely where merchants stand. If I read Crossan correctly, they are not singled out as the primary obstacle in the path toward the Reign of God. True enough, the rich, that is, those who enjoy a disproportionate share of the rewards of the existing patronage system, are subject to repeated warnings. But, within the prevailing social structures of the ancient Mediterranean, only a tiny minority of the rich are merchants. The point, in any case, is not to castigate commercial activity as such, but to challenge the refusal of openness implicit in inordinate personal possessions. The buying and selling characteristic of the marketplace is never condemned as such; even the memorable Gospel account of Jesus' physical attack upon the money changers in the Temple (Mark 11:15-16), according to Crossan, is a symbolic act threatening the destruction of the Temple, and not an expression of moral outrage against exchange relations as such

(1991: 357). The Reign of God remains indifferent to economics, astonishingly so from a modern perspective.

Our perplexity may be relieved by considering once again the precariousness of the merchant in the agrarian empires of the ancient Mediterranean. Of all the social classes identified by Lenski's model, merchants were involved in activities that stood at the farthest remove from the patronage system. Making one's living by open trading in the marketplace, in principle, is subversive of brokerages based exclusively on kinship and political connections. Though any given merchant's livelihood is likely to be embedded in such connections, his relationship to them is peripheral. In a patronage society the merchant is a liminal figure. It is not surprising, therefore, that the sayings attributed to Jesus seem to reflect a cagy ambivalence toward merchants and moneymaking. Their unscrupulous way of seizing new opportunities for profit making is not a threat to the Reign of God, but may be a curious clue as to how Jesus' disciples should prepare themselves for its coming.

The Aristocratic Bias against Business

The contrast between Jesus' ambivalence about merchants and the hostility toward business characteristic of traditional Christianity is evident as soon as one compares Jesus' sayings with the considered reflections of Greco-Roman philosophers. Crossan's analysis of the antieconomic ideology of the ancient Mediterranean underscores the dominance of aristocratic values. His most effective witnesses are the Romans, Cato, and Cicero. Cato's treatise, *On Agriculture*, presents, in Crossan's view, "a remarkably clear [moral] hierarchy: farmer, trader, thief, and moneylender." Cato observes:

It is true that to obtain money by trade is sometimes more profitable, were it not so hazardous; and likewise money-lending, if it were as honourable. Our ancestors held this view and embodied it in their laws, which required that the thief be mulcted double and the usurer fourfold; how much less desirable a citizen they considered the usurer than the thief, one may judge from this (Cato cited in Crossan 1991: 51).

Cicero's *De Officiis* adds the following advice to his son Marcus, regarding careers suitable to a gentleman:

First, those means of livelihood are rejected as undesirable which incur people's ill-will, as those of tax-gatherers and usurers. . . . Vulgar we must consider those also who buy from wholesale merchants to retail immediately; for they would get no profits without a great deal of downright lying; and verily, there is no action that is meaner than misrepresentation (Cicero cited in Crossan 1991: 52).

Even so, Cicero is willing to make some concession to wholesale merchants, because of the scale of their commercial activities. Even for this moral rigorist, sometimes nothing seems to succeed like success:

Trade, if it is on a small scale, is to be considered vulgar; but if wholesale and on a large scale, importing large quantities from all parts of the world and distributing to many without representation, it is not to be greatly disparaged. Nay, it even seems to deserve the highest respect, if those who are engaged in it, satiated, or rather, I should say, satisfied with the fortunes they have made, make their way from the port to a country estate, as they have often made it from the sea into port (Cicero cited in Crossan 1991: 52-53).

Successful merchants may become respectable by ceasing to be merchants and buying into the landed aristocracy. Crossan deftly suggests the difficulties involved in carrying off this disguise, by reminding his readers of the antics of Trimalchio, as immortalized in Petronicus' *Satyricon*. "Aborted capitalists," like Trimalchio, were to remain a "social anomaly" in the patronal world of the ancient Mediterranean.

However vivid these testimonials to aristocratic prejudice, traditional Christianity's antibusiness bias may be rooted still more deeply in the convictions expressed by Plato and Aristotle. In the course of Book II of Plato's *Republic*, Socrates is depicted in conversation with Glaucon and Adeimantus concerning the virtue of justice. Just as it is useful to decipher small print by looking at the same letters writ large, so justice in an individual might better be grasped by considering justice in the *polis* as a whole. Thus begins Plato's exercise in constructing model cities. Socrates' first attempt, however, is not to Glaucon's liking; for it is of minimal size and lacking in everything but the basic amenities. What follows, then, is a description of an alternative: "a luxurious city," based on unrestricted economic expansion fueled, in turn, by the feverish pursuit of a variety of sensual pleasures. The image is a chilling one, for the luxurious city, made possible through unfettered commercial activity, eventually must resort to war in order to keep up with its own appetitiveness.

Let us listen in once more on Socrates and Glaucon:

And the country which was enough to support the original inhabitants will be too small now, and not enough?
Quite true.
Then a slice of our neighbours' land will be wanted by us for pasture and tillage, and they will want a slice of ours, if, like ourselves they

exceed the limit of necessity, and give themselves up to the unlimited accumulation of wealth?

That, Socrates, will be inevitable.

And so we shall go to war, Glaucon. Shall we not?

Most certainly, he replied.

Then, without determining as yet whether war does good or harm, thus much we may affirm, that now we have discovered war to be derived from causes which are also the causes of almost all the evils in States, private as well as public.

Undoubtedly (1937: 636-37).

What other lesson could one draw from, say, the Pelopponesian war that had cast such a pall over Plato's generation? Athens' unprecedented commercial expansion had led to imperialistic pretensions that finally provoked that self-destructive conflict among the Greek city-states. Plato knows where business leads: once the marketplace has become the engine of economic development, gratifying all the desires that can surface within a "luxurious city," the result is moral catastrophe.

In Book I of the *Politics*, Aristotle provides a theory of economics that frames the aristocratic prejudice against business in terms of a natural law. In contrast to Socrates' strategy of understanding justice in individuals by examining it first in the *polis* as a whole, Aristotle begins his observations on the *polis* by examining the chief form of association that is constitutive of it, namely, the *oikos* or patronal household. His economics, as the term itself suggests, thus is essentially a theory of household management. Property, for example, is defined first in relationship to the household, and not with reference to exchange relations in the marketplace. As "an instrument of action" intended to maintain a household, property or wealth—contrary to the musings of Solon—does have a fixed or natural limit.

Never mind that Aristotle is able to reconcile such a limit with legitimating both slavery and warfare as natural arts of acquisition. Nor that household management generally is focused on developing the skills necessary to maintain the *padron*'s rule over his slaves, women and children. Crucial here is Aristotle's contention that observing such natural limits is incompatible with making one's living by commercial exchange:

There are two sorts of wealth-getting, as I have said; one is part of household management [i.e., agriculture], the other is retail trade: the former is necessary and honorable, while that which consists in exchange is justly censured; for it is unnatural, and a mode by which men gain from one another. The most hated sort, and with the greatest reason, is usury, which makes a gain out of money itself, and not from the natural object of it. For money was intended to be used in exchange, but not to increase at interest. And this term interest, which means the birth of money from money, is applied to the breeding of money because the offspring resembles the parent. That is why of all modes of getting wealth this is the most unnatural (Aristotle 1984: 1997).

Aristotle's dubious assumption of fixed limits in nature, namely, that "nature makes nothing incomplete, and nothing in vain," thus leads him to take a dim view of exchange relations, precisely because they have the capacity of transgressing such fixed limits.

Christian Betrayals

That Cato and Cicero swallowed the philosopher's argument so completely should not come as a surprise. Harder to understand is how and why classical Christianity eventually acquiesced in it. There are some very large issues at stake here that would require a treatment as thorough and insightful as Crossan's analysis of the historical Jesus. If his reconstruction of Jesus' message regarding the Reign of God is on the right track, then the emergence of Catholic Christianity in late Mediterranean antiquity smacks of a massive betrayal, however unwitting, of Jesus' commitment to an unbrokered and unconditional egalitarianism.

The nature of this betrayal, or accommodation to prevailing Mediterranean norms, if you will, has been vividly presented in the writings of Elisabeth Schüssler Fiorenza (1983). The so-called *Haustafeln* reaffirmed in the deutero-Pauline epistles dramatizes a process in which Christians will come to accept the basic institutions of the patronal society as a venue for spiritual growth, and not as a fundamental obstacle to the Reign of God. Crossan's reconstruction, however, challenges us to consider also the economic logic implicit in these institutions. The ideology that declared the naturalness of the master's rule over slaves, the subordination of wives to husbands, and children to their fathers, also condemned commercial activity as unnatural. It is hard for me to see how, in the name of renewed faithfulness to the historical Jesus, Christians can liberate themselves from the social prejudices of the ancient Mediterranean aristocracy, while clinging uncritically to its self-serving view of economics.

Were Christians to complete this effort at consciousness-raising, the path taken by Bruce Barton might deserve a second look. Is there some subterranean affinity linking the historical Jesus' gestures of open commensality and open healing and the world's emerging preference — after the collapse of Christendom, and its secular surrogates — for open markets? There may be. But Barton's identification of Jesus' social program with modern marketing management is just as much a betrayal as the deutero-Pauline acceptance of the patriarchal household, or the current tendency of some to equate the conventions of suburban respectability with Christian "family values." The truly radical challenge implicit in Jesus' social program, if I read Crossan correctly, is to continue performing the Reign of God, knowing all the while that every serious performance must fall short in one way or another.

It thus becomes possible to speak—as the U.S. Catholic bishops, for example, spoke in their recent pastoral letter on the economy—of "business people, managers, investors, and financiers follow[ing] a vital Christian vocation when they act responsibly and seek the common good" (O'Brien and Shannon 1992: 606). Measured against the historical Jesus' proclamation of the Reign of God, a Christian vocation in business is no more a betrayal of that radically egalitarian vision than is a Christian vocation in education, health care, or politics, or in the various forms of ecclesial ministry. No more, and no less. The radicalism of Jesus' critique of all brokered relationships is evaded, whenever any one of these institutions is arbitrarily singled out for being especially resistant to the Reign of God.

This conclusion, I contend, does not let business off the hook, morally speaking. On the contrary; it ensures that business is to be held accountable to the same standards that inform Christian praxis in every field of human interaction. Perhaps the only way to maintain an honest brokerage is to hold it continually accountable to the vision of brokerless Kingdom. The effort to judge business practice fairly by the praxis of the Reign of God is especially urgent, given the pressing needs of the world's poor. As the events of the past few years in China, Mexico, and the former republics of the Soviet empire have demonstrated, liberation from poverty means liberating poor people to develop their own comparative advantages in the global economy. Surely, it would be tragic, were Christian commitment to an outmoded form of social analysis to impede, rather than enhance, the poor's access to the marketplace. Such obscurantism seems difficult to reconcile with either open commensality or open healing and, in any case, is totally unnecessary, given the capacity for transcending all paradigms implicit in the social program of the historical Jesus.

11.

Responses and Reflections

JOHN DOMINIC CROSSAN

> and the viper
> said
> *"the fountains of myself are a vision*
>
> *I will not behold"*
> —A. R. Ammons, *Diversifications*

Early influences as permanent prejudices? I grew up among the first generation of postcolonial Irish in the protected lee of the foundering British Empire. Schooling, in that situation, bred strange anomalies. High school, for example, was in Donegal, a county connected to the Republic by a narrow sliver of land and surrounded on all its non-Atlantic sides by Northern Ireland, then as now a part of Britain. It was a boarding school, not from social privilege but from geographical necessity since Donegal's small towns required some centralized institution. Still, even with all instruction in Gaelic, the curriculum was adopted bodily from the elite private schools of England. In Irish History class, I learned what awful things Britain had done to Ireland. *Against* empire, therefore? But in courses on the Greek and Roman classics, with texts chosen by British education to prepare its youth for imperial administration, I learned, say from Caesar's *Gallic Wars*, to admire the syntax and ignore the slaughter. Even of our ancient Celtic ancestors. *For* empire, therefore?

On festive occasions when the boarding students were released to visit their local relatives, I usually went to a paternal uncle-in-law who, when he was a little drunk (that is, on all festive occasions), would show me from a well-greased rag beneath his bed, a Luger used not in the fight for Irish independence but in the Irish civil war which immediately succeeded its partial acceptance. From all of that pedagogical confusion I hold two truths with equal and fundamental certainty. One: the British did terrible things to the Irish. Two: the Irish, had they the power, would have done equally terrible things to the British. So also for any other paired adversaries I can imagine.

The difficulty, of course, is to hold on to both those truths with equal intensity and not let either one negate the other, and to know when to emphasize one without forgetting the other. Our humanity is probably lost and gained in the necessary tension between them both. I hope, by the way, that I do not sound anti-British. It is impossible not to admire a people who gave up India and held on to Northern Ireland. That shows a truly Celtic sense of humor.

Jesus Christ and Constantine

Despite trying to hold with equal intensity those twin foundational truths just mentioned, I prefer, when I read Marc Ellis' paper, to let *him* speak both of the Holocaust, on the one hand, and of the Palestinians, on the other. Although anyone can speak out against injustice anywhere, my primary responsibility as both historian and Christian is, first, not to confuse those roles and, second, to analyze the injustice of *my own* tradition's inaugural moments. Here, then, are three theological and three historical presuppositions to any discussion, especially with Marc Ellis, but also with anyone else involved in this book.

First, I see every religion I know or can even imagine as inherently triadic, triangular or, yes, trinitarian. There must be a *transcendent referent*, be it place or state, power, person or order, be it gods or goddesses, Goddess or God, mandate of heaven, nirvana, or nothingness. There must, also, be a *material representation*, be it person, place, or thing, be it oasis or clearing, desert or storm, book, temple, community, or empty space. There must be, finally, an affirming, accepting, or *believing individual/community*.

Second, I understand Jesus as Christ, as divine, or as God *only* within that framework. The term can never be essential or substantive but only relational and interactive. It means that at least one person sees in Jesus the manifestation of God. It means no more and no less than for another Jew to see the Temple or the Torah as divine or "as God."

Third, when I said all of that on a recent radio interview, the host kept repeating, "Yes, Yes, but was Jesus *really* divine?" We were at impasse, but the difference was at least clear. He wanted "divine" to be substantive and objective; I insisted it was relational and intersubjective. And there we catch a glimpse of that lethal deceit that corrodes the soul of Christianity, hardens its heart, and sickens its spirit: the claim that *our* faith is in a fact while *your* faith is in an interpretation, that *our* myth is history while *your* myth is lie. We may and must do comparative mythology, compare the advantages and disadvantages of finding divinity here rather than there, in this rather than in that, but nobody, not a Christian or anyone else, can pull *fact* on the other, can deny that we are all standing on faith, that is, on the bedrock of foundational interpretation.

To those three general theological presuppositions, I append three particular historical ones about the first two common-era centuries. First, any reconstructed historical Jesus must be understood within his contemporary Hellenistic Judaism, a Judaism responding with all its antiquity and tradition to Greco-Roman culture undergirded by both armed power and imperial ambition. But that contemporary Judaism was, as modern scholarship insists ever more forcibly, a richly creative, diverse, and variegated one.

Second, by the end of the second century of the common era, two hundred years after Jesus, *rabbinic* Judaism, like *catholic* Christianity, was deeply involved in retrojecting its ascendancy onto earlier history so that it would later be as difficult to discern any earlier plurality in one as in the other. By that time those two great religions had emerged as distinct products of a common matrix, as twin daughters of a common mother. Each claimed to be the only legitimate heir and each had texts and traditions to argue that claim. Each, in fact, represented an equally legitimate, equally valid, equally surprising, and equally magnificent leap out of the past and into the future. It would, in truth, be difficult to say, had Moses woken from slumber around 200 CE, which of the two would have surprised him the more.

Third, and now the terror begins, it was Christianity which eventually obtained the political, economic, and military support of the Roman Empire and was able to promote its claim and persecute its opponent in a way never open to Judaism.

Against that background, then, I debate two points with Marc Ellis. I am not yet convinced that there is something intrinsically more violent or oppressive in Christianity than in any other religion. I know how bad the history is and desire neither to ignore nor escape it. But if Judaism had become the official religion of the Roman Empire, would it have acted any better or worse than Christianity? So I still want the cost-accounting to be primarily with Constantine and, of course, with all the pre-Constantinian imperialization that prepared Christianity for that Pyrrhic victory.

Second, to see Jesus as Messiah or Son of God or divine does not, *in itself*, negate the reconstructed historical Jesus presented in my book. Those titles are, of course, interpretive and interactive rather than objective and substantive but, within that framework, all depends on how they are understood. Jesus' Kingdom of God was not a monopoly personally dependent on himself but an empowerment freely available to all who were ready to live like he did. Maybe it was already dangerous to shift the focus, as Jesus himself *did not*, from communal Kingdom to personal King, but it still depends on whether that leader is understood as holding a power dependent on his presence or announcing an empowerment present before and after his absence.

One final example. When the Julian (Julius Caesar) Calendar was introduced across the Roman Empire under Augustus, inscriptions in the province of Asia, say from Priene in 9 BCE, spoke of Augustus' birth as *good news* about the advent of a *savior* and a *god* who brought *peace* to a wartorn empire. How, against that background, should one judge the angelic annunciations to Mary and the shepherds in Luke 1:28–35 and 2:8–14 where Jesus' birth is *good news* about the advent of a *savior* and *son of God* accompanied by *peace* on earth? Do you celebrate the daringly paradoxical vision that equated or replaced the birth of Caesar Augustus (mentioned in between at Luke 2:1 in case one might miss the point) with that of a poor Jewish peasant child? Or do you shudder slightly knowing that Jesus would eventually become Augustus and what once was paradox would then be fact? How early does that cost-accounting with Constantine have to begin?

The Syncretic Jesus

Could, however, that conjunction of Christ and Constantine be but an example of what Jeffrey Carlson calls "the syncretic self"? He suggests, and he is surely correct, that, while there is no,

"common essence" shared by all religions, in terms of "content" of the elements selectively appropriated ... there is a structural, formal constant: Each of our "inventories" shows the influence of *many* places and times. We are all, and each, intrinsically plural.

I would, for example, define my own "essence of Christianity" in similar fashion not as some *unchanging content* but as an enduring *formal dialectic* between, as he underlines, an historically-read Jesus and a theologically-read Christ. Yet that only makes the question more pressing: is that conjunction of Christ and Constantine not simply the fourth century's perfectly valid syncretic selfhood?

I leave aside for now the question of content, of any possible discrepancy between a Jesus who resisted the *systemic* evil of imperial power and a ruler who must incarnate it even in his own newly Christianized self. I focus only on *form*. Even if it was ever justifiable for Jesus and Constantine to converge, then the same syncretic principle that justified its combination would eventually, there and/or elsewhere, justify alike its dissolution. When, much earlier, for example, 1 Timothy 3 models Christian leadership on Roman paternal power, *patria potestas* (a male, settled-down householder, married with children) or *1 Clement* 37 models it on Roman military power, *imperium militiae* ("not all are prefects, nor tribunes, nor centurions, nor in charge of fifty men, but each carries out in his own rank the commands of the emperor and of the generals"), I abstract for now from questions of *content*, of, that is, the appropriateness of those models, in order to underline the relativity of any such models to their own time and their own place. If we grant that the syncretic self involves an inevitable *formal* dialectic between tradition and environment, why should that single and almost accidental Roman acculturation be deemed transcendentally normative for all future Christian experience?

Cost-accounting with Constantine must be conducted on two levels. One is that of *content* and that is the more obvious one intended at the end of my opening article. What was gained and lost in that historical conjunction? However, Jeffrey Carlson has drawn attention to a far more significant level, that of *form*. If syncretism is inevitable, that single ancient fourth-century example, whether rated as good or bad in final content, cannot be definitive for all Christian futures. Not only must any syncretic acculturation be assessed for benefits and losses, but no syncretic acculturation can be normative beyond its own time and place. How do other alternative and contemporary syncretisms, say in South America today, give modern robes to a Christianity for whom the Greek pallium or the Roman toga were but inevitably passing fashions from antiquity?

Imposing Discoveries

Brandon Scott situated *The Historical Jesus* within the trajectory of my earlier writings in terms of a preference for the Saussurian synchronic over the Darwinian diachronic: "With one notable exception, Crossan has followed Saussure." I find that insight extremely helpful in understanding my own work especially as I never thought of it in those terms before. Scott's own paper, however, is not just a synchronic analysis of my synchronic *The Historical Jesus* but is actually an interaction of the synchronic and the diachronic. He locates that book within the growth and development (Darwin) of my own writings as a general system (Saussure). I think that the major characteristic of my own work has been a similar interaction, a refusal to allow either diachrony or synchrony to dominate and an attempt, always, to place them in tensile juxtaposition. Although I would not, without Scott's perceptive comments, have seen my work this way, I find, in the light of those comments, that the dialectic of Darwin and Saussure is more characteristic than the predominance of either over the other. That would be as true of *In Parables* as of *The Historical Jesus*. In the former case, for example, I was equally interested in the parables of Jesus as a poetic genre (synchrony) and as a redactional development (diachrony). I was invited, when that book was still in manuscript, to a seminar with Norman Perrin, David Tracy, and Paul Ricoeur, at the University of Chicago Divinity School. I was strongly encouraged (from the audience, I think) to write about the parables and forget all this speculative reconstruction about the historical Jesus, to keep the title (*In Parables*) and forget the subtitle (*The Challenge of the Historical Jesus*), to discuss, in other words, synchronic genre and ignore diachronic transmission. I knew immediately, but more instinctively than theoretically, that I was not going to change anything basic but simply add an opening paragraph in the Preface (p. xiii) to keep happy those who wanted genre but not history, synchrony but not diachrony. I see now more clearly, after Scott's analysis, what was at stake, but I rephrase it to suggest that dialectic was probably then, as always, my Beatrice.

I also remember a very unnerving conversation with Norman Perrin about my just published *Raid on the Articulate: Comic Eschatology in Jesus and Borges* at the last AAR-SBL Annual Meeting before his death. He asked me for a Curriculum Vitae to propose me for Nathan Scott's vacant chair in religion and literature at the Divinity School since, as he put it, "you are now moving out of New Testament." All components of that suggestion left me breathless, but the misunderstanding much more than the compliment, and it warned me then, and consciously, not to let literature dominate too much over history. Later, the book's sales were a second warning. What I saw then I would now rephrase, in Scott's terms but my interpretation, not to let synchrony predominate too much over diachrony. The generative power was in their balanced interplay.

I am equally grateful for a second major element in Scott's paper: his accurate analysis not just of my method's validity but even more importantly of its flexibility. I emphasize here more than I did in the book that the method has two separable aspects, *formal procedures* and *material investments*, and I discuss them now in that sequence.

My collegial challenge is to agree on the former, whether or not one can ever agree on the latter. Formal procedures are like due process in law (innocent until proved guilty) and should be discussed separately and before material investments (so-and-so has been judged innocent or guilty). These are all formal moves: inventory, stratigraphy, attestation; everything plurally attested in the earliest stratum must be kept unless there are extremely serious arguments against it, or, nothing singly attested will be used even from the first stratum. They can and must be debated as formal rules but they are separable from material investments. Another scholar could accept all of those forms and still diverge completely on whether, say, the *Q Gospel* exists at all or the *Gospel of Thomas* is an independent attestation and, if so, belongs in what stratum.

What excited me most, in imagining those formal procedures, was that I myself did not know what would be plurally attested in my first stratum until I had run the database. After I had established what was plurally attested in the first stratum, I still thought that I would use this formal principle of discrimination: retain as original what best explains later multiplicity in the transmission. You can see that idea in two 1988 articles: "Divine Immediacy and Human Immediacy: Towards a New First Principle in Historical Jesus Research," *Semeia* 44 (1988):121–40; and "Materials and Methods in Historical Jesus Research," *Forum* 4/4 (December 1988):3–24. But, by the time I came to write *The Historical Jesus*, I had decided that such a principle was still too subjective and preferred this one: nothing plurally attested in the first stratum can be omitted without extremely strong arguments. Such an argument (for example, would a prayer officially memorized from Jesus' lips be found only in the *Q Gospel* and *Didache* trajectory?) lost me the Lord's Prayer as original with Jesus although I cannot imagine a better summary of his program than: *kingdom* of God, *on earth* as in heaven, and, those twin specters that stalk peasant subsistence living, too little *bread* and too much *debt*. None of that, I emphasize, establishes a spurious objectivity but rather a self-conscious and self-critical subjectivity.

I need to be a little blunt about material investments. It is usually unwise to accuse one's colleagues of prejudice for this or that opinion since they can simply reverse the accusation against oneself for holding its opposite. But to those who hold that *all* the extracanonical materials discovered in the last hundred years are late and dependent, I ask now: what might we ever discover that you would accept as early and independent? Tell us now, before we discover any more, what principles you apply to make your decision? The standard principle is quite simple and it is what we would use for a plagiarism case in a modern court of law: if personally redactional rather than generally traditional order or content from a New Testament Gospel is found in a newly discovered extracanonical one, the latter is dependent on the former. If none such is found, it is still possible, since one cannot prove a negative, that it is dependent but has simply removed those personally idiosyncratic materials that are the original author's fingerprints. One should not, however, presume such dependence but, in proper methodology, take independence not as fact but as working hypothesis and proceed to test that presumption. One tests it, however, only by accepting it hypothetically.

Much of what has been discovered is, of course, fragmentary (*Gospel of Peter, Egerton Gospel, Secret Gospel of Mark*), but when the first full and complete discovery, the *Gospel of Thomas*, is declared to be dependent by some scholars, I ask once again: what could ever be discovered that you would accept as independent? More bluntly: is canonical bias dictating historical judgment?

I am very grateful to Scott for insisting that my judgment on sources important for my case, such as the *Q Gospel* or the *Gospel of Thomas*, are not just marginal delusions but consistent with, and of course derived from, the best contemporary work on those documents. I am thinking not only of long-term research by James Robinson and Helmut Koester but also of recent doctoral dissertations such as that of John Kloppenborg on the *Q Gospel*, Steve Patterson on the *Gospel of Thomas*, and Jon Daniels on the *Egerton Gospel*. But all of that recent and excellent study on the *words* of Jesus, on what he said or was said to him, serves only to underline that we are in a very sorry condition with regard to the *deeds* of Jesus, with regard to what he did or was done to him. I am firmly convinced that the transmission of Jesus' *words* (aphorisms, parables) and *deeds* (miracles, passion) proceeded on radically different principles and trajectories and that we need to explore that divergence much more profoundly.

One example will suffice, from the *Gospel of Peter*, a fragmentary account of the passion and resurrection. Here is the situation. Helmut Koester, in his magisterial *Ancient Christian Gospels*, a book noted by Scott, and myself, in *The Cross That Spoke*, agree on two very fundamental facts. First, the passion narrative arises from prophecy historicized rather than history memorized; second, there is only a single source for all our five accounts. Third, we disagree on the reconstruction of that original source. I find it now embedded in the *Gospel of Peter* and I termed it the *Cross Gospel*, to which others responded that it was the Crossan Gospel; Koester finds it in the common materials of the *Gospel of Peter*, Mark, and John.

However, that third-step disagreement is almost trivial compared to those former first- and second-step agreements. Those are what count and what must be established in the sequence: first, second, third steps. My position on the *Cross Gospel* is, if you will, idiosyncratic, but I would happily bracket it forever to get agreement or even guaranteed consideration of those much more basic first two points. In the beginning was prophecy not narrative, and at the end was a single narrative from which nobody thereafter ever managed to escape.

At the end of his paper Scott hazarded a guess on what comes next for me: "to do for the gospels what he has done for the fragments of Jesus tradition." Yes and no. On the one hand, Koester's *Ancient Christian Gospels* has finally and superbly rewritten Bultmann's *History of the Synoptic Tradition*. On the other, the *earliest* layers are still as obscure as ever, the layers from deep in the life of Jesus to immediately after his execution. I have a manuscript promised to HarperSanFrancisco for December 1996 whose present title is *After the Crucifixion: The Search for Earliest Christianity*. I want especially to see what was there in the early thirties before Paul ever arrived on the scene. That project is just starting, but it is already ridden with dialectic: words and deeds, orality and literacy, itinerant and householder, prophecy and history, and, especially, synchrony *and* diachrony.

Heroism and Feminism

Catherine Keller notes that I never "perform any ritual of social location." She is absolutely correct. If somebody asks me directly, as she and Robert Ludwig do, I try my best to answer as honestly as I can. Hence, those opening comments on whether my Irish background had anything to do with my book's interpretation of Jesus. But what exactly would an inaugural or even repeated admission of being a live, white, middle-class, European, heterosexual, male, scholar, etc., actually accomplish?

First, to be sure, some sweet but irrelevant revenge for types not included in those categories. Second, the political rectitude of such formalized admissions seems often to excuse one from any further interest in justice or equality. Admit what you are and then go ahead and do what you want. Third, the more one multiplies such admissions, the more one trivializes any consensual ethical possibilities. All becomes admitted prejudice but thereafter little changes in the arrangements of power, prestige, and privilege. Fourth, if I deconstruct my own book with such admissions, when and where do I deconstruct the admissions themselves? I prefer, therefore, that somebody else do it to me. That somebody else say: you see it that way because you are such and such, but I see it this way because I am so and so.

I have, by the way, read several published reviews of my book that dismiss it with the first half of that sentence without having the concomitant grace to apply its second half to themselves. It is surely dishonorable if not dishonest to use postmodernism or deconstruction to sap another's foundations but never at all to subvert one's own. I do not imply at all that Catherine Keller does that to me. She emphatically does not do so, but I am replying to her question why I spend no time "textually situating oneself-in-context in relation to context and text." That is best done, I think, in mutually self-critical dialogue rather than in confessional monologue.

Finally, if I were to do such "social location" it would require, as Catherine Keller admits, much more than a few general typological names like white, European, male, or middle class. That "the vast generic emptiness of categories . . . [be] painstakingly filled" might well require an autobiography of me before I could attempt a biography of Jesus. My paternal grandparents, for example, were lower-class peasant farmers and my maternal grandparents were middle-class urban shopkeepers. When I stayed at their respective homes in the very early forties (I was born in 1934) the former were still living well outside the nearest town, Letterkenny in County Donegal, in a white-washed thatch-roof cottage (for real, not for tourist entertainment) with open fireplace for cooking, no internal plumbing whatsoever, chickens and one goat for animals, donkey and trap for transportation, and sometime town-jobs for added support. The latter lived in a market town, Ballymote in County Sligo, above and beside their shop in a house whose internal plumbing was adequate then even by contemporary standards now.

Does that early experience with my paternal grandparents explain why I made Jesus a peasant? Conversely, then, why did that other equally early experience with my maternal grandparents not make him a shopkeeper, running a carpentry business out of his home in Nazareth? I agree, on the most profound level, with Catherine Keller, that "our *logos*, our *logoi*, reveal themselves only by incarnation into our scandalous particularities," but the depth and breadth of those particularities (even without introducing Freud) would fill the space available for any other subject, would invite dismissal because of them or concentration exclusively on them, and, as all becomes autobiography, nothing would ever change in a world of inequality and injustice. Confession replaces criticism and the public display of internal organs obviates the need for the public scrutiny of ethical decision. Or, to be absurd, since my high school, St. Eunan's College in Letterkenny, had as heraldic shield a hand holding a cross surrounded by the Latin motto, "In this sign you will conquer," does a covert dislike for boarding school surface as an overt distrust of Constantine?

Catherine Keller is also correct that "there is virtually no dialogue with feminist sources" in my book. That invites some honest scholarly (and not just social) "location." So here it is. My book intended programmatically to initiate a Third Quest for the historical Jesus by ignoring the Second ("new") Quest as an almost total failure: one scandalized reviewer telephoned me to ask whether I realized that I had never even mentioned Bultmann. I did not have time, space, or concern to attack it; I hoped radically to replace it.

I wanted to start all over again with Albert Schweitzer at the end of the First ("old") Quest and try to write a book that might be the Schweitzer for the twenty-first century as he was for the twentieth. At the end of his 1906 study he had a now-famous line: "He comes to us as One unknown, without a name, as of old, by the lake-side." I framed the summary of Jesus' life in my book's Overture with "He comes as yet unknown" (xi) at the start and "as of old beside the lake" (xiii) at the end. That was, for those with eyes to see, a delicate indication that I was attempting a new Schweitzer. For those who missed it, no great importance. The book's future depends much less on my intentions than on readers' reactions.

I explain later in discussion with Frans Jozef van Beeck what made it, for me, a Third Quest. Because, therefore, of those intentions and plans, other recent studies of the historical Jesus with which I might agree on this point or that, were mentioned in passing and then ignored. I deliberately avoided saying I accept this, I do not accept that, since present methodology in research rather than past history of research was my primary interest. That applies alike to feminist and masculinist authors.

But there is a special problem with "feminist sources" *on the historical Jesus*? Where are they? Why are so few women interested in that area of research? For post-Christian feminists, there is no problem. Or is there? Why are so few Christian feminists focusing on the historical Jesus or on questions of inventory, stratigraphy, and attestation, on, that is, the precise cartography of Christianity's *earliest* re-oppression of women?

Finally, Catherine Keller asks also whether my reconstructed Jesus can avoid the trap of "heroic individualism." She notes that,

> the events upon which Crossan focuses our attention seem to flow unilaterally from Jesus' own extraordinary, if not ontologically unique, set of talents and projects. He is the one who models and generates

mutuality. Jesus himself *does* the sharing. Brock, by contrast, reads in Mark evidence of a more foundational mutuality—that is, she points to several instances in which Jesus *learns from* and is *empowered by* the women who risk relationship with him.

First, of course, there is the inevitable paradox of anyone teaching others that they can do things for and by themselves. Even one who raises a voice and says "we can do this together" could be accused of "heroic individualism." But that is surely different from claiming that *you can do it only in and through me*. Recall, then, those missionaries sent out by Jesus in the *Q Gospel*. They were not told to go out and tell people about Jesus nor to go out and send people back to Jesus. Instead, in the mutuality of healing and eating the Kingdom of God was made present on earth here and now in Lower Galilee. Anyone could do it, any time, any place. It was not present in Jesus alone, nor even in the interstices between Jesus and his first followers, but in the interstices between the processes of free healing and shared eating.

I must admit that I cannot imagine any more "foundational mutuality" than that one grounded as it is on the body's most basic necessities. Second, I have not read Rita Nakashima Brock's book but if, for example, she was thinking of the interchange between Jesus and the Syro-Phoenician woman, I had to bracket it methodologically because it only has a single independent attestation. Furthermore, it is too much coincidence for me that the only two miracles explicitly performed by Jesus for Gentiles are done at the request of a male for his son (or servant) and a woman for her daughter, are performed at a distance, and include in each case a stunning interchange between petitioner and Jesus. I am not convinced, in other words, that either the miracle for the Caphernaum centurion or for the Syro-Phoenician woman, including or especially those striking dialogues, goes back to the historical Jesus. They validate the later Gentile Mission by having Jesus participate in it indirectly, as it were, from a distance.

Brock, of course, is writing about christology, and can use such cases as valid canonical examples. I am writing about the historical Jesus, and cannot. More importantly, I need not. "Foundational mutuality" is there already at the level of the historical Jesus and it begins as it must with *bodily* mutuality. The perfectly appropriate reaction against the heroic, mythical, salvific, individualistic Christ should not result in a less than human response to the historical Jesus. It is profoundly human, as Catherine Keller knows from her visit to El Salvador, both to have Romero's poster on the wall and to have Marta say "The people themselves are Christ."

Dysfunctional Infallibility

Robert Ludwig's comparison between the pathology of familial dysfunction and the contemporary state of Roman Catholicism seems sadly and chillingly correct. I am in complete agreement with his analysis and with his hope that reconstructing Jesus could serve as initial therapy for its restoration. Because of that basic agreement, I take up only two minor points for discussion.

First, he, like Catherine Keller, asks me to be less ambiguous and more self-conscious about how my own autobiographical and theological presuppositions have influenced my reconstructed Jesus. Presuming what I just said about the difficulties of autobiographical self-location except as ritualized humiliation, I focus here on theological presuppositions.

I have never read any of the theologians mentioned by Robert Ludwig— not Rahner, Schillebeeckx, or Küng (I finished my doctorate in 1959!); not any of the South American liberation thinkers; not any of those other contemporary writers whose analyses he summarized for us. I take no particular pride in that accomplishment. I have been for over thirty years so involved in earliest Christianity in its historical, then its literary, and now its social-scientific aspects, that I have had no time to read systematic theology. Nor do I see much possibility for doing so in the near future.

I am, of course, absolutely aware of the theological implications of historical Jesus research but I do not think they are driving the process as far as I am concerned. Thus, for example, when I raise theological questions in my book's Epilogue, it is unwise to presume, as Frans Jozef van Beeck does, that they were there as motive power at the inception. On the one hand, there is only a single thing more pathetic than the dogmatic search for the historical Jesus and that is the antidogmatic one. On the other hand, there are very few jobs open as curators of Hellenistic museums, so that historians of earliest Christianity know that their focus derives from interests outside the academy and will have repercussions outside the university. What that entails for me is the responsibility of dialogue with those interests *in and when* they request it. But it also entails, even more fundamentally, an attempt to discipline my formal methodology so that being *for or against* dogmatic or ecclesiastical interests does not dictate results and prejudice conclusions.

I have argued, for example, that both the nature miracles and the risen apparitions of Jesus are concerned with questions of leadership in the earliest communities, with the origins of Christian authority rather than the origins of Christian faith. Did those conclusions come from my own difficulties with Roman Catholic authority in the sixties? Read the race to the tomb in John 20:1-10 and decide for yourself: even if such presuppositions are somehow involved, did Crossan, because of them, make up what was not there or see what was? That, maybe, is the far more difficult question. Do presuppositions dictate validly the choice of subject and interest or dictate invalidly the choice of result and conclusion? If, for whatever reason, I have sympathy with peasants, does that mean that I forced Jesus into a status he never had or that I deliberately chose to write about the illiterate peasant Jesus rather than the literate retainer Paul?

The second point is Robert Ludwig's quotation of the phrase "fundamental option for the poor." What Jesus made, in my understanding, was not a fundamental option for the poor but a fundamental option for justice. The Kingdom of God is in opposition to systemic injustice. The radical egalitarianism or ethical radicalism of Jesus was a profound rejection of the systemic evil and *structural* violence of his social situation, one of both patriarchal and imperial oppression.

I distinguish emphatically personal or individual evil (brutalizing your slave by rape) from systemic or structural evil (living by and within a slave economy). From the former viewpoint, the good and kind owner is innocent; from the latter viewpoint, only the slave is innocent. Take, for example, Jesus' aphorism, "Blessed are (we, you, the) poor (*ptochoi*) in spirit." Leave aside, first, Matthew 5:3's spiritualizing addition of "in spirit" and stay with the *Q Gospel's* version as in Luke 6:20b, "Blessed are (we, you, the) poor." Next, the Greek word for poor is *penes* but for destitute is *ptochos*, so that the proper translation of the saying is: "Blessed are (we, you, the) destitute." That distinction between poverty and destitution was very clear to everyone concerned, in the first as in the twentieth century.

So how could Jesus possibly declare that (we?) *destitute* are blessed? Is it simply some romantic delusion about the charms of vagrancy and beggary? Not quite. In a situation of systemic evil, only the expendables are guiltless before God. Try it, for our city streets today: Blessed are the destitute as *only* the homeless are innocent. Not romantic delusion, but precise judgment.

Those two levels of evil cannot be confused nor can either be used to ignore the other. Systemic evil cannot justify individual evil nor can individual goodness obscure systemic evil. The fundamental option cannot be for the poor or even for the destitute. That would be too easy. It must always be *for* justice and, thus, for whatever that entails; and *against* whatever that demands.

Is Jesus' Vision Open to Criticism?

After mentioning three current models for theology (postliberalism, deconstructionism, revisionism), Sheila Greeve Davaney proposes her own fourth one, pragmatic historicism or constructive historicism, and asks, at the end of her paper, "Are not Jesus and his vision also open to criticism, and what does that mean for how one understands being a Christian and a theologian?" She concludes with the invitation: "So, let that theological conversation begin!" I could respond to her question and invitation on two levels, first the high abstraction of crosscultural anthropology and then the thick historical specificity of earliest Christianity. But, since Charles Strain raises a similar question, I hold my second response for the next section.

There is, apart from those two levels of individual or personal and systemic or structural evil just discussed, a still more terrible third level or depth of evil, the obscene grinning face of ecological or cosmic evil. What would have happened if, by some magnificent divine fiat, Jesus' vision of radical egalitarianism had been immediately realized in that first common-era century? Here is the terrible answer from one of the major components of my anthropological model, Gerhard E. Lenski's *Power and Privilege: A Theory of Social Stratification* (1966). He ends his two chapters on ancient agrarian empires with "A Note on Distributive Justice" (pp. 295-96).

> On the whole, agrarian societies give the impression of gross injustice in the distributive realm. As we have seen, a small number of individuals enjoyed immense luxury, consuming in a single day goods and services sufficient to support large numbers of the common people for a year. At the same time a considerable portion of the population was denied the basic necessities of life and was marked out by the social system for a speedy demise. It does not take much imagination to conceive of a more equitable method of distribution.
>
> However, when the demographic factor is introduced into the analysis, we suddenly discover that the problem was never so simple as it sometimes seems to those of us who live in the comfort of a modern industrial society. Despite the ravages of war, famine, plague, and other disasters, and despite the influences of infanticide, abortion, monasticism, and prostitution, those segments of the population which were at, or above the subsistence level continued to produce more offspring than could be employed except by a steady reduction in privilege. Thus, barring an effective method of controlling fertility, which no agrarian society ever discovered, there seems to have been no alternative to the existence of a class of expendables, as harsh as such a statement may sound to modern ears.

That was a long citation deliberately given in full. I do not propose lauding Roman imperialism for avoiding ecological disaster because, just as *systemic* does not justify *personal* evil, so neither does *ecological* justify systemic evil. But all three levels, layers, or dimensions must be faced both together and separately. Any dialectic between our vision of Jesus-then and Christ-now will have to take all three dimensions into account. And those considerations continue into the next section.

Working the Linkages

Charles Strain raises a single powerful question for both Christian liberation theology and socially engaged Buddhism: must and how must "egalitarian community and social structure . . . be woven together in ways that transform"? I return now to that thick historical specificity of earliest Christianity to see what happened to Jesus' program as it moved into first actualization in the *rural* environs of Galilee. We are seeking, in other words, the first *rural* Christians.

I presume that many of Jesus' first followers were destitute. They were probably members of peasant families pushed down the terribly slippery slope from small freeholding to tenant farming to day laboring and were staring, next, at agricultural enslavement or the various forms of economic expendability necessary as the safety net for aristocracy's privilege. The dispossessed became more and more numerous as more and more land slipped, especially through debt, from being a family inheritance for those who lived upon it to being an entrepreneurial possibility for those who lived elsewhere. No wonder that, when the Jesus movement later created a prayer to sum up its vision, it concentrated on bread and debt, on too little of the former and too much of the latter, as the precise specifications of what the Kingdom was all about, *on earth* as in heaven.

Notice, however, that those missionaries of the Kingdom are not simply a caste of itinerant beggars. I emphasize this in dialogue with the brilliant work of Gerd Theissen who speaks of "itinerants" and "sympathizers" as if we had a calculated imbalance of spiritual marathoners and supporting gatoraders rather than a situation of strict mutuality and balanced reciprocity. There was, from the beginning, a reciprocity or dialectic of healing and eating built into the program itself. There was, in other words, a gloriously ambiguous dialectic of itinerant and householder within it from the very start. Recall all that was said in my opening paper about the *Q Gospel's* missionaries and especially about the symbolic catechesis of their dress code. The Cynic missionaries carried a knapsack to assert their self-sufficiency; the Jesus missionaries carried none to assert their codependency. Imagine, then, what happened when Jesus or one of those missionaries first walked down the alley and knocked on the courtyard door of a peasant home. Focus closely on that interaction of itinerant as representing "egalitarian community" and the householder as representing "social structure." We are not, of course, speaking here of social structure on the level of village, city, state, or empire but even or especially with household we face the basic unit of social institutionalization and there the problem already begins. Does the itinerant demand that the householder depart? Must all householders become itinerants? If yes, then where is the household left for the itinerant to stay in? I insist, by the way, on the paradoxical nature of that dialectic and I do not want to solve it, but to let its inevitable tension serve as the crucible for the earliest Jesus movement. Since Jesus was not slowly training a peripatetic seminar of students in the theory of the Kingdom (*pace* Mark's Gospel) but sending out instant missionaries to practice the Kingdom's presence in a program terribly simple to understand, *the dialectic of itinerant and householder is the atomic unit of the Jesus movement.* And, I repeat, it is necessarily, gloriously, and explosively paradoxical from the very first moment of its conception.

I look now at that dialectic in process, at the voice of the itinerants in the *Q Gospel* and at the response of the householders from the *Didache*, a text whose earliest layers may well be as old as those of that former, say in the fifties of that first century. The *Q Gospel's* missionaries were warned, as we saw in my opening paper, to expect either acceptance or rejection. The negative response is clear enough and ends any future interaction. But what did the positive response entail? Were all householders expected to up and leave so that the mission was to develop a caste of itinerants? If they did, there were no householders to stay with. If they did not, were they truly accepting the itinerants' message? Here was the ineluctable dilemma: if the itinerants were rejected, they failed; if they were accepted, they also failed. You can hear their reproaching voice in the earliest stratum of the *Q Gospel* at Luke 6:46, "Why do you call me 'Lord, Lord,' and not do what I tell you?" or, again, in the double image at 6:47–49.

> Every one who comes to me and hears my words and does them, I will show you what he is like: he is like a man building a house, who dug deep, and laid the foundation upon rock; and when a flood arose, the stream broke against that house, and could not shake it, because it had been well built. But he who hears and does not do them is like a man who built a house on the ground without a foundation; against which the stream broke, and immediately it fell, and the ruin of that house was great.

This is not a question of rejection or acceptance but, presuming initial acceptance, of hearing but not doing. Householders were remaining householders.

On the other hand, read the *Didache* to hear the voice of the householders answering back. It is trying with exquisite tact and delicacy neither to deny the valid witness of the itinerants' symbolic catechesis nor to let it destroy their own continuing householder status. Those latter have, for example, as is clear from *Didache* 4:9-11, both children and slaves. The document returns, again and again, in 10:7, in 11:7-12, and in 13:1, 3-7, to the problem of containing but not eliminating the itinerants, whom it calls simply, prophets. It not only speaks of accepting true and denying false itinerants/prophets but, in 11:11, it establishes a crucial new response to true prophets: do not judge but do not imitate:

> But no prophet who has been tried and is genuine, though he enact a worldly mystery of the Church, *if he teach not others to do what he does himself;*
>> shall be judged by you:
>> for he has his judgment with God,
>> for so also did the prophets of old.

That "worldly [cosmic] mystery of the church" is, at its widest, their entire itinerant witness and, at its narrowest (possibly), the "two by two" itinerancy of female and male unmarried missionary companions. The householders have worked out a compromise whereby they can both accept and not accept the itinerant's radical challenge. One listens to the itinerant but remains a householder. Does that mean nothing has been achieved and all is serene hypocrisy? Here is *Didache* 1:5–7:

> Give to everyone that asks you, and do not refuse,
>   for the Father's will is that we give to all from the gifts we have
>   received.
> Blessed is he that gives according to the mandate;
>   for he is innocent.
> Woe to the one who receives;
>   for if anyone receive alms under pressure of need he is innocent;
>   but he who receives it without need shall be tried as to why he took
>   and for what,
>   and being in prison he shall be examined as to his deeds, and he
>   shall not come out thence until he pay the last farthing.
> But concerning this it was also said, "Let your alms sweat into your
> palms until you know to whom you are giving."

Something surely has been achieved. Not the radicality of total dispossession advocated by itinerants who had nothing in any case but householders with palms sweating to give alms from what they had.

Excuse the brevity of that example, which is actually an agenda for future research. The dialectic between itinerant and householder, between *Q Gospel* and *Didache*, between, in Strain's terms, "egalitarian community and social structure," goes back indelibly to the inaugural program of the historical Jesus himself. The absolute idealism of Christian radical egalitarianism or of Buddhist dependent co-arising must be accepted as one pole of a dialectic, as a challenge over against all forms of institutionalization. "If truth be told, dialectics are," as Strain notes, "rarely even," but that is what theologians are supposed to do: to keep them as even as possible because the pathology of absolutism stalks either pole of the dialectic when left to itself.

Your Own Face in a Deep Well

That title indicates the most basic criticism of my book made by Frans Jozef van Beeck. He asks at the start and finish of his article: is Crossan's picture of Jesus yet another mirrored face seen at the bottom of a deep well? Yet does that question not destroy any possibility of historical reconstruction? Does it not a priori invalidate the entire process? For how could

I or anyone else disprove its allegation? On the one hand, I am not myself a Mediterranean Jewish peasant, so I have clearly not projected my own face onto Jesus, but on the other hand, no matter what reconstruction I presented, van Beeck could have made that same criticism, at least on the level of sympathy if not of identity.

Two immediate questions, then. First, how does Frans Jozef van Beeck know that I agree with or even like my reconstructed Jesus? I never said I did, although I have admitted elsewhere that I could not follow his program. Does he presume I agree with Jesus because he himself believes that historical Jesus research must produce a reconstruction acceptable or agreeable to the investigator? Second, if reflected faces are inevitable, what is then left for Frans Jozef van Beeck who considers the historical Jesus important for Christian faith? What is left is either the Marcion or Tatian options from the second century, when the problem of multiple gospels about one Jesus first became painfully obvious. Either eliminate three versions with Marcion, or laminate all four together with Tatian. So the historical Jesus is simply a *Reader's Digest* condensed version of the canonical foursome. And they are protected from the face-in-well dismissal, I presume, because Frans Jozef van Beeck would claim "conservative community control" in those cases. But notice that singular. Precisely what confronts us is multiple communities producing a wide variety of gospels, now inside and outside the canon. It is those data that force the problem, and they cannot be obscured by any general statements about orality or textuality, suspicion or reconstruction. The effect, even if not the intention, of casting a priori doubt on any reconstruction (the face-in-well defense) is to preserve as historical the condensed diatessaron of the canonical Jesus.

The next most serious and pervasive problem is Frans Jozef van Beeck's refusal to criticize the book on its own terms, and here misunderstandings and even monstrosities multiply at an alarming rate. What happens, in effect, is that he constantly pulls it back into the First and/or Second (New Hermeneutic) Quest for the historical Jesus without realizing that it is actually proposing a Third Quest, if one wants to use those Arthurian terms.

First, I deliberately and epigraphically quoted Renan, Schweitzer, and Klausner, as classically divergent Catholic, Protestant, and Jewish interpretations of Jesus. I intended to play them, both against one another, and against myself, and not just to place myself, as he suggests, "in this company." Was it really not clear, for example, that my Jesus' Galilee was somewhat different from Renan's "green hills and clear fountains" (p. 225)?

Second, forget the Old Quest in reading my book. It looked for a positivistically definitive historical Jesus. I explicitly stated, "that there will always be divergent historical Jesuses, that there will always be divergent Christs built upon them, but ... that the structure of a Christianity will always be: *this is how we see Jesus-then as Christ-now*" (Crossan 1991: 423). That must, of course, be debated, but it does not help to describe it, with

Frans Jozef van Beeck, as either Enlightenment or Romantic thinking. It is, as Jeffrey Carlson correctly commented, *"not* the nineteenth-century quest for the historical Jesus ... not the Enlightenment's dream of value-free objectivity, nor liberal theology's dream of the unchanging essence of Christianity." This does not make it correct, but it locates it where it is: in the late twentieth-century's postmodernism.

Third, the New Hermeneutic is equally unhelpful as immediate background. My underlining of the social and the political is exactly the opposite to its emphasis on the personal and the existential.

Finally, and this is where my method, almost totally ignored by Frans Jozef van Beeck, becomes constitutive. This Third Quest is programmatically different on three fronts: its *materials* involve both intra- and extra-canonical documents; its *methods* integrate a crosscultural anthropological or social-scientific, a historical, and a literary level or vector; and its *philosophical bases* are more postmodern than positivistic, rationalistic, romantic, or existential. My book intended to launch a third quest (lower case) and that was why method is so vital to it. Method does not make it right, but method is where Frans Jozef van Beeck must meet it and never does. He responds instead to the earlier history of Jesus research and not to the book before him.

There is, however, one place where his point is well taken and it requires some explanation. He says:

> Crossan can write — in what must have been a moment of inattention to the demands of both critical scholarship and sensitivity — that the prescription behind these [passion] narratives is, "Hide the prophecy, tell the narrative, and invent the history" (Crossan 1991: 372). This slogan begs for disagreement, because ... the hermeneutic of suspicion has turned into an open charge of fraudulence. Instead of befriending the texts, which are his allies, the critic has turned against them.

That is quite fair and accurate but why did I turn against the texts and why in only this one place? The context ["The Passion as Narrative," pp. 367-91] was arguing that our canonical passion accounts are not history memorized but prophecy historicized. I was condensing in that section much of my earlier book *The Cross That Spoke: The Origins of the Passion Narrative* in which I proposed a fourfold sequence of historical, prophetic, narrative, and polemical passion traditions (pp. 406-7). The point is that, for example, the darkness at noon during the crucifixion in Mark 15:33 comes not from history remembered but from prophecy fulfilled, from Amos 8:9, "On that day," says the Lord God, "I will make the sun go down at noon, and darken the earth in broad daylight." Thus, the *historical* (there was no darkness) is mediated though the *prophetic* (there will be darkness) into the *narrative* (there was darkness) passion. So far, so good. But then I gave one example of the final stage, the polemical passion, from Cyril of Jerusalem in his *Catechetical Lectures* 13.25 (*The Cross That Spoke*, 406-7):

> Do you seek at what hour exactly the sun failed? Was it the fifth or the eighth or the tenth? Give the exact hour, O prophet, to the unheeding Jews; when did the sun set? The prophet says: "On that day, says the Lord God, I will make the sun set at mid-day" (for there was darkness from the sixth hour) "and cover the earth with darkness in broad daylight."

I commented: "The unfairness of such anti-Jewish polemic is now quite obvious. Of course the narrative passion agreed in detail with the prophetic passion. It had been quarried from its contents" (407).

What happened, as I condensed the much longer argument of *The Cross That Spoke* into the far shorter section on the passion in *The Historical Jesus*, was that any mention of the polemical passion was omitted, but my anger at its injustice showed through that comment picked up by Frans Jozef van Beeck. I was wrongly retrojecting what was done with those passion texts onto their original creation. I make no apology, however, for that bitter comment as a judgment on what later anti-Jewish polemics did with those prophetic "fulfillments." The penultimate chapters of our Gospels could not have been written without Jewish texts as their foundations and yet they have been used to brutalize Jewish people thereafter. It is bad enough to beat people over the head; it is worse to do so with their own stolen sticks.

Economic Empowerment

Dennis McCann's "thesis is that Christianity's perennial bias against moneymaking in general and modern business in particular rests less on the teachings of Crossan's Mediterranean Jewish peasant and more on the aristocratic prejudices of Plato and Aristotle" so that "solidarity with the oppressed, undertaken in the name of the historical Jesus, may require an openness to forms of economic empowerment that Plato and Aristotle would never approve of." That invites me into areas of economics and business, where my ignorance is close to total, so what follows may not be a very adequate response.

Apart, for a moment, from dreams of radical egalitarianism or finding hidden treasure, how, in that first common-era century could a poor individual *become* very, very wealthy—how could one move strikingly up the economic ladder? A free rural peasant, even with an extended family living and working on a fifty-acre farm, would be lucky not to go under but to break even or possibly stay comfortable through the generations. A free urban artisan might have to buy every morning what he had to sell that day or not eat at all until he sold it. How, then? Who, then? The answer was already clear from fictional Trimalchio, but here it is again, from Paul Veyne in *From Pagan Rome to Byzantium* (82):

> Freed slaves . . . [s]et up in business as artisans, shopkeepers, or merchants . . . accounted for less than 5 percent of then total population; yet they formed a group that was highly visible socially and very important economically. Although not all shopkeepers were freed slaves, all freed slaves were shopkeepers and traders.

Here is one place where life could begin as a destitute enslaved foreigner and end as a millionaire Roman citizen. I intend absolutely no romanticization of slavery, but if, at its worst, Roman slavery was just as bad as its antebellum American counterpart, at this its best it had there no counterpart at all. Owners gave slaves money to trade with, divided the profits between them, and let them eventually buy their own freedom. Or else, on their deathbeds, they freed them and sometimes even made them heirs. So, from profit or piety, they became free, automatically Roman citizens, and, depending on the circumstances, possibly even wealthy. And if not immediately, then maybe soon.

Patronal connections, business interactions, and capital investments might well continue on individual and familial levels for quite some time. No doubt, this happened especially in Rome where a landed aristocracy needed foreign slaves much more skilled in trading than themselves to use and expand their excess cash. But it is fascinating to watch the social anomalies spawned endlessly by this process of slave manumission. It was, first of all, an imperial admission that, when one really wanted something done, the carrot was better than the stick, and that was probably not best thought about too much. It was, second, a challenge to rethink the relationship of land and commerce, but that was best not thought about at all.

None of that was of any help to peasants being squeezed by debt off their lands and down the slippery slope from small freeholders, to tenant farmers or sharecroppers, and on to day laborers and destitutes. It was clearly better to be a slave in the right place than a peasant in the wrong one. But, in terms of McCann's challenge, there would have been many people in the first century for whom liberation meant precisely manumission and for whom business ability was the salvific key that unlocked their fetters.

I do not minimize at all the fact that the Trimalchio factor was probably far more an urban than a rural, and an Italian than a provincial phenomenon. Neither do I minimize the dichotomies between rank and status as against wealth and prestige that such freed slaves had to undergo. But even or especially if the historical Jesus met few such people, as early Christianity spread across the Roman Empire it may well have met more and more of them important to its success. Let me conclude with another quote from Paul Veyne (123):

> Why was commerce almost universally devalued until the industrial revolution? The key to the mystery lies in the fact that commercial wealth belonged to the newly rich, while old wealth was based on land. Inherited wealth defended itself against upstart merchants by imputing to them every conceivable vice. No merchant, however, steals from his customers with the practiced ease and sanctioned right that the aristocrat does from the peasant.

Concluding Remarks

I conclude, where I began, with: early influences as permanent prejudices? But *all* of us must hear together the hiss of the viper from the epigraph that preceded that beginning. This conclusion, in any case, lets me do what I love to do, study texts closely and comparatively to see changes, redactions, and implications. I do so in dialogue with Frans Jozef van Beeck once again, but now tongue in cheek. He was kind enough to send me a first version of his article before the second one, which he summarized at the symposium. The first version concluded by describing me as "a capable, quite original, *Catholic* New Testament professor with the soul of a leprechaun" (my emphasis). The second one changed only one word in that finale: "a capable, quite original, *rather skeptical* New Testament professor with the soul of a leprechaun" (my emphasis). I leave aside whether "Catholic" and "quite skeptical" are simply synonyms, or whether the change from one to other represents promotion or demotion in stature. I want, instead, to hold on to that former combination: Catholic with the soul of a leprechaun. There is actually a word for that conjunction: it is Celtic Christianity, which is not exactly the same as Roman Christianity. For, when Rome had fallen to the barbarians, it was on the foggy, soggy, boggy shores of Ireland that the scriptures were preserved and studied, copied and decorated with a serpentine convolution that Roman *gravitas* could never have imagined.

In honor of that process I give the last word to an Irish monk working in Greek, Latin, and Gaelic, far from home in the monastery of St. Gall in northeast Switzerland in the eleventh century. On the page in question of what is now termed the Codex Boernerianus he had copied the Greek text of 1 Corinthians 2:9–3:3 and written the Vulgate Latin translation word-for-word above each line. But then, down at the bottom, in slightly smaller letters, he wrote this poem in Gaelic about making a pilgrimage to Rome:

> To come to Rome, [to come to Rome]
> Much of trouble, little of profit,

The thing you seek here,
If you bring not with you, you'll find not.

Great folly, great madness,
Great ruin of sense, great insanity,
Since you have set out for death,
To be in disobedience to the Son of Mary.

A most appropriate final word, in more ways than one, to a symposium on the historical Jesus, Mac Maire or Son of Mary, and to reflections on how a Jewish peasant became an imperial Christ.

References

Abe, Masao. 1985. *Zen and Western Thought*. Ed. William R. LaFleur. Honolulu: University of Hawaii Press.

Aitken, Robert. 1984. *The Mind of Clover: Essays in Zen Buddhist Ethics*. San Francisco: North Point Press.

Appadurai, Arjun. 1990. "Disjuncture and Difference in the Global Cultural Economy," in *Global Culture: Nationalism, Globalization and Modernity*. Ed. Mike Featherstone, pp. 295-310. London: SAGE Publications.

Aristotle. 1984. *The Complete Works of Aristotle: The Revised Oxford Translation*, Vol. 2. Ed. Jonathan Barnes. Princeton: Princeton University Press.

Attridge, Harold W. 1992. "Reflections in Research into Q," *Semeia* 55:223-34.

Barton, Bruce. 1925. *The Man Nobody Knows: A Discovery of the Real Jesus*. Indianapolis: Bobbs-Merrill.

Berryman, Phillip. 1987. *Liberation Theology*. Oak Park, IL: Meyer Stone Books.

Bianchi, Eugene C. and Rosemary Radford Ruether, eds. 1992. *A Democratic Catholic Church: The Reconstruction of Roman Catholicism*. New York: Crossroad.

Bordo, Susan. 1990. "Feminism, Postmodernism, and Gender Skepticism," in *Feminism/Postmodernism*. Ed. Linda J. Nicholson. New York: Routledge.

Bossy, John. 1987. *Christianity in the West 1400-1700*. Oxford and New York: Oxford University Press.

Bradshaw, John. 1988. *Healing the Shame That Binds You*. Deerfield Beach, FL: Health Communications, Inc.

Brock, Rita Nakashima. 1991. *Journeys by Heart: A Christology of Erotic Power*. New York: Crossroad.

Brown, Delwin. 1994. *The Boundaries of Our Habitations: Tradition and Theological Construction*. Albany: State University of New York Press, forthcoming.

Casanas, Joan. 1983. "The Task of Making God Exist," in *The Idols of Death and the God of Life*. Ed. Pablo Richard, pp. 113-49. Maryknoll, NY: Orbis Books.

Charleston, Steven. 1990. "The Old Testament of Native America," in *Lift Every Voice: Constructing Christian Theologies from the Underside*. Ed. Susan Brooks Thistlethwaite and Mary Potter Engel. San Francisco: HarperSanFrancisco.

Clifford, James. 1988. *The Predicament of Culture: Twentieth-Century Ethnography, Literature and Art*. Cambridge: Harvard University Press.

Crosby, Michael. 1991. *The Dysfunctional Church: Addiction and Codependency in the Family of Catholicism*. Notre Dame: Ave Maria Press.

Crossan, John Dominic. 1973. *In Parables: The Challenge of the Historical Jesus*. New York: Harper & Row.

———. 1975. *The Dark Interval: Towards a Theology of Story*. Niles, IL: Argus Communications.

———. 1976. *Raid on the Articulate: Comic Eschatology in Jesus and Borges*. New York: Harper & Row.

————. 1979. *Finding Is the First Act: Trove Folktales and Jesus' Treasure Parable.* Semeia Supplements. Philadelphia: Fortress Press.

————. 1983. *In Fragments: The Aphorisms of Jesus.* San Francisco: Harper & Row.

————. 1985. *Four Other Gospels: Shadows on the Contour of the Canon.* Minneapolis: Winston Press, Seabury Books.

————. 1986. *Sayings Parallels: A Workbook for the Jesus Tradition.* Foundations and Facets. Philadelphia: Fortress Press.

————. 1988. *The Cross That Spoke: The Origins of the Passion Narrative.* San Francisco: Harper & Row.

————. 1991. *The Historical Jesus: The Life of a Mediterranean Jewish Peasant.* San Francisco: Harper SanFrancisco.

————. 1992. "Why We Must Seek the Historical Jesus," *The Boston Sunday Globe*, 26 July.

————. 1993. "The Ethics of the Historical Jesus." Unpublished manuscript of an address given at Capital University, Columbus, Ohio, 24 January 1993, 14 pages.

Daly, Mary. 1973. *Beyond God the Father.* Boston: Beacon Press.

Davies, Stevan L. 1983. *The Gospel of Thomas and Christian Wisdom.* New York: Seabury Press.

————. 1992. "The Christology and Protology of the Gospel of Thomas," *Journal of Biblical Literature* 111:663-82.

Downing, F. Gerald. 1984. "Cynics and Christians," *New Testament Studies* 30:584-93.

————. 1987. *Jesus and the Threat of Freedom.* London: SCM Press.

————. 1988a. *Christ and the Cynics: Jesus and Other Radical Preachers in First-Century Tradition.* JSOT Manuals 4. Sheffield: Sheffield Academic Press (JSOT Press).

————. 1988b. "Quite Like Q. A Genre for 'Q': The 'Lives' of Cynic Philosophers," *Biblica* 69:196-225.

Droogers, André. 1989. "Syncretism: The Problem of Definition, the Definition of the Problem," in *Dialogue and Syncretism: An Interdisciplinary Approach.* Ed. Jerald Gort, Hendrik Vroom, Rein Fernhout, and Anton Wessels, pp. 7-25. Grand Rapids: Eerdmans.

Dudley, Donald Reynolds. [1937] 1967. *A History of Cynicism: From Diogenes to the 6th Century A.D.* Hildesheim: Olms.

Ellis, Marc H. 1991. "Jewish Progressives and the Ecumenical Dialogue," *University of Dayton Review* 21:47-64.

Evron, Boas. 1981. "The Holocaust: Learning the Wrong Lessons," *Journal of Palestine Studies* 10:15-26.

Faure, Bernard. 1991. *The Rhetoric of Immediacy.* Princeton: Princeton University Press.

Goodwin, Barbara. 1992. *Justice by Lottery.* Chicago: University of Chicago Press.

Grant, Jacquelyn. 1989. *White Women's Christ/Black Women's Jesus.* Atlanta: Scholars Press.

Gutiérrez, Gustavo. 1983. *The Power of the Poor in History.* Maryknoll, NY: Orbis Books.

————. 1987. *On Job: God Talk and the Suffering of the Innocent.* Maryknoll, NY: Orbis Books.

————. 1988. *A Theology of Liberation*, 15th Anniversary Edition. Maryknoll, NY: Orbis Books.

Harvey, Van Austin. 1966. *The Historian and the Believer*. New York: Macmillan.

Hengel, Martin. 1977. *Crucifixion in the Ancient World and the Folly of the Message of the Cross*. Philadelphia: Fortress Press.

Hobsbawm, Eric John. 1965. *Primitive Rebels: Studies in Archaic Forms of Social Movement in the 19th and 20th Centuries*. New York: Norton [Originally published in 1959 as *Social Bandits and Primitive Rebels*].

———. 1973a. "Peasants and Politics," *Journal of Peasant Studies* 1:3-22.

———. 1973b. "Social Banditry," in *Rural Protest: Peasant Movements and Social Change*. Ed. Henry A. Landsberger, pp. 142-57. New York: Barnes & Noble.

———. [1969] 1985. *Bandits*. 2d Ed. Middlesex: Penguin Books.

Hyers, Conrad. 1989. *The Laughing Buddha: Zen and the Comic Spirit*. Wolfeboro, NH: Longwood Academic Press.

Jacobson, Arland Dean. 1992. *The First Gospel: An Introduction to Q*. Sonoma, CA: Polebridge Press.

Johnson, Elizabeth A. 1992. *She Who Is: The Mystery of God in Feminist Theological Discourse*. New York: Crossroad.

Johnson, Luke Timothy. 1992. "A Marginal Mediterranean Jewish Peasant," *Commonweal* 24 (April):24-26.

Johnson, Samuel. 1905. "Cowley," in *Lives of the English Poets*. Vol. 1. Ed. George Birkbeck Hill, pp. 1-69. Oxford: Clarendon Press.

Jones, Ken. 1989. *The Social Face of Buddhism*. London: Wisdom Publications.

Kähler, Martin. 1988. *The So-called Historical Jesus and the Historic Biblical Christ*. *Fortress Texts in Modern Theology*. Philadelphia: Fortress Press.

Kapleau, Philip. 1980. *The Three Pillars of Zen*. Garden City, NY: Anchor/Doubleday.

Kelber, Werner H. 1983. *The Oral and the Written Gospel: The Hermeneutics of Speaking and Writing in the Synoptic Tradition, Mark, Paul, and Q*. Philadelphia: Fortress Press.

Kermode, Frank. 1967. *The Sense of an Ending*. New York: Oxford University Press.

Kierkegaard, Søren. 1978. *Søren Kierkegaard's Journals and Papers*. Vol. 5. Ed. and trans. Howard V. Hong and Edna H. Hong. Bloomington: Indiana University Press.

King, John Edward, ed. and trans. 1927. *Cicero: Tusculan Disputations*. Loeb Classical Library. Vol. 18 of 28. Cambridge: Harvard University Press.

Klausner, Joseph. [1922] 1945. *Jesus of Nazareth: His Life, Times, and Teaching*. Trans. Herbert Danby. New York: Macmillan.

Kloppenborg, John S. 1987. *The Formation of Q, Trajectories in Ancient Wisdom Collections*. Studies in Antiquity and Christianity. Philadelphia: Fortress Press.

———. 1988. *Q Parallels. Synopsis, Critical Notes, and Concordance*. Foundations and Facets Reference Series. Sonoma, CA: Polebridge Press.

Knitter, Paul F. 1987. "Toward a Liberation Theology of Religions," in *The Myth of Christian Uniqueness*. Ed. John Hick and Paul Knitter, pp. 178-200. Maryknoll, NY: Orbis Books.

Koester, Helmut. 1980a. "Apocryphal and Canonical Gospels," *Harvard Theological Review* 73:105-30.

———. 1980b. "Gnostic Writings as Witnesses for the Development of the Sayings Tradition," in *The Rediscovery of Gnosticism* (Proceedings of the International Conference on Gnosticism at Yale, New Haven, CT, March 28-31, 1978. Vol. 1), pp. 238-56 (discussion: pp. 256-61). The School of Valentinus. Studies in the

History of Religions: *Supplements to Numen* XLI/1. Leiden: Brill.

———. 1990. *Ancient Christian Gospels: Their History and Development*. London: SCM Press & Philadelphia: Trinity Press Int.

Kundera, Milan. 1986. *Life is Elsewhere*. Trans. Peter Kussi. New York: Penguin Books.

Küng, Hans. 1976. *On Being A Christian*. Garden City, NY: Doubleday.

———. 1988. *Theology for a Third Millennium: An Ecumenical View*. Garden City, NY: Doubleday.

———. 1990. *Reforming the Church Today*. New York: Crossroad.

Lake, Kirsopp, ed. and trans. 1912–13. *The Apostolic Fathers*. 2 vols. Loeb Classical Library. Cambridge: Harvard University Press.

Larson, Ernie and Parnegg, Janee. 1992. *Recovering Catholics: What to Do When Religion Comes between You and God*. San Francisco: HarperSanFrancisco.

Lenski, Gerhard E. 1966. *Power and Privilege: A Theory of Stratification*. New York: McGraw Hill.

Lessing, Gotthold Ephraim. 1957. *Lessing's Theological Writings*, selected and introduced by Henry Chadwick. Stanford: Stanford University Press.

———. 1968. *Gesammelte Werke*, 2d ed., Vol. 9. Ed. Paul Rilla. Berlin and Weimar: Aufbau-Verlag.

Levine, Daniel H. 1992. *Popular Voices in Latin American Catholicism*. Princeton: Princeton University Press.

Lohfink, Norbert. 1990. *Lobgesänge der Armen: Studien zum Magnifikat, den Hodajot von Qumran und einigen späten Psalmen*. Mit einem Anhang: *Hodajot-Bibliographie 1948-1989* von Ulrich Dahmen. *Stuttgarter Bibelstudien*, 143. Stuttgart: Verlag Katholisches Bibelwerk.

Mack, Burton. 1987. "The Kingdom Sayings in Mark," *Forum* 3:3-47.

———. 1993. *The Lost Gospel: The Book of Q and Christian Origins*. San Francisco: HarperSanFrancisco.

Macy, Joanna. 1979. "Dependent Co-Arising: The Distinctiveness of Buddhist Ethics," *Journal of Religious Ethics* 7:38-52.

May, Gerald G. 1988. *Addiction and Grace: Love and Spirituality in the Healing of Addictions*. San Francisco: HarperSanFrancisco.

McBrien, Richard P. 1981. *Catholicism: Study Edition*. Minneapolis: Winston Press.

McCann, Dennis P. and Strain, Charles R. 1985. *Polity and Praxis: A Program for American Practical Theology*. Minneapolis: Winston Press.

Meier, John P. 1991. *A Marginal Jew: Rethinking the Historical Jesus*. The Anchor Bible Reference Library. Garden City, NY: Doubleday.

Meyer, Marvin W. 1992. *The Gospel of Thomas: The Hidden Sayings of Jesus*. San Francisco: HarperSanFrancisco.

More, Thomas. 1992. *Care of the Soul*. New York: HarperCollins.

Murnion, Philip. Ed. 1983. *Catholics and Nuclear War: A Commentary on "The Challenge of Peace."* New York: Crossroad.

Newman, John Henry. 1877. *Essays Critical and Historical*. London: Basil Montagu Pickering.

Nhât Hanh, Thích. 1987. *Being Peace*. Berkeley, CA: Parallax Press.

———. 1991. *Peace is Every Step*. New York: Bantam Books.

Niebuhr, Reinhold. 1963. *An Interpretation of Christian Ethics*. New York: Seabury Press.

Oakman, Douglas E. 1986. *Jesus and the Economic Questions of His Day*. Studies in the Bible and Early Christianity 8. Lewiston, NY: Edwin Mellen Press.

O'Brien, David J. and Shannon, Thomas A. 1992. *Catholic Social Thought: The Documentary Heritage*. Maryknoll, NY: Orbis Books.

O'Brien, Herbert and Swidler, Leonard, eds. 1988. *A Catholic Bill of Rights*. Kansas City: Sheed & Ward.

Ogden, Schubert M. 1982. *The Point of Christology*. San Francisco: Harper & Row.

Ong, Walter J. 1970. *The Presence of the Word: Some Prolegomena for Cultural and Religious History*. New York: Simon & Schuster.

———. 1982. *Orality and Literacy, The Technologizing of the Word. New Accents*. London and New York: Methuen.

Panikkar, Raimon. 1978. *The Intra-Religious Dialogue*. New York: Paulist Press.

Parnegg, Janee. 1992. See Larson, Ernie.

Patterson, Stephen John. 1988. *The Gospel of Thomas within the Development of Early Christianity*. Ann Arbor, MI: University Microfilms International [Ph.D. dissertation, Claremont Graduate School].

———. 1990. "The Gospel of Thomas: Introduction," in *Q-Thomas Reader*. Ed. John S. Kloppenborg, Marvin W. Meyer, Stephen J. Patterson, and Michael G. Steinhauser, pp. 75-123. Sonoma, CA: Polebridge Press.

———. 1991. "Paul and the Jesus Tradition: It Is Time for Another Look," *Harvard Theological Review* 84:23-41.

Peck, M. Scott. 1978. *The Road Less Traveled: A New Psychology of Love, Traditional Values and Spiritual Growth*. New York: Simon & Schuster.

Pelikan, Jaroslav. 1987. *Jesus Through the Centuries: His Place in the History of Culture*. New York: Harper & Row.

Perrin, Norman. 1967. *Rediscovering the Teaching of Jesus*. New York: Harper & Row.

Plato. 1937. *The Dialogues of Plato*. Vol. 1. Trans. B. Jowett. New York: Random House.

Pope John Paul II. 1990. "Uproot Racism, Syncretism: Address of Pope John Paul II to a Group of Brazilian Bishops Completing their 'ad limina' Visit," *The Pope Speaks* 35:409-13.

Pye, Michael. 1971. "Syncretism and Ambiguity," *Numen* 18:83-93.

———. 1978. *Skillful Means*. London: Duckworth.

Rahner, Karl. 1951. "Chalkedon—Ende oder Anfang?" translated as "Current Problems in Christology," *Theological Investigations*. Vol. 1, pp. 149-200. Baltimore: Helicon Press, 1964.

———. 1978. *Foundations of Christian Faith*. New York: Seabury.

Ribuffo, Leo. 1981. "Jesus Christ as Business Statesman: Bruce Barton and the Selling of Corporate Capitalism," *The American Quarterly* 33:206-31.

Rothschild, Fritz, ed. 1990. *Jewish Perspectives on Christianity*. New York: Crossroad.

Ruether, Rosemary. 1975. *New Women/New Earth*. New York: Seabury Press.

———. 1983. *Sexism and God Talk*. Boston: Beacon Press.

———. 1992. See Bianchi, Eugene C.

Sale, Kirkpatrick. 1991. *The Conquest of Paradise: Christopher Columbus and the Columbian Legacy*. New York: Penguin.

Sanders, E.P. 1985. *Jesus and Judaism*. Philadelphia: Fortress Press.

Sanon, Anselme T. 1991. "Jesus, Master of Initiation," in *Faces of Jesus in Africa*. Ed. Robert J. Schreiter, pp. 85-102. Maryknoll, NY: Orbis Books.

Sayre, Farrand. 1948. *The Greek Cynics*. Baltimore: Furst.

Schillebeeckx, Edward. 1979. *Jesus: An Experiment in Christology*. New York: Seabury.

———. 1980. *Christ: The Experience of Jesus as Lord*. New York: Seabury.

Schreiter, Robert J. 1989. "Teaching Theology from an Intercultural Perspective," *Theological Education* 26:13-34.

Schüssler Fiorenza, Elisabeth. 1983. *In Memory of Her: A Feminist Theological Reconstruction of Christian Origins*. New York: Crossroad.

———. 1992. *But She Said*. Boston: Beacon.

Schweitzer, Albert. [1906] 1968. *The Quest of the Historical Jesus: A Critical Study of Its Progress from Reimarus to Wrede*. Trans. W. Montgomery. New York: Macmillan.

Schweizer, Eduard. 1971. *Jesus*. Richmond, VA: John Knox Press.

Scott, Bernard Brandon. 1989. *Hear Then the Parable: A Commentary on the Parables of Jesus*. Minneapolis: Fortress Press.

Scott, James C. 1976. *The Moral Economy of the Peasant: Subsistence and Rebellion in Southeast Asia*. New Haven: Yale University Press.

———. 1977. "Protest and Profanation: Agrarian Revolt and the Little Tradition," *Theory and Society* 4:1-38, 211-46.

———. 1985. *Weapons of the Weak: Everyday Forms of Peasant Resistance*. New Haven: Yale University Press.

———. 1990. *Domination and the Arts of Resistance: Hidden Transcripts*. New Haven: Yale University Press.

Shannon, Thomas A. 1992. See O'Brien, David J.

Sobrino, Jon. 1978. *Christology at the Crossroads*. Maryknoll, NY: Orbis Books.

———. 1982. *Jesus in Latin America*. Maryknoll, NY: Orbis Books.

Steinem, Gloria. 1992. *Revolution from Within: A Book of Self-Esteem*. Boston: Little, Brown and Company.

Stevens, Wallace. 1990. "Notes Toward a Supreme Fiction," in *The Collected Poems of Wallace Stevens*. New York: Vintage Books.

Stout, Jeffrey. 1981. *Flight from Authority: Religion, Morality, and the Quest for Autonomy*. Notre Dame: University of Notre Dame Press.

Strain, Charles R. 1977. "Ideology and Alienation: Themes on the Interpretation and Evaluation of Theologies of Liberation," *Journal of the American Academy of Religion* 45:473-90.

———. 1985. See McCann, Dennis P.

———. 1992. "Alienation," in *A New Handbook of Christian Theology*. Ed. Donald W. Musser and Joseph L. Price, pp. 23-25. Nashville: Abingdon Press.

Stuke, Horst. 1963. *Philosophie der Tat*. Stuttgart: Ernst Klett.

Swidler, Leonard. 1983. "The Dialogical Decalogue," *Journal of Ecumenical Studies* 20:15-18.

———. 1988. See O'Brien, Herbert.

Temme, Jon H. 1987. "Indigenous Christologies: Perspectives from the Early Church for the Modern Church," *Trinity Seminary Review* 9:28-39.

Theissen, Gerd. 1987. *The Shadow of the Galilean: The Quest of the Historical Jesus in Narrative Form*. Philadelphia: Fortress Press.

Tracy, David. 1981. *The Analogical Imagination: Christian Theology and the Culture of Pluralism*. New York: Crossroad.

Turner, Victor. 1974. *Dramas, Fields, and Metaphors: Symbolic Action in Human Society*. Ithaca, NY: Cornell University Press.

Tyrrell, George. 1909. *Christianity at the Cross-Roads*. London: Longmans, Green and Co.

Vaage, Leif Eric. 1987. *Q: The Ethos and Ethics of an Itinerant Intelligence*. Ann Arbor, MI: University Microfilms International [Ph.D. dissertation, Claremont Graduate School].

van Beeck, Frans Jozef. 1989. *God Encountered: A Contemporary Catholic Systematic Theology*. Vol. 1, *Understanding the Christian Faith*. San Francisco: Harper & Row.

van den Berg, J. H. 1974. *Divided Existence and Complex Society: An Historical Approach*. Pittsburgh: Duquesne University Press.

Veyne, Paul. 1987. *From Pagan Rome to Byzantium*. Trans. Arthur Goldhammer. Vol. 1 of *A History of Private Life*. Cambridge: The Belknap Press of Harvard University Press.

von Balthasar, Hans U. 1990. *Mysterium Paschale*. Trans. Aidan Nichols. Edinburgh: Clark.

Waskow, Arthur. 1978. *Godwrestling*. New York: Schocken.

Weil, Simone. 1952. *The Need for Roots: Prelude to a Declaration of Duties Toward Mankind*. Trans. A.F. Wills. New York: Putnam.

Whitehead, Alfred North. 1917. *The Organisation of Thought: Educational and Scientific*. London: Williams and Norgate.

———. 1978. *Process and Reality: An Essay in Cosmology*. Ed. David Ray Griffin and Donald W. Sherburne. New York: Macmillan.

Wilder, Amos. 1964. *Early Christian Rhetoric*. New York: Harper & Row.

Witherington III, Ben. 1990. *The Christology of Jesus*. Minneapolis: Fortress Press.

Wyschogrod, Edith. 1990. "Man-Made Mass Death: Shifting Concepts of Community," *Journal of the American Academy of Religion* 58:165-76.

Yee, Gale A. 1992. "Jezebel," *The Anchor Bible Dictionary*. Vol. 3. Ed. David Noel Freedman, pp. 848-49. Garden City, NY: Doubleday.

Contributors

Jeffrey Carlson (coeditor) is Associate Professor of Religious Studies at DePaul University in Chicago, Illinois, where he has taught since 1989. He is the author of several articles on Christian theology and religious pluralism and the forthcoming book *The Syncretic Self: The Nature of Religious Identity* to be published by Orbis Books. His contributions include the "Introduction" (with coeditor Robert Ludwig) and his essay, "Crossan's Jesus and Christian Identity."

John Dominic Crossan is Professor of Religious Studies at DePaul University since 1973. His book, *The Historical Jesus: The Life of A Mediterranean Jewish Peasant* (1991), is the focus of this book. His most recent publication is *Jesus: A Revolutionary Biography* (1994). Previous books include *In Parables: The Challenge of the Historical Jesus* (1973), *Four Other Gospels* (1985), *The Cross that Spoke: The Origins of the Passion Narrative* (1988), and *Sayings Parallels: A Workbook for the Jesus Tradition* (1986). His contributions to this volume include the lead essay, "The Historical Jesus in Earliest Christianity," and the concluding "Responses and Reflections."

Sheila Greeve Davaney is Associate Professor of Theology at Iliff School of Theology, Denver, Colorado. She is the author of *Theology at the End of Modernity* (1991) and *Divine Power: A Study of Karl Barth and Charles Hartshorne* (1986). Her essay in this volume is entitled "A Historicist Model for Theology."

Marc H. Ellis is Professor of Religion, Culture, and Society Studies at the Maryknoll School of Theology in Maryknoll, New York, where he has directed the M.A. program in Theological Studies since 1980. He is the author of *Beyond Innocence and Redemption: Confronting the Holocaust and Israeli Power* (1990), *Toward a Jewish Theology of Liberation: The Uprising and the Future* (1988) as well as several other books. His essay in this volume is "The Brokerless Kingdom and the Other Kingdom: Reflections on Auschwitz, Jesus and the Jewish-Christian Establishment."

Catherine Keller is Associate Professor of Constructive Theology in the Theology School at Drew University, where she has taught since 1986. She is the author of *From a Broken Web: Separation, Sexism and Self* (1987) and the forthcoming *Open Apocalypse: Toward a Constructive Theology of Relation*. Her essay in this volume is entitled "The Jesus of History and the Feminism of Theology."

Robert A. Ludwig (coeditor) is Director of University Ministry at DePaul University, where he also teaches in the Religious Studies Department. He is the author of *Christian Origins: An Exploration of the New Testament* (1983) and *Grace and Christ: Fundamental Theology and the Meaning of Human Existence* (1984). His contributions to this volume include the "Introduction" (with coeditor Jeffrey Carlson) and his essay, "Reconstructing Jesus for a Dysfunctional Church: Crossan's Christology and Contemporary Spirituality."

Dennis P. McCann is Professor and Chairman of the Department of Religious Studies at DePaul University, where he has taught Catholic Studies, Religious Social Ethics and Business Ethics since 1981. He is the author of *On Moral Business: Theological Perspectives on Business, Ethics and Economics* (forthcoming, with Max Stackhouse), *New Experiment in Democracy: The Challenge of American Catholicism* (1987), and editor of a special symposium edition of *The Journal of Business Ethics*, titled *Religious Studies and Business Ethics: New Directions in an Emerging Field* (1986). His essay is entitled "Doing Business with the Historical Jesus."

Bernard Brandon Scott is the Darbeth Distinguished Professor of New Testament at Phillips Graduate Seminary, Enid, Oklahoma. He is the author of several books, including *Hear Then the Parable: A Commentary on the Parables of Jesus* (1990), *Jesus: Symbol-Maker for the Kingdom* (1981) and *The Word of God in Words: Reading and Preaching the Gospels* (1985). His contribution to this volume is the essay "to impose is not / To Discover: Methodology in John Dominic Crossan's *The Historical Jesus.*"

Charles R. Strain is Professor of Religious Studies at DePaul University where he has taught American religion, religion and culture, and Japanese religion since 1976. He is co-author (with Dennis P. McCann) of *Polity and Praxis: A Program for American Practical Theology* (1985) and editor of *Prophetic Visions and Economic Realities: Catholics, Protestants and Jews Confront the Bishops' Letter* (1989). His essay in this volume is entitled "Sapiential Eschatology and Social Transformation: Crossan's Jesus, Socially Engaged Buddhism, and Liberation Theology."

Frans Jozef van Beeck, S.J. is John Cardinal Cody Professor of Theology at Loyola University of Chicago since 1985 and the author of *God Encountered* (1989), *Loving the Torah More than God?* (1989), *Catholic Identity After Vatican II* (1985), and *Christ Proclaimed* (1979). His essay in this volume is entitled "The Quest of the Historical Jesus: Origins, Achievements, and the Specter of Diminishing Returns."

Index